THIS GREAT ESCAPE
THE CASE OF MICHAEL PARYLA

Andrew Steinmetz

THIS GREAT ESCAPE

The Case of Michael Paryla

BIBLIOASIS

WINDSOR, ONTARIO

FIRST EDITION

Library and Archives Canada Cataloguing in Publication

Steinmetz, Andrew
This Great escape : the case of Michael Paryla / Andrew Steinmetz.

Issued also in electronic format.
ISBN 978-1-927428-33-7

1. Paryla, Michael, 1935-1967. 2. Paryla, Michael, 1935-1967—In motion pictures. 3. Great escape (Motion picture). 4. Actors—Germany (West)—Biography. 5. Actors—Canada—Biography. 6. Jewish actors—Germany (West)—Biography. 7. Jewish actors—Canada—Biography. I. Title.

PN2658.P359S74 2013 791.4302'8092 C2013-901998-7

Edited by Dan Wells
Copy-edited by Alice Petersen
Typeset by Chris Andrechek
Cover Design by Gordon Robertson

Biblioasis acknowledges the ongoing financial support of the Government of Canada through the Canada Council for the Arts, Canadian Heritage, the Canada Book Fund; and the Government of Ontario through the Ontario Arts Council.

PRINTED AND BOUND IN CANADA

The story that I am about to tell, a story born in doubt and perplexity, has only the misfortune (some call it fortune) of being true.

—Danilo Kiš

What the hell kind of great escape is this? No one escapes!

—Louis B. Mayer

For Sonya and Emil

Breakfast between Zurich and Bern
Michael Paryla, August 1957

The Case

Appell

Appell is taken early and late. Each day in rows we stand in the compound and are counted. But counting is for children and numbers no great matter. Escape is hidden within. Like death from the living by the miracle of birth. How shall I put it? Escape is like an order from above issued from inside. Searchlights may sweep the forest at night all night, seismographs sunk in the earth may record prisoners digging. Despite it all, Michael, I have compiled the following case history with the pen that hangs on a string like a worm around our necks.

Escape Construction

Breakdown of Materials	Tom, Dick & Harry (1944)	Michael (1967)
Bed boards	4,000	0
Bed Covers	192	1
Beading battens	1,370	0
Blankets	1,699	1
Pillow cases	161	2
Towels	3,424	0
Chairs	34	0
Single tables	10	0
20-man tables	52	0
Benches	76	0
Double-tier bunks	90	0
Knives	1,219	0
Spoons	478	0
Shovels	30	0
Forks	582	0
Lamps	69	0
Electric Wire (feet)	1,000	0
Rope (feet)	600	0
Bed bolsters	1, 212	0
Water cans	246	0
Milk (Glasses of)	0	½
Barbiturates (Medicine bottles)	0	1
Whiskey (750 ml bottle)	0	½
Alarm clocks	0	1

Screenplay

1963. *The Great Escape*—The Mirisch Company Inc. Presents

INT. TRAIN COMPARTMENT—DAY. The door opens and a Gestapo agent enters. He glances at the identity cards offered by a pair of SS officers. Not of interest, not on his list. In total there are 76 escaped prisoners from Stalag Luft III and Hitler has ordered a nationwide manhunt, *eine Großfahndung*. The Gestapo agent moves forward and then stops when he comes face to face with the actors Richard Attenborough and Gordon Jackson, escaped POWs disguised as businessmen on the train. There is something about *them*. He studies their papers closely and questions them in German and in French. He hands the props back, and moves past them into the coach ahead.

The train slows down as it swings into the turn of a steep gradient. At 2:14:34 run time, the Gestapo agent finds the actor David McCallum, and flips through his passbook. McCallum is cast as Flight Lieutenant Ashley-Pitt, better known as Dispersal to his POW buddies. (The ensuing brief exchange between the Gestapo agent and Ashley-Pitt does not match James Clavell's draft screenplay of April 26, 1962; it was improvised or it followed the 'final' shooting script, of which there were more than seven in circulation on the set during the making of the movie.)

Gestapo (standing): Sie reisen für eine Firma?

Ashley-Pitt (seated): Ja. Für mein Geschäft.

Gestapo: Danke.

Ashley-Pitt: Danke.

Are you traveling for your company? Yes, for my business. Thank you. The Gestapo man exits the coach and the door slides shut behind him, and that's the last an English audience sees of this actor alive. He's had perhaps a minute of screen time in one of the most watched war movies of all time, but is not credited for the role, a bit part. Shortly after the film was made he died, aged 32, from a drug overdose in Hamburg. Watched by millions yet completely unknown, eclipsed by Hollywood stars. And there's a further irony. He was a refugee from Nazi Germany, partly Jewish and the son of one of Austria's most celebrated left-wing actors, playing a Gestapo agent, a role reprised on thousands of television repeats.

In fact, watching television is how I came to know of my 'cousin' Michael. Alive but not living, stranded in the no-man's-land of a motion picture. His character is staged and scripted, but I was spellbound nonetheless—Michael was convincing. Fedora and trench coat. Elegant. Blond. His smooth transitions. His lively walk, his coat unbuttoned, his fashion bespoke the casual flair of some fresh-as-the-breeze fascist. This image, I now understand many years later, is counterfeit, a convenient archetype, manufactured by the American film director John Sturges and his sidekick Bert Hendrickson in Costume Design and Wardrobe. But it is him, close enough to the real thing. So what to call him? Historicized? Father's cousin? My first cousin once removed? The family used *Michi*. As in, Michi broke Mama's heart.

MICHI'S DIARY

I HOLD IN MY HANDS HIS OLIVE *Tagebuch* from the summer of 1949, when he was fourteen. He writes from Lahr, from inside a Displaced Persons camp located in the French zone of post-war Germany. Michi in transit with his mother, Eva, and stepfather, Antoine Stehr, bound for Canada. The diary is slim, composed in German. Folded and tucked within the pages—a letter never sent, addressed to Georg, a school friend. There are not many entries, but I have enough work, overturning each heavy, capitalized noun in German, and then inspecting the underneath for the imprint of his mind, in English. I rely on others and the *Collins German Dictionary* to find his voice.

20.8.49

This great trip began one week ago. Everything went head over heels. We had to leave Mainz in two days. Now we are sitting in Lahr. I am in a refugee camp for the first time. We have to wait here until we can go to Naples.

21.8.49

Today is Sunday. I have received a pair of shoes with crepe soles. I wore them for the first time today. They are my first shoes with crepe soles. Tonight there is a dance at the YMCA. Maybe we will go.

22.8.49

There was a dance on Sunday and today. But we went only on Sunday. Instead, we wanted to go bathing. It was a nice walk to the lake. On the way back we passed Lahr's water purification plant. The man explained everything to us. In the field we saw a mole. It was the first time I had seen a mole roaming free. When we returned to camp everything was closed. The dance was stopped. We soon learned that diphtheria had broken out in the camp. Now we have to wait for developments. We will probably have to stay here longer.

23.8.49

Bad things are happening to us. If the cultures are good USA and Australia will go tomorrow. But for Canada we still know nothing. Many rumours are circulating that we have to stay here until mid-September. But I do not believe this. The food in the camp is awful. Every noon: potatoes with noodles. Every evening: pea or bean soup.

24.8.49

Another child is sick today. We are locked up for longer. The transports are not going yet.

27.8.49

I have written nothing for two days. But nothing worth saying happened in these days. Tomorrow the gate will be opened again. USA and Australia leave next week. At least that is what is being said. But there is no information about Canada. Today we had spinach for lunch. That was quite amazing. Yesterday I had to help with the cleaning. That is why it tasted so good.

29.8.49

The stupidest of stupid things is that I cannot go bathing because of my hand. But the doctor said it will be alright by tomorrow or the next day. Then there will be a celebration.

3.9.49

Again I have not written for two days. But that is not terrible. Nothing happens here. Yesterday we were registered. We are supposed to get going next week. I hope that this is true. It is not very nice to sit here in Lahr for so long. My hand is good again. I have been bathing. Today I may go again.

7.9.49

Today Australia went. We were at the train station as the train left. My friend also left. Things are now also certain for us. We go on the 14th, and in fact we are leaving with USA to Bremen. This is good.

8.9.49

The days are very boring. I do not have a friend anymore. They are all gone. I find life in the camp increasingly worse and unbearable because mother's nerves are not so strong and I get yelled at a lot.

11.9.49

I made myself a ping-pong net and play a lot of ping-pong. I can do it quite well; but I want to get a lot better.

17.9.49

On the 14th we left Lahr. On the 15th we were in Bremen. On the 22nd we go further. Here in Bremen the camp is first class. Everything goes quickly and clean.

Young master Michi is a gentleman by the sounds of it. At fourteen, his passport is stamped "Displaced Person of Undetermined Nationality". You might ask, how did he get himself into such a diplomatic mess? A bit of history.

Michael Paryla was born in Vienna on November 27, 1935. His parents had fled Germany to Austria in 1933, immediately following the Reichstag Fire, to save their skins. They both were actors. His father, Karl Paryla, was Austrian but earned his first important engagement at the Reinhardt Theatre in Darmstadt. Karl was politically active, a communist, and had married Michael's mother, Eva, against the wishes of his family. Eva was a *Mischling*. Raised Lutheran, she had a Jewish background.[1] When she was a teenager, Eva had a small role playing a prostitute in the first touring production of Bertolt Brecht's *The Threepenny Opera*. Her acting teacher, in Breslau, had been a young Max Ophüls, a German-born film director who later made films in France and Hollywood.

After the occupation and annexation of Austria into Nazi Germany, in March 1938, the family fled Vienna for Zurich. Michael was three years old.[2] In Zurich, his father's theatre and political connections helped the family avoid detention in a Swiss Displaced Persons camp. But soon after arrival, his parents separated. Michael stayed in an apartment with his mother and attended a Waldorf school, where Rudolf Steiner's mystical

---

1 'Jewish background': it won't be the last time I use this phrase and I'd like to clarify what it means to our family with a genealogical note, but it seems early for that, especially since full disclosure entails relaying information that came to be known by some very recent genealogical research. Michael, maybe even his mother Eva, would have been unaware of certain of these facts: you see this is the thing about German families with Jewish backgrounds, there is often a lot of background to the background, which gets in the way and becomes a foreground screen. For now may it suffice to say that this is my background, too: baptised Protestant and raised in a secular family, on my father's side there are Jewish roots and a German past. My mother's side is Swedish.

2 There is, hidden away on a high shelf, out of Michi's reach, a story regarding the family's escape from Vienna, immediately after the Anschluss. Like the background to his Jewish background, there is a time to tell this tale, but that time is not here yet.

philosophy of anthroposophy would form the backbone of his early childhood education. Toward the end of the war, Eva volunteered with the Red Cross, helping to plan a massive relief effort in aid of post-war refugees. Michael's father, meanwhile, pursued his acting career. Karl Paryla made his mark in the World Premiere of Bertolt Brecht's *Mother Courage and Her Children* (1942) and *Life of Galileo* (1943) at the Zurich Schaulspielhaus, one of the most important theatres in the German-speaking world.

In 1946, Michael, aged eleven, accompanied his mother and his stepfather on a train journey back to Germany. They settled in the Russian Zone of post-war Berlin. His stepfather, Antoine Stehr, also had political connections on the left. His mother found work as a broadcaster at Radio Berlin. The family had difficulty surviving the cruel post-war conditions. The city was in ruins. There were cold winters and food shortages. New arrivals, the family made do with ration cards and goods from the black market.

In her book *Tearing the Silence: On Being German in America*, the German-born American writer Ursula Hegi observes that parents of her generation were silent about the war and the Holocaust. Intentionally or not, they implicated their own children in that silence. Her parents' generation, Hegi writes, "tried to create for their children *eine heile Welt*—an intact world". How different was Eva's approach and her decision to leave Zurich for Berlin after the end of the war with an eleven-year-old boy. As an inhabitant of Soviet East Berlin, Michael grew up with evidence of the Allied air raids all around him. He was not at all presented with *eine heile Welt*. He was presented a jigsaw puzzle. Berlin itself was in quarters: Russian, French, British, and American.

It was with a sense of obligation that Eva and Antoine had returned to Germany. They embraced the reconstruction and the declaration of a new beginning. Eva, many years later, explained her decision in context of a civilian mission: it was her obligation and duty as a citizen, who, importantly, had not spent the wars years in Germany—i.e. as someone who had not been poisoned or corrupted by the Nazis, having lived in exile since 1935—to help rebuild the country. Eva's kind had not rotted under the Third Reich. So it was idealism and pride that motivated Michael's parents to take up residence in black-market-dominated post-war Berlin. The buildings and the infrastructure had been destroyed, the morale rubbed out in the dust. Crime was rampant. Berlin's grey citizens eked out an animal existence. During the harsh winter of 1947, it's been recorded that wolves from the surrounding forest entered the city to forage for food. Posters went up on walls warning people of wolf attacks.

Under these circumstances the family adopted Romeo, a German shepherd. Where did they find Romeo? Not from the Humane Society, certainly. Making room for a pet in their lives seems more than a bit indulgent, but then a German shepherd could have come in handy in those conditions, as security in the wild west of post-war Berlin.

In July of 1948, shortly after the Allied sectors had been put in a stranglehold by the Soviets, the family and family dog were airlifted to West Germany from embargoed Berlin, via Gatow, an air base under the British Command.[3] They touched down in Baden-Baden. By the next summer, the family was moved to a refugee camp in Lahr, on the western edge of the Black Forest. Here, a diphtheria outbreak threatened the family's chances of emigration.

---

3   …and family dog--that is correct. Blockade or no blockade, Michael's mother Eva was never short of powers of persuasion. Eva went out of her way to convince an RAF officer that she and her family 'could not leave' Berlin without Romeo. When she journeyed alone to the air base Gatow with Romeo to seek a spot for her dog for the airlift, the SBO allegedly told her, 'If I had a dog like yours, I couldn't leave him behind either,' and dutifully supplied a pass for Romeo's transport.

In his letter dated September 9, 1949, an exuberant Michael Paryla, on the verge of immigration to Canada, writes to a friend:

Dear Georg!

I have a lot to tell you. You will be surprised that I am in Lahr. This is how it happened. In the summer of 1948 I travelled to my father in Vienna. While I was there, my parents received their exit permits to leave to West Germany. I could not get out of Vienna quickly. My parents were in Mainz. But everything went broke in Mainz. My parents could not earn enough. Shortly before Christmas, I also came to Mainz. Maybe you heard about this from Anja, if you still have contact with this young lady. This summer I wanted to come to Switzerland, to visit my first teacher in Zurich. That would have been nice. But as usual something unforeseen happened. Of course, our exit visa, on which we had been counting for one year, and in which we no longer believed, arrived out of the blue. We have been sitting here in a camp in Lahr for three weeks. This is not at all nice. But on Wednesday we are finally leaving for Canada.

Now be well. Greetings to you, your parents and grandmother. Your Michi.

The forwarding address he gives is 262 York Street, Ottawa, CANADA, printed all capitals.

Unnecessary Travel Lengthens The War

BAVARIA FILM STUDIOS, *Munich. October 2010*

I STAND AT THE BOX OFFICE, outside the museum opposite the active studios, under a grey but clearing sky.

"*Morgen.* I have a question."

"Welcome." A young man is working the window.

"Inside the museum ... "

"Yes?"

"Is there an installation from *The Great Escape*?"

"*Nein.* But *Das Boot* you can see." His two female co-workers are momentarily intrigued by their first visitor of the morning, a foreigner and not a Facebook friend.

"*Aber keinmal* Great Escape?" I leverage the little German I know.

"*Das Boot* is more modern." His co-workers join, reinforcements, to have a closer look.

"Yes, I know. *Aber ... * But ... " And then I divulge the keynotes of my visit to all three–and why I have come so early on a weekday morning to disturb their social media quiet time. The movie was a Hollywood blockbuster. A member of my family had a small role in it. Unfortunately, he died young, in Hamburg, a long time ago.

"We're sorry," the woman in the black hoodie seems genuinely touched. She has an open, friendly face, oval-shaped, and plump freckled cheeks. She looks at her female counterpart who has cropped and dyed spiky hair, then inquires, "What was his name?"

"Michael Paryla."

The young women exchange bewildered glances, then black hoodie says, "We don't know him."

"He is buried in Waldfriedhof." I offer a local reference, this might make him real.

"That is near to this place." The black hoodie is onside, but her female colleague has moved away, gone into a small office. Looking for clues in her laptop or cell.

"The prison camp scenes were filmed here in 1962." I decide to push the film angle.

"Yes, we know." The young man takes over. His tone is poised between passive and aggressive.

"The tunnel scenes were filmed inside." I point to the studio buildings and sound stages behind the metal fence surrounding the film city. For a moment, I consider telling them about Wally Floody, a Canadian like me and former mining engineer and prisoner of Stalag Luft III. Floody was a wartime Spitfire pilot. He was hired as a technical advisor on the film set. Charles Bronson's character Tunnel King is partly based on Wally Floody. But never mind.

"It's too bad," the young man reflects. "But no one knows the history of 'this' place." He shakes his head.

I have travelled a long way to be told exactly what I expected to be told. I'd done my homework in Canada. I had learned about *Das Boot* from Das Google. But that didn't stop me from coming here, accepting an unwilling audience, holding out for a surprise. I have three at the window again, crowded inside the box office, which reminds me that the Mirisch Brothers released *The Great Escape* in an era when the POW film genre had finally become trapped by its own success. Prisoner escape stories conveniently supplied a reliable narrative and dramatic vector, but during the post-war decade there had been a glut of POW films, many based on bestselling memoirs like Paul Brickhill's.[4] Instead of lecturing them on a topic about which I'm far from an expert, I tell my gatekeepers a little more about Michael and his part in the movie. I point in the vague direction of Waldfriedhof and acknowledge his grave is that way. Are they at all interested? *Over there, he is buried under the tall trees in a mossy cemetery*, I might say, since I know this from a letter Michael's father penned on April 21, 1967. I could spout verbatim from the private correspondence—the poignant documents written in the days and months after Michael's death—but turn off the tap. I'm a very curious customer as it is.

"Why don't you visit his grave?" the man, sounding bold and on the edge of rudeness, suggests. "It's too bad, but there is nothing inside about the movie and there is no archivist here, no film historian."

As for the past, they are it. Not one born before 1990.

"I found a web page," I say, ignoring his forward suggestion, "made by an American. It pinpoints a football field near the studio lot, bordering the forest, where the model prison camp might have been built."

"Yes, we know about this, a man was here from America last year. He asked many questions like you and made this web page, probably. But he really didn't know what he was talking about. He was just like you," the young man informs me, which means the American was guessing.

"Are you sure there is not a film historian on site?"

"Too bad, but no. We are sorry."

I sigh good-naturedly but at the same time show my disappointment. How can they not be better organized? They're

---

4   In England alone around 75 feature films were released between 1950 and 1959 about the Second World War, among which the prisoner of war genre figured prominently. Some of the best known prisoner of war films of that era include: *The Wooden Horse* (1950); *Three Came Home* (1950); *The Password is Courage* (1952); *Stalag 17* (1953); *The Colditz Story* (1955); *A Man Escaped* (1956); *The Bridge over the River Kwai* (1957); *Danger Within* (1959).

Germans. Nonetheless, they have apologized for a situation out of their control.

"Over there by the train tracks," spiky hair points, "is a film institute, but it is only educational and for teachers and students." She slides her hands into her pant pockets. "They won't know your film there, either."

"We are it for knowledge," says the young man. (They are ganging up on me now. Needlessly beating a dead horse.) "Your film was years ago. There is no consciousness of the film here, which is too bad, and not good."

He holds up his palms, and backs away from the window. More denial than asked for. Still, I won't shoot.

"Thank you for your help."

I walk along the road bordering the studio lots and the forest. He said 'your film'. It's not my film—it's Michael's. Michael was given a minute on the train, to play Gestapo opposite Richard Attenborough and Gordon Jackson and David McCallum and James Garner et al. My film? *Das Boot* is what the people are served today. WWII U-boats. The Battle of the Atlantic. Visitors demand entry to the claustrophobic world of a submarine crew, never mind the shenanigans of a group of Allied prisoners of war. There is a guided tour in English at 1 PM. The cost is 11 Euros. I have no interest in the professionalism of these submariners, thirty-thousand of which perished undersea. I won't go in.

I'm here to find out more about the other movie, and to follow as closely as I can in Michael's footsteps. But I'm finding that it's not an easy task. Like the type of prisoner who was brought to Stalag Luft III in spring of 1943, Michael was a serial escapist most of his life, beginning in 1935, when he exited the womb in Vienna disguised as happiness itself, in the eyes of his mother Eva, and his father, Karl.

*

About a kilometre from the box office I find the football pitch. No sign of Stalag Luft III here though. The field is unremarkable: white goal posts and bald spots in the grass where play is heaviest. Office workers in short sleeves and dress pants, from a neighbouring low-rise, are out kicking a ball during an early lunch hour. I stand by the touchline and take photographs in the direction of the forest, then a couple more from the opposite side, facing the studio lot and high fence along its boundary.

If not exactly here, then somewhere close, the director John Sturges began filming in the summer of 1962. In order to build a complete replica of Stalag Luft III, the film crew sought and received permission from the German Minister of the Interior to fell a considerable number of trees in the Grünewald, a forest bordering the studio's back lot, on the agreement that they replant two-to-one when the shooting was done. It took Sturges and crew six weeks to build a replica of the original camp, and then another four months to shoot the movie, which wouldn't have been filmed in Germany if Sturges had not run into a labour dispute with the Screen Extras Guild back in California. The film would use a large number of extras, almost 600. Even with a four million dollar budget and his mind already set on a location in the San Gabriel Mountains, a two hour drive from Hollywood, Sturges took the entire shooting abroad. In nearby Munich, a theatrical centre, the American crew found German actors for important secondary roles: Hannes Messemer, Robert Graf, and Harry Riebauer. Stalmaster-Lister Co. directed the casting of extras. Enter Michael, stage right.

Standing by the side of the football pitch, I remember reading about the deforestation efforts of the film crew and thinking about how this mimicked the labour of the actual Russian POWs who, in 1942, were sent out on a work detail to cut down trees beyond the Vorlager, the forecamp, in preparation for the construction of Stalag Luft's North Compound. The trees in question would have been gaunt Silesian pines native to forests in the north-east, altogether different from the ones in the Grünewald. Early in the movie, there is a goofy set-piece involving actor John Leyton as Willie 'Tunnel King', in which a number of escape-happy Hollywood POWs hide in wagons laden with cut branches, but are found out at the perimeter fence by pitchfork-yielding goons.

Correction. It was not out here that filming began in 1962, but inside the sound stages. That spring and early summer in Bavaria the weather was foul. Rainstorms would not let up. Sturges had wanted to shoot his movie chronologically, starting with the opening scene: the POWs' arrival at camp by a convoy of covered trucks. He even brought in flamethrower trucks in an attempt to bake the mud and dry out the studio lot. The heavy artillery did little good. Meanwhile, the stars had assembled and were waiting to shine, having taken up residence in Munich. (Except for McQueen, who waited for no one. McQueen was having a riot, out riding his motorbike, destroying farmers' fields, or else he was tearing around in his Mercedes-Benz 300 SL Gullwing; the local authorities rigged a speed trap in his honour, and, inevitably, confiscated his licence.) One day, early in June, Sturges called for a meeting of cast and crew. No more time to waste. He had given up filming exteriors. The crew would begin filming in the middle of the picture. Indoors to the sound stages they went, and began with the tunnels. Next, the scenes inside the barracks. Actors James Garner and Donald Pleasance were given their calls.

Less than fifteen minutes later, I'm headed back to my friends in the box office, shouldering my laptop, smoking a cigarette for effect. Michael was a smoker. Prisoners of all stripes often are. Like Sturges, I'd planned to spit out the book chronologically, but as it is my hard drive is crammed with research notes, transcriptions of family letters, photographs and multiple drafts of the endless permutations of my book so far. There have been days aplenty in the past decade that I have wanted to hire a flamethrower truck and melt the beast in its smooth white silicon crèche, then turn the nozzle on myself. Turns out some of us are fire retardant. *The Last Escape* was the original working title of *The Great Escape*. Maybe that's the title I'll use for this.

"What about the train station?" I throw this out, offhandedly. They must know the routine from the American who came before me.

"Yes," black hoodie admits. "The other guy, he too talked about a train station."

"Is it near here?" I'm thinking of the scene two-thirds through the movie where a handful of escaped prisoners are piled up, none too inconspicuously, on the station platform. In this scene Michael makes his entrance. He arrives by motorcade to Neustadt Station and then proceeds to board the Hollywood gravy train. From what I have read, it was filmed in the vicinity.

"It might be Pullach," the young man ventures.

"Not Geiselgasteig?" Geiselgasteig is referenced all the time—in books and documentaries about the film—but the Germans wouldn't know the place if they were standing on it. Maybe it's my pronunciation.

The two women turn and enter the small back office. Cue the water bottles. Cut to black hoodie mouthing my mangling of 'Geiselgasteig'. The spiky blonde is sucking a pencil. Smoke and mirrors.

"Pullach. You must take the S-Bahn two stops in the direction of Munich and then cross by foot over the Isar on Großhesseloher Brücke and then you will walk several kilometres, yes, through the forest. Once in Pullach ask for directions to the train station. They have a very old one, it could be what you are looking for."

I go. But before leaving I ask my friends at the box office if I may take a photograph of all three, together?

"Why of us?" Humbled and suspicious, modestly and falsely incredulous.

"To help my memory," I say. "Your faces will help me remember details from this day and this place."

Michael (bottom left, looking on with undisciplined hair) in an August Everding production of *L'Affaire Dreyfus* by Hans Rehfisch. The play focuses on the 1894 trial for treason of Alfred Dreyfus, a Jewish artillery officer in the French military. Falsely accused and eventually pardoned, the Dreyfus Affair roused virulent anti-Semitic feelings in France. (Date unknown)

Leaving, I walk to the S-Bahn stop and wait by the tracks, breathing a mixture tar and creosote fumes. It's not yet noon. The day is warming up.

The train arrives and I step on. It is only a seven minute ride to Großhesselohe. I ring the bell and get off and begin walking, crossing over the tracks, following signs to the Brücke. The streets are quiet and the houses of Großhesselohe—half-timbered palaces, fenced and gated—are monstrosities. All of FC Bayern must be shacked up here in the south of Munich, and who knows perhaps a number of War Criminals as well. But where the hell is the bridge?

The signposts and hand-painted directions have led me deep into a residential neighbourhood. I do realize that I must cross the Isar to reach Pullach, but I can't find the bridge, nor any sliver of the river. I'm hot and lost on a fruitless search for a station that's probably not the one I want anyway.

After twenty minutes of wandering and wondering, I spot a gardener over the fence, raking leaves.

"*Bitte, Helf. Eine Frage?*" My throat is dry and my voice sounds hoarse and very weak. I've not had the chance to talk much the last couple of days, discounting internal monologues and my brief chat with the box office crowd, and the timbre of my voice sounds pathetic. My speech has the ring of 'Bite elf, I'm a fag?' nowhere close to 'Please, help me, I have a question?'

Michael lived in Munich from 1956 until his death ten years later. In the first months after arriving from Canada he stayed with his aunt, Irene, and worked odd jobs while he pursued a career in the theatre. Finding work in the theatre often meant travelling and taking a temporary residence in Bremen or Berlin or Hamburg. But he loved Munich above all. Bavaria's cultural centre, the Bohemian atmosphere, the open air Biergartens covered in gravel and shaded by chestnut trees. These things are pervasive even today. Eventually, he bought property, but no one in my family can tell me where it was. In a letter from 1967 his father calls it a luxurious home; he complains to Eva that Michael now lives like a bourgeois, and that this bothers Karl greatly. His father also describes Michael's grave in some detail, but nowhere does he mention the irony that his son, a refugee from Nazism who plays a Gestapo on a train in *The Great Escape*, is buried in a cemetery, four stops beyond the Bavariafilmstadt, the film studio where a substantial part of the movie was made in 1962.

It makes perfect sense to me now that I am walking the streets that Michael's house would have been nearby, conceivably an address in this very suburb. Why hadn't I thought of it before? Which means I haven't been walking aimlessly—methodically drawn into the thick of it, is more like it. Why else would Michael have been buried far to the south of Munich, unless he and his Frau Margaret had been living in the vicinity? This proximity to the studios would have eased him into an audition for the film. I keep walking and as I am connecting the dots and inventing my own dots, I have begun taking photographs of houses, of Michael's untold houses. I'm certain of that. It's uncanny. I am getting close to him. Roll camera. It makes good sense that Michael resided within shouting distance of his grave and the film studio, or maybe, maybe I am looking at things backwards.

The groundskeeper comes to the gate, opens it, and steps onto the street.

"Bite elf, I'm a fag."

I try English, then my best French. In the days of the escape, during the Second World War, RAF officers were often multilingual. The first escapees sent out of the tunnel had been selected, from among hundreds of candidates inside Stalag Luft III, because they spoke German fluently. But forget that—no use, the gardener is Romanian and a foreigner like me. For passport, he shows me his hands, calloused palms and fingers, the international sign of the worker.

I unlatch my shoulder bag and pry out my notebook and a pen. I make a drawing and then begin block-lettering B-R-U-C-K-E. But the gardener is distracted by the white slab of my laptop, which is peaking from my bag. *MACBook,* international sign of the knowledge-worker aristocracy. *Isn't the answer in there?* he seems to be saying, staring hard. *Why not use that?*

Momentarily, he points down the street, sends me off on my way. His trailing voice, *Links, rechts, links, rechts*, left, right, left, right.

*

After crossing the bridge it is still five kilometres to Pullach through the forest. Links und rechts and around I go for over an hour-and-a-half. The sun is blazing and the ground is afire with red and yellow leaves. Cyclists rush past, and old women chatting and marching briskly overtake me on the path. The forest is well-tended, the earth track swept, and I keep coming upon the same piece of river and railway tracks, as if I might be walking in a big circle, but no, here is the edge of a town, which must be Pullach.

On a street corner, I hail a man passing on his bicycle. As he comes to a stop, a boy slides off the front handlebars.

"Can you help me?" I ask in English, skipping the elf routine.

His son stands aside and the man partially dismounts, holding steady the front and back wheel.

"Yes, I hope so," says he. He speaks German, French and English, and everything else besides.

I explain what I am looking for: I describe Neustadt in the film and ask the way to Pullach Station.

"Pullach Station is that way," he points straight down the road. "But you do not want Pullach. Let me see your film." He gestures to my laptop. "Let me see the station in there."

No problem. It takes me several minutes to turn on my computer and cue the movie. Meanwhile, he asks where I am from. Canada. When I answer, the boy studies his father's face to verify if Canada is a good place. I gather it is, as the boy cracks a smile even as his father is explaining "his situation". He has six children and no car. He is always on the tram, the man tells me, for transportation, and therefore he is familiar with almost every station south of Munich.

"Where are you from?" I ask, suspecting he is Roma.

"Hungary."

"I have been to Budapest. I went in—"

"Yes." He interrupts. He knows all about my visit to Budapest in 1989. He remembers my important trip to Berlin. It's boring to have Westerners paint impressions of the Eastern Block. He doesn't have the slightest interest in the fictions travelers take to heart. I've been chastened. "Germany looks like a nice place on the surface," he offers, "and it looks as if everything works well here, but it's not the case." He's seen most of the country. "*Hier ist es Schlecht*. You understand? Here it is bad, unpalatable. Especially the schools," he says. "I must fight the government to put my children in the right schools."

"That's bad," I mutter to him and his boy. We are getting seated just as naturally and comfortably as you can, on a patch of grass between the paved sidewalk and a residential fence, to view a WWII action film.

Prim pedestrians move on. Nobody is curious about us. I start the movie and the gypsy and his son watch intently as Michael steps out of the Mercedes at Neustadt Station. Trench coat, fedora. Handsome devil.

"There." The father points. "See: two tracks and the station shelter with the tile roof. This is not Pullach. This is not even Munich."

He does not remark on Michael. He hasn't noticed him.

"You won't find that station here in the south, even the landscape is wrong."

I tell him that I have read many articles about the making of the movie and almost all of them mention nearby Geiselgasteig as the area where the old train station is located.

"No. It's not the case."

To make certain he is not mistaken, I play the movie segment once more. The boy has taken an interest at least. How many action movies has he watched like this, I wonder? Laptop, sitting in the grass, the bicycle on its side: we might have invented the green drive-in theatre right here. Not many is my guess. Movie stars, potentially, are ordinary people to him. Like Michael is to me. I sense the boy is getting excited, his curiosity physical. I watch him as he watches Michael at Neustadt. I wish I could show him the scene on the train where Michael actually has some lines, but that comes a little later on.

Instead, I narrate more about my family, how they originally came from Breslau, in Silesia, a strip of land in the northeast, and how in Michael's case family history and film history shadow each other in a curious way. I don't actually say aloud 'in a curious way', yet as I am addressing them I am simultaneously plugged into an internal monologue and fear, for a moment, that I might finally have grown incontinent 'in a curious way'. The stark egonomics I have lived under for years have produced a fallacy based on the false pretence that the entire world shares my thoughts and concern and interest in Michael's story. But that's enough. I must keep to the facts. And although I get the sense neither are listening carefully— not the boy, certainly not his father—I persist because I feel it's important where Michael is concerned that they learn a little more than what meets the eye. It's important to me, anyway. I'm beginning to ease into our family's exodus story set in 1935, when the boy's father notices something, a placard on the station house at Neustadt.

"Look there."

I pause the film.

"*Unnötiges Reisen verlängert den Krieg.*" He shakes his head. "It's nothing."

At Pullach station, I wait with a handful of commuters for the train to Munich.

It's propaganda. *Unnecessary travel lengthens the war.*

The Seagull

*When I see the curtain rise on a room with three walls, when I watch these great
and talented people, these high priests of the sacred art depicting the way people eat,
drink, make love, walk about and wear their clothes, in the artificial light of the
stage... when I'm presented with a thousand variations of the same old thing, the same
thing again and again—well, I just have to escape, I run away.*

The Seagull Act I

THERE ARE PARTS OF MICHAEL'S STORY I could never find in
Europe. Even so, the seven years he spent in Canada, from
1949-1956, seem very remote. I knew nothing of the family's first temporary address in Canada, in Ottawa, until I
discovered his diary, and then, the other day, drove from my
residence down to 262 York Street only to find it no longer
exists. Where once there stood a row house, there is now a
four-way stop. A bland intersection, one block down from
busy Rideau Street.

Within a year of arriving in Canada, Michael's family settled
in Sault Ste. Marie, on the shores of Lake Superior. His stepfather Antoine Stehr, a biologist, found a position at the Forest
Insect Laboratory to study Spruce budworms. His mother
Eva, no longer involved in the theatre, entered the ring of dog
breeding, kennel clubs, and conformation shows. Meanwhile,
Michael attended Sault Ste. Marie Collegiate Institute from

1949 to 1955, and later McGill University, where he studied chemistry but failed miserably.

His first dramatic role came in the fall of 1955, at the age of twenty. Michael played Konstantin Trepliov in Anton Chekhov's *The Seagull*, in the McGill University English Department's December production at Moyse Hall. It was an occasion, the first ever production of the play in English in Montréal. Archival material indicates that Soviet officials were in attendance:

> The embassy of the Soviet Union is interested in securing nine tickets for the Saturday evening performance of "The Seagull" by Chekov, Dec 3, 1955 and I am sending herewith the cheque for paying to the tickets. The Soviet Embassy would appreciate any information you could send answering "The Seagull" performance, producing by the McGill University. Thank you very much for your kind consideration. Yours very truly, E Novikov. First Secretary.

Not long ago, I began to compile an oral history of Michael's adolescent years, based on conversations with former classmates, using as a reference point his arrival in Canada in 1949. I supplemented the memories of friendships formed in high-school with the remembrances of family friends and acquaintances. I interviewed two of Michael's cousins; my father, Nicolas, and my aunt, Sybille. My father Nicolas had stayed with Michael et famille in Sault Ste. Marie from 1954-55, when he was fifteen and a new immigrant to Canada from South America. My conversations with Michael's mother were had in the summer of 1994, the year Eva was diagnosed with pancreatic cancer.

*

EVA (Mother)
It's too late. It's too late to talk about him.

MCGILL DAILY

The tremendous current popularity of Chekov, and in particular of his once ridiculed drama *The Seagull*, seems to prove that audiences have caught up with this influential writer. This will be the first dramatic offering this year by McGill students, who have become well known in this city for good productions of classic drama. *The Seagull* will be followed next term by a revival of Shakespeare's *Much Ado About Nothing* which is scheduled for the first week of March.

Anton Chekov's *The Seagull*, December 1, 2, 3 at Moyse Hall, Arts Building. Set design and direction by Stephan Porter. All parts played by students and members of the faculty of English. Curtain time 8.30.

KEN (High-school friend)
I am going to use the name Mike because that is how we all knew him and it may say something about him that he used this North American contraction. It is likely that he was Michael, or whatever the German version is, at home, and that he used that when he went back to Europe. Relationships between teens were much different in the fifties than they are now, and maybe we did not communicate nearly as much to each other as young people do in these Facebook times, but Mike was definitely the friend with whom I had most contact and he and Eva had a very great influence on my life.

He was fourteen when he arrived in 1949. He lived two doors down from us on Wellington Street. The railway was literally in his backyard. The CPR Station and the Express Office was out his back door. There were two tracks and steam engines were used. It was noisy. At night the boxcars shunting back and forth kept the neighbourhood awake. During the summer, Mike and I and your father worked together unloading Canada Post boxcars crammed with parcels.

We walked to and from school each day and home for lunch. Mike never talked about the past. He showed up in the Soo, and socially he fit right in. He was self-confident, extremely good-looking, a handsome teenage boy, not at all introverted. He didn't study very hard, but he did well at school. He got high marks without much effort. And he learned clarinet; I remember music was important in his family. He was athletic and good at sports but never joined one of the school teams. I don't know why. Instead he preferred to play basketball with some older kids at the YMCA. He picked up basketball quickly. Basketball was 'American'. He wanted to master that aspect, I think, being an ordinary kid.

Eva coached him not to talk about the war. His mother was worried he might get picked on, because he was German. The family didn't want to attract attention, or cause trouble. They didn't want to awaken any kind of racism. I've got to think they lived in fear of that eventuality. So Eva had coached him to never enter a dispute of any kind. Michael would never debate an issue at school. He wasn't shy, but you couldn't get him into an argument. He avoided confrontation.

My parents were very much into the activities of the United Church that was just a block down Wellington Street from our houses. Mike and his family were not religious. My uncle was in a church-sponsored minstrel show, and I asked Mike if he would come. Mike handled that by saying that he would not be going; nothing more. There was a bit of culture conflict there. There was a large and active Young Peoples group, to which Mike did not become included even though the rest of us did. He was genuinely curious about why my family would go to church at all. He listened carefully when my father would explain the roots of our faith. When Mike was satisfied he understood, he would say something like, "Okay, I get it," and leave it at that. He would move on to something else, leaving no doubt what his opinion was. It was a very effective way to influence others and he had mastered that skill at a very young age.

On the other hand, I would not describe Mike as a leader. I doubt if he was ever chosen as a team captain or class president. He was a year or two older than most of us, but he preferred to stay under the radar. In the summer, Mike and I did some camping and fishing. We'd borrow a boat or canoe. In the good old days there were thousands of places to just put up a tent. Lois' parents had a cottage and we could go there. One time we brought home smelt and Eva cooked them in a sort of stew with the heads still on. Saturday football games were a big deal. We might decorate my parent's car and get into the parade and there was always a big bunch of us, including Mike.

NICOLAS (Cousin)

I'd been sent at the age of fifteen from Colombia to live with my aunt Eva and Antoine and Michael in Ontario. Everything was new—so many first impressions—and Michael and I were very different. I: compulsive, over-serious, probably humourless, on my guard, in Canada to study and do well, confident that I could do well—better than he. Awkward. He: making a point of being relaxed, trying to look in no doubt, to be hip, sloppy, not a good student—but mostly, I think, because he was utterly undisciplined and uninterested. Because I think he was smart.

Michael was tall, slim, very loose like a noodle. He smiled and laughed a great deal. Happy-go-lucky.

LOIS (High-school friend)

We were teenagers then, and not too bright ones either. But I remember he was good-looking, well built, just a good guy. He was a friend, and I liked him. Jane, who was my real best friend, had a crush him. So did Jenny Folds, the girl across the street. She really had a crush on Mike. It was always Mike. I knew him as Mike. We never talked about Germany. I don't know why we didn't, but we didn't. To me he was Canadian. We knew Eva and Antoine had come from Germany, we knew that, but it didn't figure.

He never mentioned his biological father. I never knew about the family being actors. I never knew about that stuff. He was in something at high-school and it was Ken who told me it was *The Mikado*. He wouldn't have been on stage even, because it was puppets, but he did the voice. Ken apparently saw Eva, Mrs. Stehr, later, but after high-school I didn't see Mike at all. And after they moved from Wellington Street, I never spoke to Eva, or Mrs. Stehr, again.

But anyway, we were friends, the whole gang of us in that neighbourhood did things together. We danced, all of us, but he was a great dancer. I loved to dance with him when we went to the dances after ball games. I had my own girl-friends and we would probably meet up at football games and basketball games.

KEN

The thing I remember most about them is their family dog, named Romeo, and how traumatized the family was when they had to put him down. It had hip dysplasia, and it was obvious to everybody who knew the family that that dog was suffering. He should have been put down earlier than he was. But the family just couldn't cope with destroying it. There was some story about how it had saved them once. Mike said that the dog had been involved in his escape from Germany. It must have been during or just after the war. In Berlin, the dog had come to their rescue and helped them. They loved that dog. It was so hard for them to see it go, to betray it, in a sense. They suffered to an unusual degree over that, the whole family did. Eva, Antoine, and Mike.

After Romeo, Eva took up the breeding of Siamese cats and she had the poodles, one of which won top bitch (of all breed) at the CNE in Toronto. Eva knew what she was doing. The kittens were selling for $50 dollars at a time when no one paid anything for a cat. One day, Mike and I were trying to calm Eva while working to save a kitten who'd got caught in the heating ducts. There was so much time and effort involved in both the physical grooming and the training. The rest of us could play with cats and dogs, but there were limits. Mike enjoyed animals but that side of him was eclipsed by Eva's enthusiasm.

You couldn't call Romeo an ordinary animal. He was a big German shepherd, and he was maybe the only piece of their past which they didn't hide. Romeo was their signature. Losing him was like losing part of their identity, an identity which both shamed them, and made them proud. You could understand that dog in a lot of different ways.

TREPLIOV (*Konstantin Gavrilovich Trepliov, the Russian Hamlet at the heart of Chekhov's play.*)
A psychological oddity—that's my mother. Oh, there is no doubt about her being very gifted and intelligent: she's capable of weeping bitterly over a book. You mustn't praise anybody but her, you mustn't write about anybody but her, you must acclaim her and go into raptures over her wonderful acting.

BUDDY (Family friend)
He died when Woodstock was on—Woodstock, the rock n' roll concert. He died in New York. Correct? Well you see that was years ago. The best person to talk to about Michael would be Janine Blum. She was good friends with Michael in the Soo. They were in the same class at high-school, a few years ahead of me. I was pretty close to his parents, Eva and Antoine, later, in the early sixties, and I remember when he died; Eva was pretty traumatized by that. It was an accidental death, correct? He had been taking sleeping pills and had started drinking and the combination was one of those accidental deaths. I don't recall Eva talking much about Michael. They might have been estranged or something. I'd been aware of him in high-school, but it was years later that I got to be friends with Eva. As I said, the best information you can get is probably from Janine.

KEN
Janine Blum was his girlfriend. Her father didn't approve of Michael, who came from a lower social standing. So that was a bit of a problem. Anyway, he soon left to Montréal. At McGill, I heard he studied chemistry. I don't know. I wasn't at McGill, Michael and me had gone different ways by then. But I remember hearing that the wife of one his professors at McGill had a thing for him. She was a much older woman, and apparently this professor found out and Mike got worried and then rejected her—Michael rejected this woman—and she then retaliated somehow and made trouble for him. I don't know where I heard that.

I learned that he had died from Eva, but there was some mystery and I never found out what it was. Eva seemed really angry. She would not speak about him. After his death, even ten years later, when I saw her now and again, she seemed really, really angry still.

LOIS

I didn't see much of him when he started going with Janine. I didn't know her. She was a year ahead of us. Therefore I really didn't know her, but she was a good-looking girl, a very nice kid. I didn't see much of him then after grade eleven. I'd still see Mike a little bit, I'm thinking of when we got our results at the end of grade thirteen and each one of us were asking the other one how they did. I saw Mike that day. It might have been the last time.

*

Almost a half-century after their courtship, I drove to Almonte to visit Michael's former girlfriend Janine Blum. It was uncanny—if that is the right word: but not entirely a surprise to me—to learn that Janine lived so nearby. Canada is a vast country. Why Almonte, only forty kilometres to the west of Ottawa, where I lived? Because it was too good to be true, that's why. Because now I could not pass up making a visit, though we had never before met and I was reluctant to impose and break the silence.

Outside the house, I met her husband, a former diplomat. He left Janine and I alone to chat. Two hours later, when I was leaving that same afternoon, I promised to return, very soon. There was so much to discuss. And yet my parting words were tinged with a variety of regret. There was always that moment, when talking—whether on email, by phone, or in person—that you felt strongly that a return visit was in order and would be necessary; since never more than now, after learning a little more about him, did it become more apparent how coarse was my familiarity and how modest my level of understanding and knowledge was. But how much did I want to know?

Encountering Janine for the first time, I was reminded of Eva, Michael's mother. Self-possessed, articulate, stylish. In retrospect, to find similarities between a boy's mother and first girlfriend is, I don't know, merely obvious. I was very close to Eva in my teenage years and by proxy of the inverted past, I felt immediately at ease with Janine—discussing Michael, times they had shared, and the manner of his death—when maybe I shouldn't have.

I remember when I visited Eva several months before her death, she had been fascinated that I was writing a novel based on her life story.

"When do you work?" She had asked, pointedly. "Morning or night?"

I responded, "at night, always at night," and she seemed to comprehend what that all meant. "Be careful," she cautioned me, making an exaggerated gesture by covering her mouth with both hands, but I made nothing of it. Talking to me she was thinking of Michael. That's obvious to me now. But at the time, when I was in my mid-thirties, nothing was obvious to me.

I never did return to Almonte after my meeting with Janine, and not because of the distance. Almonte is basically a suburb of Ottawa. Instead, I planned a trip to the McGill Archives, where I spent an afternoon in a small bright room searching through yearbooks and the student newspaper, *The McGill Daily*, for the first documented signs of Michael's theatrical career.

Professor Porter has done his best to bring out all the humour there is in *The Seagull*. To a large extent he has succeeded, but he has thereby sacrificed a very great deal of the drama of the play. Nina is played by Pearl Sheffy, and I have nothing but praise for her excellent performance … Michael Paryla as

Konstantin also deserves praise. When these two were on stage together the play almost invariably had all the tension that Chekov (sic) gave it."

(Peter H. Engel, Friday, December 2, 1955)

Returning from the archives, I found a second-hand copy of the Penguin Edition of the play, which until then I had not read. Soon I could not contain myself, underlining the text in pencil, decorating the margins with asterisks. Trepliov's character struck me, and when I began to notice biographical symmetries between Michael and Chekhov's Trepliov, I had to ask myself how playing the part and speaking the lines for that character might have influenced a young Michael Paryla.

It's a question I ask myself from time to time, from play to play, sometimes imagining I were him.

TREPLIOV
(*Pulling off the petals of a flower, one by one*). She loves me ... she loves me not ... she loves me—loves me not ... loves me ... loves me not. (*Laughing.*) You see, my mother doesn't love me. And why should she indeed? She wants to live. To have love affairs, to wear light-coloured blouses, and here I am, twenty-five years old already. I'm always reminding her that she isn't young any longer.

*

JANINE (Girlfriend)
I met him when I was in a play myself in high-school, in 1953, and he was not allowed to be in the play of the season because he wasn't paying attention to his marks, so that was

the school's punishment—you couldn't participate in these extracurricular things unless you kept your marks at a certain level. So I was in that play and that's how we met. Then in 1954, maybe, I went to McGill. He was a year behind me. But he came to McGill as well the next year and immediately joined the drama club. He had a chosen role in *The Seagull* and that was when he started to show his keenness. Then he tried to get into the National Theatre School and he auditioned—I remember very well, because I was with him that day—and the interview went okay but the trouble was he didn't have French and at that time they were looking for bilingual artists. Not too long after that he started focusing on the idea of training in Munich.

SYBILLE (Cousin)

I first met my cousin Michael when he came to Bogotá for the summer with my brother Nicolas, after Nicolas' first year in Canada as a high-school freshman. I thought he was very handsome and a happy, jovial fellow. A bit hyper like Eva. I liked him very much. He brought his clarinet, which he played frequently to my delight. At the end of the summer vacation—this would have been 1953—they left again for Sault Ste. Marie, Ontario, where Eva and Antoine lived. I was devastated. I saw Michael a time or two after that.

NICOLAS

He was Canadian with a difference. I do not think he felt "German", but as the years went on and he was just hanging in there—McGill was difficult for him, he wanted to study theatre, get involved in acting—well then he began to say that Canada was a desert for the arts and that if one wanted to have a career in the arts, be an artist, an actor, one had to go to Europe, and for him specifically that meant Germany.

He had failed out of McGill, wanted to act, so, Germany it was—I assume contact was made with Karl.

JANINE
He identified very well with Canada. He came young enough. And he had very good ear, also. And he never had an accent. He learned slang and the Canadian way of speaking in no time. He never had a foreign sound to him. He was very good at languages.

LOIS
The Stehr's were on one side of the house and the Palumbo's were on the other, and news travelled quick between them. And my sister, Mary, who was ten years younger than me, went around with Anita Palumbo. So she was down there a lot. Mary would have been four if Mike was fourteen when he arrived in the Soo. Well, Mary was just scared to death of dogs, and she was really scared of their dog, Romeo. And all those years he was in high-school she would have been down there at the house with Anita Palumbo, and Romeo would be around. She didn't see this—but whether Eva and Mike were having a kerfuffle or what, whether they were having an argument as teenagers do with their moms, and whether Mike lifted his arm or not, to strike his mother, which I don't think he would do—probably he was just arguing with her, but Romeo apparently bit him. Mary didn't see it happen but she heard about it, probably from Anita or Mrs. Palumbo. Romeo bit him on the face. Mike got bit on the face. That's all I'm saying.

KEN
During the war, and for some years after, anything German or Japanese was the ultimate in evil. We all knew families who had lost sons or fathers, soldiers who had been killed. At

Remembrance Day events, the students chosen to lay a wreath were ones whose fathers had died. On the other hand, there were many new immigrants from Europe who came to the Soo at this time to get jobs in the steel mill and in forestry operations. The derogatory term was DP. If any of this was difficult for Mike, he handled it perfectly.

He would have known that success required him to fit in and that would mean not exposing the past. I expect that explains the close association with his mother. He addressed her as Mutti, and often had short asides with her in German even when I was present. But there was almost no talk of life in Europe. I sometimes wondered about Mike's past but must have received the message to leave it alone. I was told that Mike's uncle got himself on 'Hitler's blacklist' and that the family had to escape, and the boat his uncle got on happened to go to South America. It was implied that Eva had similar conditions, but the fact that one of Mike's grandparents was Jewish just never was hinted at. Mike must have known the stories but said nothing. My own family's church association was odd to Mike, as I have said. When I would talk about religion, he was typically puzzled. "Okay," he would say, and change the subject.

JANINE

We had a German delicatessen in town, and a small European community, we weren't all from the country you know. Confections and things from the German delicatessen were always on hand in their house. Eva always had specialty things, and a more robust kind of bread. She took delight in things like that.

KEN

I would say that his body was magnificent. In warm weather, it was not uncommon for Mike to be wearing only underwear in the house. Mike must have been very much in demand with girls. We all had girlfriends and went to dances and parties. The only serious girlfriend that I can remember Mike having was Janine and that must have been difficult since Janine's family was upper class and Mike did not have much money to fit in there. There may have been some conflict in that regard but Mike was not too concerned that Janine's father did not approve of him. Since I had access to a car, I did more things with the two of them than might be expected, but I was never at Janine's house.

JANINE

McGill Theatre: in some ways it is very vivid, and in some ways it was very long ago. At McGill there was a coterie of theatre people and they took a shine to him. I was taking fine arts and my professor looked at all of this scene—there always is these kind of connections on the campus—you have all sorts of little intrigues: he and the theatre critic for the *Montréal Star* who had an office on campus for a reason I don't remember—they found it amusing to refer to Michael as 'The Adonis'. The theatre critic—he was an open homosexual— certainly had his eye on Michael. At the time people weren't too open—but *he* was open. Anyways they both had a lot of fun calling Michael 'The Adonis'.

We were going out but it was a hard year. We didn't have any place to be, privately. He lived in a fraternity and I was in a girls' residence. And it was a difficult period for me personally, because my mother was dying at the time. So it was a grim year. Then Michael went to the audition and it didn't work and he started to focus on going over to Munich.

LOIS

I heard that he had committed suicide. That's the way it was told to me. That would have come from Mrs. Palumbo, who lived next door to Eva.

KEN

We all liked Antoine. He was an impressive man—did things well, and with good humour. Mike had much respect for him. Antoine owned a very old Morris Mini and I taught him to drive.

TREPLIOV

Well, my father was a member of the petty bourgeoisie, as you know—although he was a well-known actor too.

JANINE

Karl was his father, but I don't think he had any influence on Michael. It had been a bitter separation—Eva herself had very little contact with him. Occasionally there must have been contact, but it was slim. I met him once. It was 1957. August in Munich. I have a very clear memory of that. Michael hardly knew his father. He established contact when he went to live and study in Germany, but he didn't see him often because Karl was often travelling and often Michael was very involved with his own work. But the morning I met him, Karl had gone to the market and picked up a basket of fresh strawberries, so we met in a park and sat and got to know one another a little bit. I remember it vividly because it was such a lovely moment—sitting in a park and eating strawberries—he'd even thought of bringing some sugar so we could dip the strawberries, using the stems and dipping into the sugar, so it was a very sweet moment. But about Michael's relationship with his father afterwards—because there would be a number of years in Munich that they would overlap in various contexts because of the theatre: I don't know anything about that time.

KEN

We listened to the music of the day but preferred classical. That was what was played in his house and it became what I preferred. I took music lessons so I thought I knew what I was talking about in that category but when I once criticized some less-than-trained musician, Mike's response was, "Listen to it, it is what is being written now."

NICOLAS
He believed that without a tradition, Canada had no conception of what art 'is'.

JANINE
His stepfather Antoine Stehr was a very serene, Zen-like person who was good at giving advice. He helped to guide Michael. Young people liked Antoine very much. They were attracted to him. A lot of people looked up to him.

Maybe I was a little closed, earlier, on talking about whether Karl Paryla had an influence on Michael. There was a love-hate attitude in the Stehr house when his name came up. Once in a while there would be a letter and Eva would have hysterics about it. It was seldom, but every once in a while there would be something. Eva would rant. But she also took a considerable pride in the fact that Karl was a director and making a name for himself in Germany, so it was complicated. That was impressed on Michael. The kind of pride in someone who does well in the arts. It had to have been. But certainly in the time I knew Michael in Canada, Karl Paryla was not a name that was discussed, he didn't know his father, really. He didn't relate to him until he actually lived over there, and I only saw that one glimpse, our visit in the park.

KEN
One day, when Mike and I were on the way home from writing the grade thirteen English Departmental Exam, Mike told me

that he had answered the questions about the Shakespeare play based on a play other than the one that we had studied. Our marks for the year were based on that exam.

We worked at the CPR rail express and freight shed one summer. The next summer we both got shift work at the steel mill. I had a motorcycle. If our shifts coincided, Mike would ride with me to work, but just getting on a machine to ride was of no interest to him. I pretty much took the bike apart and put it back together. Mike had no interest in that.

I am thinking now that he must have spent much of his time reading. Considering what he did with the English exam, a lot of his time must have been spent reading Shakespeare and others. Later on, he must have been thinking theatre while saying chemistry. I wonder if it was to keep out of Eva's way.

SYBILLE

I was in Germany the summer of 1962. I was eighteen years old. Michael lived in Munich. We spent time together. He was extremely nice and it was there that he took me to the set where *The Great Escape* was being filmed. He spent a great deal of time showing me how the tunnel scenes were filmed, and answered my many questions. There was nothing much going on the day we visited the set, and he felt bad for me. I didn't really mind. I was there to see him. One of the stars was on the set, not Steve McQueen, another one. Charles Bronson. Bronson was loud and a show-off and when Michael offered to introduce me to him, I said no way. That guy was so full of himself!

I remember really enjoying my visit with Michael. He seemed to get a kick out of showing me around. He was warm and kind and I didn't feel he felt himself to be more important than the next guy.

That was the last time I saw him. As to the circumstances surrounding his death, here is what I know. He worked very hard and was interested in serious theatre acting. He was not interested in being a Hollywood superstar. His career advanced. Working late into the night and then sleeping late into the day put his schedule at odds with the normal daily schedule. He was usually keyed up at the end of his workday and had difficulty falling asleep. His doctor prescribed a sleep aid for him. He was tapped for a leading role in a theatre production. The premier performance was very successful. He received rave reviews. The celebration of his success lasted into the wee hours of the morning. During the post-premier celebration alcohol was served. How much he drank, I don't know. Unfortunately, when he arrived home, he took his normal sleep aid. That mixed with the alcohol killed him. He was only 31 or 32 years old. He had achieved great success with this performance, so he was in no way depressed. He had arrived, so to speak. His death devastated Eva.

JANINE
He was a gifted actor. But he didn't have major roles. He had minor parts. He didn't live long enough to have more.

TREPLIOV
I'm commonplace and insignificant.

JANINE
My family name being Blum, people would naturally assume. Same as with Eva's maiden name. But it isn't always that the person with that name is Jewish. We weren't brought up that way at all, neither was my father's family brought up in the Jewish faith. Michael's name of course was Paryla, and no one would assume anything. Living in the Soo, I knew two Jewish families. You just didn't talk about it and there was nothing to talk about.

Being German or being Jewish was not an issue. But I knew. I knew about his family background.[5]

My father was accused by Eva of trying to make trouble for the Stehrs when they went to get citizenship. But that was never proven and I think it was a case of Eva having an imagination, and her paranoia. My dad didn't have a clue about influencing anybody in government. He never took an interest in politics. But then I wouldn't know for sure. I wasn't living at home at the time. I was at McGill. After I left for university I really severed ties with the Soo. I had found it stifling.

*

Trepliov (*enters, hatless, carrying a gun, and a dead seagull*): Are you alone here?

Nina: Yes alone.

---

5   'His family background'; formerly the 'Jewish background': it's time for that genealogical note, as promised, before the chorus of voices severely underestimates the historical pressures and traditional forces behind what's in a name (though I do see Janine's point: being German or Jewish did not matter to *them*, they were in love. But alas.) Emil Hermann Siegfried Steinmetz, to give him his full name (Eva's father, Michael's grandfather) was born in Breslau in 1885 to Jewish parents, Gustav Steinmetz and Bertha Keiler. Emil Steinmetz married a non-Jewish woman (Else Strohwald), an event that, interestingly, took place in Kensington, London, England in 1908. Emil himself was baptized as a Lutheran in 1916, perhaps related to the fact that he was receiving lucrative wartime contracts from the German government during WWI. He was a leather-goods manufacturer, and examples of his wartime work include military pistol holsters and the leather lining bands of officers' helmets. Emil Steinmetz left Germany in the summer before WWII started, in 1939, and spent the wartime years in Colombia, South America. Emil was estranged from his only brother, Friedrich Steinmetz, born in 1891. Friedrich, unlike Emil, did not assimilate, and instead of Colombia sought refuge in Argentina, where Friedrich appears to have died in 1970. Friedrich's daughter, Bertha Erica Steinmetz (b. 1920), never left Germany. Deported from Breslau in 1942, she perished in the Shoah. Emil Steinmetz returned to live in Germany in the 1950s and died there in 1977. He was one of the few on hand who attended Michael's funeral in Munich in 1967. I am almost certain that Michael was unaware of his uncle Friedrich's existence, unawares too that Bertha Erica Steinmetz had been murdered in Auschwitz. Information about Friedrich and Bertha Steinmetz did not become known to me until late in 2012. Obviously there has been a lot going on—many forces at play: repression, avoidance, denial, ambivalence, assimilation—which has kept our Jewish background shrouded in intergenerational darkness.

(Trepliov *lays the seagull at her feet.*)

Nina: What does this mean?

Trepliov: I was despicable enough to kill this seagull today. I'm laying it at your feet.

Nina: What is the matter with you? (*Picks up the seagull and looks at it.*)

Trepliov (*after a pause*): Soon I shall kill myself in the same way.

Because words in Chekhov onstage are directly related to actions offstage; because Arkadina heckles the outdoor performance of Trepliov's play; because Nina says she is drawn to the lake on Sorin's estate 'like a seagull'; because Trepliov loves Nina, and because Nina stars in Trepliov's tedious new-agey playlet; because when Trepliov tells Nina he loves her, Nina responds 'shhh'; because Arkadina's lover, the writer, Trigorin, becomes interested in Nina; because Nina falls for Trigorin; because Arkadina is jealous, and because Trepliov is doubly jealous; because Arkadina calls Trepliov a 'non-entity', and because Trepliov feels like a non-entity in her presence; because Trepliov's father is missing from his life, yet influential; because nothingness and emptiness and impotence are leitmotifs for Trepliov; because Arkadina wills her son into non-being so she may not grow old; because after Trepliov's first attempt to take his life, Arkadina bandages his head, and warns him—when she is about to leave the estate again—she wants no more 'bang bang'; because Trepliov fails at art and at love.

*

JANINE

The last time I saw him was in 1962, before the movie was made, but he knew that he was going to be in it and he was quite excited talking about that. The excitement for him was being with all those renowned German actors. And then he died shortly after making the film. He was in Hamburg—wasn't he?—working on a play. The story given to me was that he was given uppers and downers, because you don't sleep very well when you have an exciting play, and it goes late: you arrive home and you need to come down, but you can't mix drugs with alcohol. That was the story—'that's what happened'. And Margaret was not implicated in any of that, was she?

I could not believe how little his part was in the film. He had such a minor role.

KEN

Mike had some permanent damage as a result of mumps. It definitely had gone into the testes. He'd mentioned it on more than a couple of occasions when Eva was present. It was obvious that it had been serious. At the least, it would have been very painful and very scary at the time. However, I am certain that there was some permanent effect. I understand that in rare cases sterility can occur.

> Arkadina: You won't play about with a gun again when I'm away, will you?
> Trepliov: No, Mama. That was a moment of mad despair, when I had no control over myself. It won't happen again. (*Kisses her hands.*) You've got magic hands.

EVA

The tragedy was that he got involved with a woman who was ten years older than him. I never met her, but she had a son, who was eighteen, and they wanted to send him from Germany to Canada, to do his high-school again. And when he came to us—a young person so dishonest and misled and confused—we had to send him back. It was a catastrophe. He was a total mess. Jerry.

Knowing this boy, Jerry, I knew that this woman had to be sick. I could not do anything for Michi, he had to find out for himself, he had to untangle the knot. You know, Michael was such a straight, honest person. And he wasn't anymore. He did things later... I just shudder.

Of course Margaret, she was extremely angry when her son was sent back to Germany. Irene, my sister in Munich, tried to contact Michi about the whole business. He wouldn't listen to her or to me. We had not been in touch. Michi was in Hamburg. He had this engagement with a theatre, and he was under such pressure from that woman—so that's where he died, in Hamburg. She died the year later, from a brain tumour, on the operating table. I always knew that woman was sick.

KEN

He did not do well at school—although that surprises me. I have found a clipping from the *Star* dated August 19, 1955. It lists the students' marks from the grade thirteen examinations at the Collegiate Institute. Mike's marks were Eng. Comp. 50, Eng. Lit. 56, Alg. 50, Geom. 77, Trig 51, Botany 60, Phys. 60, Chem. 67.

TERRY (Eva's friend)

I shared a house with Eva in London, Ontario, for several years. Eva never talked to me much about Michael, and to be honest, I never encouraged her to talk about him. I figured if she wanted to tell me anything about him, she would do so on her own accord. She did however tell me that he had killed himself, and she thought drugs had something to do with it. She mentioned "the woman" but never went too deeply into it. After Eva died I did find a couple of photos of Michael and I believe I still have them tucked away somewhere. There's no doubt that Michael had what you might call "movie star" good looks, sort of a James Dean looking sort.

KEN

I saw Eva the following year. It was awkward because, although Eva seemed pleased for a visit, she told me not to mention Mike.

EVA

I would have gone to Germany, but I couldn't.

JANINE

For some reason that I never fathomed, there was a rift between Eva and Michael. I never understood what was going on there, with Margaret, his girlfriend or wife—or why Eva had removed herself from contact. She didn't hear from him for years. And then after he died, she slept beside a photograph of him, which she had on her bed table, for twenty-seven years. But at the end of her life, when my sister went to see her in hospital she wouldn't open that door. 'It's too late, it's too late.'

*

Special Consultation Room. National Library and Archives, Ottawa. On the 3rd floor, I have been instructed to wear white cotton gloves when handling the material. The material is Michael. In March 1956, he played Claudio in the English Department's production of William Shakespeare's *Much Ado About Nothing*. There are no extant reviews. This is because there are gaps in the publication schedule of *The McGill Daily*. One such hole begins early in March 1956, before *Much Ado* opened at Moyse Hall. Publication of the newspaper recommenced in May. Convocation season. But not for Michael. He dropped out of his year at McGill in April and left Montréal in the fall for Munich. To become an actor. And maybe because the advances of a married woman, the weight of a lover, the pressure of his Arkadinian mother, his father's whirlpooling void, were too much for The Adonis.

There has to be more to find out about his time in Sault Ste. Marie and at McGill, and to do this I had intended to query a few more 'names' from Michael's past, and to return to several of the known 'key players', like his good pal Ken Taylor or the straight-talking Lois Rodger. But after transcribing and reading the material through, I thought differently. I had enough. Just enough? It didn't seem right that I should go back for second looks. Second or third conversations invoked the spectre of police work, and statements under oath. Going back would entice embellishment or self-censorship, and also draw more attention upon me, more reflection upon my motives, when many of these people I talked with already had preconceived notions, having read my portrait of the lady.[6] In their eyes, I was either heretic or hagiographer, and I didn't feel comfortable in either role.

You see, almost without exception, Michael's people belonged, at one time or another, to the cult of Eva. What they remembered about Michael or Mike or Michi was often preceded by fond memories of his mother. They remembered her Whippets and Borzoi, her bridge playing and cigarette smoking, her personal style and cooking, above all her life stories—about Bimbo, the pet monkey she had as a child in Breslau; about her mother's death from tuberculosis; about her brother and father committing her to an asylum in Germany because she pursued acting; about her marrying Karl Paryla to get away from her family; learning to play accordion in Zurich; about the dangers of her post at Radio Berlin and the invitation to become a spy for the Russians. They remembered these stories, from Eva's canon, and also they remembered that which infused her voice: her larger-than-life manner of being. And, without exception, they bore witness to the profound influence Michael's mother

6   My novel *Eva's Threepenny Theatre*, published in 2008, had made the rounds.

and stepfather Antoine had had on their own lives; how each of them, each their own way, were touched by this pair. Eva took people in when people needed taking in. We need to be understood most when we don't understand ourselves. They talked to me about Eva as, I began to feel, Michael himself would never have talked about his own mother.

Eva figured in my own childhood, and always in the back of my mind was a story I'd heard about her and *The Threepenny Opera.* I didn't know much about the playwright Bertolt Brecht initially, but in my early twenties I played in a rock band in Montréal, and one night while we were in the studio making a recording I got to talking with the sound engineer about Kurt Weill. When we were done putting down tracks for the evening the sound engineer pulled out a record of Lenya performing 'Seeräuberjenny' and 'Kanonen-Song'. That was it. The world-weary killer instinct: Eva talked like that. She could put on a kind of kitsch, and roll to that droll, aloof, harsh cabaret style.

It was easy, suddenly, to see Eva as a product of Weimar Germany, manufactured by that precise period evoked by Brecht & Weill's songs. As a socialist playwright, Brecht wouldn't touch naturalism, which he considered an endorsement of the bourgeois world view. Eva was schooled in Brecht, and so it felt right that a novel based on her life story should put up with ideas of alienation and detachment in an effort to ... I don't know, bring about a little genre consciousness.

Before leaving Montréal in 1956, I like to think that *Mike* had time on his hands, time and the inclination to peruse the INCO advertisement, which appears in the May 25th edition of *The McGill Daily*: "Almost two million pounds of INCO Nickel will help brighten Canadian cars in 1956 ... more jobs for Canadians at the International Nickel Company of Canada."

Sault Ste. Marie, on the shores of Lake Superior, is not far from the INCO mines. I doubt Mike had it in him to return there.

So: Germany.

His mother did not approve. Eva didn't want him to return *there*. But she and Antoine couldn't afford to send him to New York, the only other acceptable option, in their minds, where he could train as an actor. "In Canada, it was shit." Direct quote from Eva's mouth. Michael called Canada a desert. So it was back to Europe. At least in Munich he could stay with relatives, including Eva's sisters, Irene and Melanie, and father, Emil, all of whom had spent the war years in Germany.

Despite his mother's misgivings, Michael was back on German soil, only seven years after leaving the DP camp in Lahr. He was fourteen then; he is twenty-one now. His return allowed him to renew contact with his biological father, though the relationship between the two would always be strained. Karl Paryla had lived and worked in the early years of the GDR, in East Berlin, but he retained his permanent residence in Vienna, with his second wife, the actor Hortense Raky, and their children, the actors Nicholas and Stephan Paryla-Raky.

When Janine Blum visited Michael in the summer of 1957, the couple toured the Swiss Alps. They went to see his elementary school, a Waldorf school, which Janine remembers was located in Habkern and not in Zurich after all. Habkern is a German–speaking municipality in the canton of Bern. The word is derived from the Old High German word for 'hawk' and Habkern wikipediately is 'the place where there are many hawks.' Hawks perhaps, but not a place of many people. The municipality's population in 1951 hovered below seven hundred. Whether Michael attended a school in the place of many hawks or in Zurich, place of many ultra-rich, is neither here nor there. That it drew him back, in his twenties, and he revisited his school with his girlfriend is the point. His school made an impression on him. Michael had so few places like it, that he could name home, no permanent address. Born in exile, he was essentially a refugee and of undetermined nationality since birth. Yet he remembered the Waldorf school fondly. There must have been a reason.

During their travels, in Zurich, Michael and Janine stopped in at Café Select. During the Second World War years, Café Select was a headquarters for emigrants, misfits, pacifists and anti-fascists, and it was here that Michael's stepfather Antoine often went to pass the time. Eva and Antoine found each other in Zurich. But for Michael and Janine, Zurich was no place to rest. They toured the Bernese Alps and gazed upon the Eiger and Shreckhorn, before returning to Munich and finally saying their goodbyes. Michael had no intention of returning to Canada. Janine, no plan to stay in Germany. So: heartbreak. Janine would follow Michael's successes in acting from afar, through her relationship with Eva, which stayed strong.

Michael met Margaret Jahnen by 1959. They did not marry, but the couple lived in Munich as husband and wife, with Margaret's teenage son, Jerry. Margaret goes down in history as 'that woman', an older woman. She was not Michael's first association with an older woman, if we are to believe in the advances of the wife of one of his former professors at McGill. His relationship with Margaret Jahnen led to a prolonged estrangement with Eva. (Somehow, no surprise there.) Moreover, the couple experienced money troubles and Michael worked a series of odd jobs on top of his acting gigs. Chronic financial worries and professional jealousies led to tension with his father. Soon, the only person left in his corner was Margaret, about whom the family then and now remains wilfully ignorant.

After the lean first years, his career gradually took off and he earned engagements in theatres in Bremen and in Hamburg. His acting credits include television and film roles. An extra in the film *Der Engel, der seine Harfe versetzte* (1959); Francisco in *Hamlet, Prinz von Dänemark*, a television production staring Maximilian Schell (1961); he played an extra in the film *Die Schatten werden länger*—Defiant Daughters, The Shadows Grow Longer (1961). He was Fred Nicolls in a TV production of *Der Strohhalm*, Eugene O'Neill's 'The Straw' (1964), and he appeared in *Aktion T 4* and *Aktion Brieftaube—Schicksale im geteilten Berlin* (1964). But from the beginning of his career he focused on becoming a stage actor. Early highlights include the part of Don Cesar in a production of *Ein Bruderzwist in Habsburg* by Franz Grillparzer, a play about a fratricidal quarrel, and a role in the August Everding production of *L'Affaire Dreyfus* by Hans Rehfisch, a play which focuses on the 1894 trial for treason of Alfred Dreyfus, a Jewish artillery officer in the French military falsely accused and eventually pardoned. He also found himself in the role of Cosimo de Medici in a 1959 production of Bertolt Brecht's *Life of Galileo* at the Munich Kammerspiele, the same play in which his father was cast for the 1943 World Premiere in Zurich.

Eleven years to make it. Time was short.

LETTERS TO EVA

It is very difficult for me to write this letter to you, as it contains news that will affect you just as deeply as it has affected me.

Du must allen Mut und alle Kraft zusammen nehmen, um die schreckliche Tatsache aufnehmen und ertragen zu koennen.

You need to gather all your courage and all your strength in order to absorb and deal with the awful facts.

Her lips part then bump like clouds. This is Karl Paryla's handwriting. Sounding words, knowing meaning will strike not much later.

I can't believe it yet myself and I don't know where to turn or to seek comfort. *Aber*—But—I have taken it upon myself to deliver terrible news; the worst thing that could have happened to us. *Unser Michael ist nicht mehr.* Our Michael is no more. He died last night in Hamburg.

The incident is still completely inexplicable, but I see it as my duty to immediately inform you of anything I know.

Michael was supposed to go on stage at the Thalia Theatre in Hamburg yesterday; when he didn't show up, they broke into his room and he was lying in his bed, sleeping.

Eva breaks here—numb, mumbling 'lying in his bed, sleeping'—*and follows the route upstairs from the kitchen and along the narrow hall. Pressing her skirt between her legs, she slips into his bedroom to find the sunshine amassed on the rug and the cat warm on the pillow at the head of his bed.* Aber. *Michael is no more.* But. *Memory believes. Memory is certain of a hole before Karl's letter grips her again and she slumps on her side on the bed: Michael with a fever after having his tonsils removed, Michael and his barking cough, when it was past time to turn out the light and stop him reading. When it was morning again, she would wake him, a boy of fourteen, fifteen, her fine blond boy. Her son. Her only child.*

Beside him, a half-empty bottle of whisky and a pill bottle, from which he had evidently taken sleeping pills. He suffered from insomnia and the pills had been prescribed by a doctor. He was brought to St. Georg Hospital by ambulance, where a Dr. Wuehler (with whom I've spoken on the phone) attempted resuscitation. *Herzmassage,* cardiac massage, artificial respiration. But nothing helped anymore.

Because it was already broken. His heart. Or because they broke it with force, compressing his ribs, shooting blood through four chambers, they tried to squeeze him out from underneath but the weight... it was too much, he was already so weak.

He was already so weak and exhausted that he died, without regaining consciousness, shortly after entering the hospital.

*She reads from left to right, in one eye out the other: Das Motiv eines Selbstmordes war nicht auszuschliessen, suicide was not dis-*counted, even though there was no indication to that effect. Only further investigation will shed light on the matter.

Eva rests her head on the pillow. The cat hops off the bed. The telephone rings. Antoine. Calling from the lab. What loneliness she feels. She inhales linen, a mouthful of the dry fabric sticks, the tingling cuts her tongue. Selbstmordes. Self-murder. Self-slaughter. Which is better? German or English? She can taste his scalp. He would reek like black pepper when he sweated, when she held him in her arms and kissed the crown of his head. What good is it? Michael is no more. Whosoever has seen a happy thing fall, has stood at the abyss…

I am interrupting my work here in Vienna and will drive to Hamburg and only then will I be able to gain some clarity on all the circumstances surrounding his death. All the people I questioned over the phone today, and who had been in close contact with him, tend to believe it was an accident. A combination of sleeping pills and alcohol. A few weeks ago I was able to see him for myself in Hamburg. I spent a lot of time with him and got the impression that he had matured and was on the right path. He was in great shape and great spirits. He had a respectable contract, a successful career, good prospects.

But. Eva knows he was a clown. Michael was a practical joker. At Collegiate High-school, the first year they had arrived in Canada, from Germany, his teachers had told her this; and Eva never forgot it—the expression was one she had never heard before: 'Practical joker'. 'Your son is a practical joker.' Was it something good? Maybe it was. Laughter is lucky. In any event, to Eva the expression sounded like Canada and America, it was a confirmation or a baptism.

There had been exile and immigration; and now, assimilation. Canada was a land of practical jokers and her son Michael and his new friend Ken Taylor were maybe the biggest jokers in all Sault Ste. Marie. For teenage boys, they were harmless, which she liked. They went fishing together and for 'picnics' (which also sounded very nice). They played on the railway tracks and in the schoolyard. She liked it that boys this age could be soft and that Michael and Ken were buddies. 'Buddies'. Buddies and practical jokers. Michael had matured and was on the right path, alright, alright, but Eva hadn't forgotten that Michael was a practical joker—which is to say he might have surprised them all, but not her, not his own mother— Michael had spent the war in Austria and in Switzerland, and then two years in war-destroyed Berlin, before emigrating here to the land of milk and cookies and picnics with bosom buddies. Michael had been a DP from birth. At fourteen, he was more sophisticated than any of his teachers or buddies could fathom. He was good at hiding who he was. And where he was from. He was a natural. Out there he was acting. But inside Michael was at war. Eva knew.

Also, it is in no way certain whether a sudden physical distress didn't cause his death. I will find out and let you know. His 'wife', with whom he had been living for years, was not there with him. But they were on excellent terms and they loved each other very much.

Eva, it would be easier for me than it actually is if I could tell you something about his death, and I can only ask that Antoine stands by you. It's terrible that I can only express myself in words now, and from such a great distance, and not take the two of you in my arms as friends.

Believe me, Eva, I feel your pain, along with mine. *The letter was sent Express and mailed to the wrong address. There is no indication as to when it arrived nor whether it is by this means that Eva first learned of Michael's death. Cross-Atlantic telephone calls were not the norm at the time.* My sorrowful condolences. I embrace you. Your Karl.

21 APRIL 1967 FROM VIENNA

Liebe Eva. A second correspondence from Karl sent Registered Mail. This is a lengthy letter, three pages, both sides, tightly scrawled. He waited three months to respond to her letter because he was on a Germany-wide tour that lasted several months.

I was often driving the Autobahn 8 hours per day, then stepping on stage, to perform every night, before travelling the next day to the next place in the next city. I also hesitated because I wanted to obtain more facts about Michi's death. To complicate matters, the pathologist (Professor Franz) insisted on transmitting the autopsy report in person, and so I had to wait until I could go to Hamburg strictly for this purpose.

I had a long talk with Professor Franz, and it turns out that Michi effectively was not healthy, and that scars in his myocardium decisively contributed to his unfortunate passing. He also asked me about his childhood illnesses, among other things, whether he had had jaundice. I remember that you once wrote to me worriedly about this from Canada. In his opinion, the scars or damage in his myocardium could have stemmed from an infection following an operation to the tonsils. Aside from that, there were no other critical findings. In any case, Antoine and Hermann Hans will better be able to discern the facts from the autopsy report, a copy of which I'm enclosing. The report as you will see for yourself is thorough and well done.

While in Hamburg, I also spoke in person with the doctor who was in charge of incoming patients at the hospital. Dr. Wuehler made a good impression; he is a serious young doctor. Trust me, he did everything in his power to help Michael, but, regretfully, the condition was too advanced. He made all the customary and necessary attempts, but it had been too late for Michi, the drug had been in his body for too long, total exhaustion, comatose.

At his apartment everything was as it had been after the incident. No evidence of suicide. He was alone. The door was locked from the inside.

At 6:00 (obviously PM) the alarm clock went off. Michi surely wanted to be awoken for the evening's performance.

At 8:00 PM, the theatre staff noticed he was missing. Approximately two hours elapsed before the administrative director, Rolf Mares—who I met, and is very kind and considerate—telephoned everywhere, and Margaret, who was in Munich, said (when she was contacted) to break open the apartment.

Nach deutscher Art wurde erst Polizei und Feuerwehr geholt; leider leider kein Arzt.

In German fashion, first the police and fire department came; regrettably, regrettably no doctor. This was a mistake. Perhaps he should not have been transported to the hospital. Some days ago I read an article reporting from a medical conference that said rapid transportation is no longer recommended in the case of cardiovascular collapse. On-site transfusions are apparently in order. In Vienna, a doctor comes along with the rescue crew. That was not the case in Hamburg; Michael did not come under a doctor's care until he reached the hospital.

I also thought of crime. Hamburg is a wild city. The St. Pauli borough, where Michi stayed, is known for prostitution and drugs and home to mobs from around the world. The police investigated the case, but quickly dropped the hypothesis of foul play as unlikely. In my opinion, the conduct of the police was negligent to say the least; and I'm not excluding the possibility that someone put a drug in Michael's drink, sometime during the day, in order to steal from him. One reads such stories in the newspapers all the time. Narcotics used for the sake of robbery. As a matter of fact, the police were unable to determine who had been with Michi during the final 24 hours before his death.

As far as I was informed, he didn't lead an unusual or dissolute life; on the contrary, it was built on humanity and camaraderie. That's clear. His friend Ralf Becher, a stage director in Bremen, a very proper chap, with whom Michi stayed, says that he was just always into the nightlife and was difficult to persuade to stay home once in a while. But perhaps he was neither physically nor psychologically suited for this lifestyle. Despite his success Michi suffered from insomnia. And so in terms of his health, he bit off more than he could chew.

But all in all, his career was the most important thing to him. Acting was his life's hope and purpose. This I know. This I can understand.

I have to say that, when she was with him, Margaret fostered a certain careless sense of allegiance in him. What you told me about her doesn't surprise me. Unfortunately, she would also cause rifts between Michael and us [Hortense and Karl

Paryla] every so often. But he was attached to her and viewed her expressly as his wife, even though she wasn't officially. The story with Jerry, for instance, also drove us apart. We were very opposed to her sending her child away. But she presented it all to us through rose-coloured glasses. The two of you apparently exchanged the friendliest of letters. And the scandal was that you had found Jerry to be a nutcase. Trips and telephone calls had cost a fortune. [7] Michael later came to me for money. I told him that Margaret was responsible for this whole affair. And since repayment was out of the question, all contact with Michi broke off. I didn't see him again until months later in Hamburg, and we got along very nicely and fondly.

I couldn't understand what he had against you and why he didn't write to you. What was it? What did he have against his own mother? Hortense and I always told him to write to you, and he promised he would. Regrettably, regrettably, you and I were no example. We had no contact. Perhaps together we could have influenced certain things. Perhaps together we could have done more for him? The right thing to do was once very simple. I am immensely reproachful toward myself. Certainly, a grown man is no longer a child that one can raise; certainly, one can entertain objections against one's children's partners. I always did against Margaret—swindling, magniloquent and yarn-spinning Margaret—whose character Michi obviously relished, but finally one should fight for those we love so dearly without holding back.

Nevertheless, we can't blame Margaret for our child's death. She took great care of him; he had a nice, positively luxurious

---

7   It's unclear what 'sending her child away' means in the context. Karl is possibly referring to the time Jerry spent visiting with Eva in Canada. Or had Margaret dispatched her son elsewhere; perhaps dismissed him from Michael and Margaret's home? This business of trips and money regarding Jerry remains obscure.

home of which he was very proud, and he was well-adjusted, he felt like the head of the family. They were still badly off when Jerry went to visit you; at the time, Michi worked odd jobs, and you might have viewed his existence as a dismal one—but that had since changed and he no longer lived in the jungle anymore. He had fixed contracts, in which I passionately encouraged him—though every now and then he dreamed of a fast-track star career in the U.S.

Overall, though, his life had become too middle-class for my taste. I am giving you such a detailed account of everything so that you get the right impression.

Liebe Eva, I feel your crushing pain. I think of you often and, when I do, I am frightened, my heart is filled with shock and compassion. I have three children and am very attached to them, but you know what Michi meant and always will mean to us; like you, I can hardly grasp what's happened and, now that I've gotten old, I'll never get over it.

This very child is a part of our life, a part that has since fallen away; I can find neither comfort nor solace. I will think of him and grieve with you for as long as I live. I went to see his grave today and spoke with him—as a communist I can't be religious—I spoke with his memory: his memory is alive. I held the deceased Michael in my arms and kissed him, but all I ever see is the living, cheerful Michael, and I hear him speak every day; I can't imagine the deceased Michael. He lies in a very beautiful, unusual cemetery in the woods; his wish was to be in Munich—the city held a special place in his heart. It is the Waldfriedhof in Grünewald. The forest extends seamlessly behind the cemetery; the street is called Am Wildwechsel. Tall trees tower over his grave. From here, by the moss and the tall forest trees above his resting place, I send my regards to you with this letter. Yours, Karl.

For the next while, until about mid-June, I will be in Stuttgart. Hotel Buchenhof. Otherwise, Vienna.

Bottom page, under his signature:

Eva: I had a death mask made of Michi; it turned out beautifully. Since it's made of plaster (I have a second one for you), I can't really send it over. But, if you want, I could have a bronze cast made in Vienna and send it to you. This would be much better.

Things are brittle as they are. He leaves it up to her.

15 JULY 1967, PALACE HOTEL MEGGIORATO, ABANO TERME

Liebe Eva, I am in Italy, finally enjoying a badly needed vacation and have the time to answer your letter. Marianne, with the two girls, visited us in Stuttgart; she is still the same exceptionally calming person. I was thrilled to see her again; it's a pity that Hermann Hans was not with us. It's especially a pity that they have all gone to Vietnam now. Only this morning I read in the newspaper about Vietnam. It is a war I cannot understand. Hopefully they will return from the witch's cauldron soon. Especially because you need the closeness of those dearest to you, those whose influence and sympathy are important to you especially now.

Eva flattens the letter on the table and looks straight out the kitchen window. Marianne. First a friend, then sister-in-law. Undoubtedly she was the same, the same exceptionally calming person.

*Almost an un-person. Marianne was on her way with Hermann
Hans to Vietnam, where as a volunteer psychiatrist with the American
Hospital Association he would be put in charge of establishing the Bien
Hoa Mental Hospital. Her brother knew his way around the globe of
human theatre. Hermann Hans got himself on Hitler's blacklist and
had left Germany in 1935. Hermann Hans and Marianne got themselves on a boat that sailed from Italy to South America. Colombia. Yes,
alright, but Hermann Hans had gotten himself on Eva's blacklist way
back in 1928, when he, along with her father, Emil, had committed
her to an asylum. In order to make her bend to their will. In order
to break her. In those days, many years ago, they had strongly advised
Eva to give up the theatre, and had discouraged her relationship with
Karl. She didn't listen to them, so they twisted her arm, fractured perhaps but had not broken her spirit. Karl's good manners when writing
about Hermann Hans and family represent, what? That a troubled
past is forgiven. Present lives are arduous enough.*

I spoke with Marianne at length about Michi and all con-
comitant circumstances. She also showed me letters from Michi.
But to what end? I cannot find peace anywhere. I also find it
unsettling that there is so little convincing evidence surrounding any cause or blame for Michi's death. You say you showed
the autopsy report to experts. But your judgment of the clinical finding from the St. Georg Hospital is completely aberrant.
You must believe me that Michi's health was not the greatest.
I told you, he had a previous collapse in Bremen. He suffered
a nervous breakdown that apparently significantly affected the
condition that led to his death. It is conceivable, even likely,
that this episode would have ended in death for Michael, but
fortunately in Bremen he was not alone, and he received treatment for a long while and recovered, unfortunately under the
supervision of a doctor whom I wouldn't necessarily trust. But
where are trustworthy doctors to be found?

I insisted on the autopsy report because I couldn't shake the feeling that Michi's health at the end had something to do with his breakdown. I haven't given up on investigating the situation and will continue to look into it when I work in Hamburg for a few weeks next season. I will above all raise the *decided* objections of your doctor of confidence.[8] And also I will once again try to ascertain who, if anybody, Michael was with the night he died. Establishing full clarity about all the unsettled details of his death has no value whatsoever for our poor boy, and yet it is a part of his short life, and we owe it to him to follow every trail to the end.

I fully understand that this is constantly on your mind, but I hope that you don't get any mistaken ideas. Everything I discover I will report to you. I didn't know that Antoine was so sick, and ask you to give him my kindest regards. It is a chaotic, horrible world that we are growing old into, and it is important to be surrounded by people who still make life seem meaningful.

In fourteen days I will be in Vienna again. Please do write to me about everything that troubles you about Michi's fate.

I send my deepest regards to you both, and embrace you. Karl.

There were no more letters.

---

8   No record as to what these objections were.

Cousins And Kunst

I REMEMBER MARIENPLATZ. I came here in the summer of 1981, when I was fifteen, to apprentice with my uncle Michael Friederichsen. He is a Kunstler, an artist who works his alchemy on silver, wood, stained glass, and bronze. At six foot three, Herr Friederichsen was large, a trembling hillside of emotion and eccentricity. Besides making jewelry and sculpture, he designed public fountains and playgrounds, even church interiors. His English was poor to non-existent, his laugh infectious.

When I arrived at the house that first morning, having made my way from the Heimstetten S-Bahn stop, I was wearing my John Lennon RIP T-shirt. I never took it off that summer. Herr Friederichsen glanced at the bespectacled Beatle, and shook his head, whimsically.

"Andy-boy, Ja Ja. Da ist Andy-boy."

I let my pack slide off my back.

"Isn't it?" He did not really question it, but had a way of speaking.

I reached out my hand.

Thereafter, I was his. Herr Friederichsen would not release me for a good month. He peered down at my shoes, inspected my jeans and shirt while turning me this way and that way—I felt lightweight and modest, a facile thing swayed by force of his mountainous bulk. We were doing a formal dance. And then he started to whimper, and the idling tremor culminated in girlish giggles and squeals broken only by a fragment of that phrase "*Andy-boy, Ja, Ja. Das ist.*" Herr Friederichsen was a sight who made a spectacle of anyone in his grip.

The final laugh: "*Ka-na-a-disch. Ja, Ja. Er ist Kanadier.*" He appealed to his wife, Mehtild, and present children, the twins, Markus and Andreas, who were seated at an outdoor table. The twins were partially obscured behind white geysers of cigarette smoke. "Come on now, isn't it? *Kanadisch.*"

Sure. Canadian. Full stop and applause. House down. I'm hilarious because my grandparents fled this country in '35.

"*Genau,*" the calm Mehtild eventually rescued me. "You are our guest. Stay with us as long as it is best. Yes. This is right?" The declarative sing-song of her English was both unsettling and comforting.

"*Prima.*" Herr Friederichsen would always give his blessing this way. Prima.

Herr Friederichsen alone did not smoke. Soon I would take up the habit; the twins Markus and Andreas, two years my senior, would get me into the game—toss juggling apples and bean bags while nursing a Marlboro; setting fire to newspaper boxes on street corners; swimming in the local quarry. They were natural at nudity and delinquency, the twins were, very agile naturists. I was easily influenced.

"*Ja. Ja.*" He started up again, shaking his head in large disbelief. "*Das ist Andy-boy.*"

I spent a month learning at the big man's elbow, making my copper bowl, a bronze candle holder, a silver cross—Herr Friederichsen showing me how it is done. Impatient, I would force my work, and rush the process, while he whistled a popular tune. Often it was 'Bridge Over Troubled Water', which played on American Forces Network Europe.

In my spare time, when I was not apprenticing to become a *Künstler* in the family way, I hung out with my cousins, and on weekends we would take Herr Meyer, a life-sized doll—half-scarecrow, half-mannikin—for a ride on the S-Bahn. Herr Meyer slouched in his seat without our support and, having arrived at our destination, we'd inquire of him, "What's wrong with you, Herr Meyer? Come now. Have you beans in your ears?" He would be carried through the underground and up the escalator, where, gradually, Meyer would emerge with us into sunlight and that grand public city square, Marienplatz.

Ah, Marienplatz. Herr Meyer was our prop. We lunched with him and brought him shopping for second-hand clothes. One afternoon, we waited at the Heimstetten S-Bahn station for the train. Suddenly Markus or Andreas—it doesn't matter which—lifted Herr Meyer off the bench and launched him headfirst onto the tracks. We ran like hell, and likely never made it to the square that day.

That same summer in Munich I met another cousin, Stephanie. Cousin Stephanie was a surprise—her name, which I fancied from the beginning; the strong cigarettes, the green necklace, her cropped hair, and the cobra neck. Stephanie was confident, disinterested, responsibly detached and unique: she was European. Visiting from France, where she lived, she snick-ered when I spoke my Québec French, and grimaced at my T-shirt's decorative sparkles. John Lennon in his oval spectacles was trapped under a coating of plastic that made my stomach bead with sweat. Stephanie was unimpressed. I felt that heavily—her disdain for kitsch—and yet, however forbidden and arrogant the fruit which had fallen from the family tree, I was attracted. Stephanie: absently pinching the strap of her brassiere and letting the white elastic snap, staccato against her skin. Stephanie: pout-ing as she mixed her mother-tongue French with a smudge of German and polished off an ice cream on... Marienplatz.

Cousins. I am idling today at a table in an Internet café near Marienplatz, thinking about cousins—Michael Friederichsen and Michael Paryla and my father Nicolas are cousins—and making connections between past and present, when I—*der kanadische Schriftsteller Andrew Steinmetz*—receive an email from Sandra Asche of the Thalia Theatre. Fräulein Asche writes from Hamburg, where, "Deep in the basement of the theatre, I found the answer to your question. In Hamburg, he stayed on Mühlendamm Strasse."

Interesting. Mühlendamm Strasse is in the St Georg district of Hamburg, and not in St Pauli, the neighbourhood Karl Paryla describes as Michael's in his letter to Eva dated January 20, 1967. But maybe forty years ago St Pauli and St Georg were the same or almost the same thing; perhaps like cousins. I reply to Fräulein Asche that I am coming by train to Hamburg in several days to visit the city's theatre archives which are held at Hamburg University. *Click.* Fräulein Asche has offered to give me a tour of Thalia Theatre, where at the time of his death Michael was performing two plays in repertory, Shakespeare's *Measure for Measure* and Shaw's *The Apple Cart*. *Click.* I don't have his Hamburg address—not yet, and maybe never—but things are falling together nicely. I've not been in Germany two days and already the email from Fräulein Asche and the name of his street unearthed from the depths of the old Thalia Theatre. What other shred of Michaelmania is to be found in the basement of that theatre, I wonder? Lennon once bragged he was born in Liverpool, but grew up in Hamburg. What ghosts haunt the stage and back-corridor dressing rooms and mirrors? I'll go have an unsentimental look at the place. I'll snoop around Mühlendamm Strasse and the St Georg Hospital, where Michael was transported by ambulance on the evening of his emphatic escape.

Ultimately, I'd like to find out *if it was an accident*. Why knowing should matter is not obvious. The truth is maybe secondary to the necessity to know. When the case of Michael is discussed among family, typically we rely on a number of phrases. 'Michael died from an overdose'—we always say this, but always pause before adding—'It was an accident.' Sometimes a variation: 'He was drinking and taking sleeping pills'—pause—'Most probably it was an accident'. Eva had her ideas, which she kept mostly to herself, divulging instead anger. Karl had doubts. Was it an accident? I'm not implying that I expect to dig up the truth—that's not realistic, probably not possible—though, like POW escape stories, the labyrinthine search for truth provides a convenient narrative vector. It gives my quest a theatrical core. And true enough, as I travel, by the day I feel more and more implicated, as though something important is happening of which I am equal parts witness and creator. Before setting out, I took acting lessons. Just a couple. They'll come in handy later, I feel.

For as long as I can remember, I knew two things about him. Michael had acted in a famous war movie and he'd died young. It was all that I knew, this was the sum of my knowledge about him, but it was enough for the mind to play with for years. Discrete facts—war movie; died young—but I inferred causality. He died young because he had appeared in that movie. Now that was something for the unconscious to turn over and over without a care in the world for proof.

Eventually I found out the movie's name, but for many years I had only a slippery hold on what his role was. Growing up in the 1970s, I had no easy access to viewing the movie unless it was broadcast on television. I had read a fair amount of Second World War history, and I did watch my share of war movies on TV. *The Great Escape* was not one of them. I saw it for the first time in my late teens. Already I had learned that

Michael appears in the train scene. That he plays a German. But after watching the movie, I really couldn't be bothered with him. He wasn't a star by a long shot, and I was too immature to appreciate that Being Not McQueen made Michael someone just as interesting to follow on screen, and off. I had yet to learn that just possibly every ordinary human life is heroic, and the fact that most ordinary lives are forgotten makes them that much more heroic.

After Eva moved to Québec in the late seventies, closer to my home, I overheard somewhere that Michael had in fact died of an overdose. Eva didn't talk much about Michael. She kept mum about him. He was a taboo subject. I must had heard 'overdose' from a different source. My parents probably. Only when Eva moved away years later, and years after that when I went to see her in London, Ontario, to record her oral history, did I become acutely aware of Michael. His absence at her death made me recognize that his death was the tragedy of her life.

To me, overdose could only mean suicide, and the idea that someone in my family had committed suicide was enthralling. I romanticized his death, for a while anyway, just as I had for a time romanticized two of my great uncles, my grandmother's brothers Abelard and Hrolf, who'd fought in the Third Reich. All romance ended when I learned a dark secret about Hrolf Kramm. It was Eva who told me about that.

This visit to Munich I am staying near Rosenheimer Platz with my 'cousin' Joerg Hahn. Herr Friederichsen, Joerg's uncle and my former mentor, is on vacation in Turkey. Shame. Herr Friederichsen was one of a handful in attendance at Michael's funeral in 1967. I would have liked to have taken him on the road when I go to visit Michael's grave in the south of Munich, an event I'm keeping for last.

Joerg reminds me a lot of his uncle. Large, barrel-chested, inflammatory, histrionic for sure, but gentle and kind and jovial too. His sparse ginger beard crowns an oft-raised chin, lending him a somewhat gallant air. Joerg works at NBC Universal's German subsidiary of The History Channel. He tells me it's his first 'real' job, after studying political science at university. A curious choice, since best I can tell Joerg is a self-hating German, the real thing. But perhaps The History Channel is perfect motivation and gets him out of bed early.

After two days, I have surmised that the only thing that Joerg likes (loves fanatically) about Germany is German soccer. Everything is permeated with "The fucking German way we do things here." The fucking German way (The FGW) is a daily complaint, the caption to the scowl Joerg wears when reading the morning newspaper, a ritual which can be relied on for the discovery of yet another example of national imbecility. Today, it was Chancellor Merkel's plans to expand the national nuclear energy program. More generally, The FGW refers to the culture and social customs. The tasteless fruit of an oppressive past. An entrenched, sycophantic regard for titles and status. The childlike awe of rules and regulations supported by punctuality, efficiency, rigidity, cleanliness, arrogance, persistence, responsibility.

Today, a tourist day for me, Joerg has offered to show me around his office and then the university quarter and the Kunstareal. I check my watch. I have another forty minutes to waste at the Internet café. We're not meeting until after lunch. Where would I be in a situation like this without Das Google? Likely line-dancing, maybe with the American war veterans inside the Hofbräuhaus, which is not far from Marienplatz. If Herr Meyer were around to accompany me I'd consider a side-trip. It's probably best that Meyer has moved on. I had better stay on topic, and make use of my time, which means investigating the reception of the movie inside Germany. Something I've always wondered about.

The German premiere of *Gesprengte Ketten* was 29 August, 1963. Only two months earlier U.S. President John F. Kennedy delivered his *'Ich bin ein Berliner'* speech, before a half a million people, on the steps of the Rathaus Schöneberg. The Cold War was in full swing. *Gesprengte Ketten*. This is how the parents of the kittens working the box office at *Baviaria filmstadt* might have known it. Black hoodie and spiky displayed no interest in the movie, and no consciousness of the reception it had received in its own day. They just didn't care about it. But I wonder how it might have resonated with the previous generation. In 1963 the Berlin Wall was under construction and many 'second cousins' in Stalag Luft East wanted to escape. Officially known in the East as *Der Antifaschistische Schutzwall*: The Anti-Fascist Protection Rampart, the barrier underwent constant evolution in design from the wire fence model of '61 to the concrete model of '75, finally adopting high-tech guard towers and electronic kill traps as more sophisticated means of entrapment became the rage. While it's true that the Anti-Fast-Exit Shit Wall was intended to protect the population in the Eastern Bloc from dispiriting fascist elements in the West (elements which would hinder the creation of a communist utopia), the partitioned elements in the East were magnetically drawn to the Berliner Mauer, as though the citizens of the GDR were prisoners in their own country, and their own state an enemy of the people. How do you like that? Five thousand defected during the years of the Wall, and around two hundred citizens were killed trying to escape. Turns out Stalag East Germany bred serial escapists.

In the USA, the movie was a box office success upon release, and yet the Oscar nod came for best editing. *Lawrence of Arabia* was the big winner that year. *To Kill a Mockingbird* was one of five strong nominees for Best Picture. At the Golden Globes, *The Great Escape* faired better. It was nominated but did not win in the best motion picture category. The movie was seen by critics as overly long and too focused on the mechanics of the escape at the expense of character development. And there are no women! In the UK it was castigated for historical inaccuracies. The movie focuses on a group of mostly American POWs, but no American was part of the actual escape.

Enough. Research is commendable, but while I am sitting around I could also snag selfies and update my blog, promote an online presence. From the café I might tweet #Michaelparyla. Instead, I order a third espresso, having decided what is best for me: to sit out the inconsequential pageant and pass on the production of the stuff overweened dreams are made of. Frankly what many agents and publishers call self-promotion feels like a demotion. Feels like a ruse. I've got no followers, obviously. Neither has Michael, and he doesn't care. His IMDb STARmeter ranking is abysmal. I should remain strong and act more like him, and not care: I don't but I do, whereas he *really* doesn't care. No ambiguity about it. Michael's in no position to ponder book sales. Now, if the boy snagged selfies and blogged or tweeted from the grave, he might catch a wandering eye. #Michaelsgreatescape. That'd be a different story. His Twitter account could put us in a different category.

Die Deutsche Film-und Medienbewertung Wiesbaden (FBW: not to be confused with The FGW) was formed in 1951 and is Germany's foremost film institution. On the FBW web site, *Gesprengte Ketten* gets a yellow star and the recommendation *Prädikat Wertvoll.* Michael was in Munich at the time of the release, but there is no record of his impression of the film then, or ever. If he sometimes dreamed of a fast-track career path, then his part in the movie, opposite the American and British stars, must have felt like just the ticket. But it wasn't to be.

What about the German audience of today? Black hoodie
and spiky. What would they make of *Gesprengte Ketten?* That's
an online mystery tour for another day.

After a short tour of the building, we land in the stock-
room near the reception area, where Joerg plays Santa Klaus and
showers his cousin with NBC Universal paraphernalia—pen
flashlights, mugs, lanyards.

"For the kids," he says. When I look on absently at the
flimsy loot, he stresses, "For *your* children."

I put some of it away, thank him and we are on our way. Joerg
sets the pace. He surges ahead, and I have trouble keeping up. He
doesn't seem to have noticed that I'm shot after three espressos.
The caffeine has wound me up and hollowed me out. I could use
a nap around now, but the siesta is not The FGW.

We make our first stop in the museum quarter at the *Alte
Pinakothek*, one of the oldest picture galleries in Europe. On
the massive front lawn of the museum, schoolchildren are
playing unorganized soccer. The sight of at least ten separate matches delights Joerg, and me as well. His team is FC
Nuremberg. He tells me he was a season ticket holder for several years, but the travel from Munich to Nuremberg, a distance of around 200 kilometres, became too much even for a
fanatic like him. Joerg's passion for the Bundesliga puts him
in a different league from my cousins Markus and Andreas,
who, when I was visitor in 1981, exhibited acute unease with
any display of nationalism, especially within the arena of com-
petitive team sports. Their disdain for the German national
team, *die Deutsche Fußballnationalmannschaft*, a team which
I myself idolized (especially the player Pierre Littbarski)
approached visceral. Markus and Andreas frowned upon on
my Bundesliga fandom, and instead showed a quiet pride
in the feats of athletes who played individual sports—for

example, in later years, the tennis players Steffi Graf and Boris Becker, though Boris was a bit much. His game relied on a thunderous serve and brute force.

"You see there." Joerg points to indicate the mottled brick-work façade of the museum, a patchwork which delineates where Allied shelling blew out half of the original wall. "Boom!" His chagrin is raw. Joerg is pleased to act as my guide, but seems impatient and somewhat irritated with the landmarks of the past.

Entering the south end of the English Gardens, he points to a monumental building partially concealed from view.

Before elaborating about the building's significance, he pantomimes: plucks index finger from his mouth, aims at the side of his head.

Rolls his eyes, and pulls the trigger. *Pow.*

"*Hause der Kunst,* do you know it?"

I don't know it.

"It's an example of Nazi architecture. The museum was built to showcase 'true' German works of art according to the National Socialists. Today it's also a nightclub, a discotheque, which I think is much better."

Hause der Kunst was a hothouse of propaganda. The inau-gural exhibit in 1937, called *Große Deutsche Kunstausstellung:* Great German Works of Art, was intended to stand in civilizing contrast to a concurrent and travelling exhibition of degenerate 'un-German' works of art. Here, for 'un-German', substitute 'Jewish Bolshevist' or 'avant-garde'.

"Roland had his own sculptures inside. Is this news? He must have been working there, during the war."

It is news, but not entirely surprising news. The Roland in question is Joerg's grandfather. Roland Friederichsen is mar-ried to Melanie, Eva's sister and Michael's aunt. During my apprenticeship in Munich thirty years ago I had been shown photographs of a bronze bust Roland Friederichsen made to honour a eugenicist named Frobanius. What did I know then about eugenics? Less than I knew about working in bronze. Before the war, the story goes, the eugenicist Frobanius had measured the dimensions of Melanie's cranium and designated it Aryan, meaning Eva's sister Melanie could remain safely in Germany during the war despite her *Mischling* status. Eventually she would marry Roland Friederichsen.

Meanwhile, the other half of the family, including Michael's mother Eva and her siblings Hermann Hans and Irene, were considered to be hybrids, persons of mixed Jewish blood, according to the Nuremberg Laws. All of this is well-trod and suppressed family history, and neither Joerg nor I have much taste for discussing it now. Not him, a representative from The FGW half of the family; and not me, a representative from the *Mischling* side of the family, the side that left Germany just in time not to be swallowed by its own kind.

We walk on, through the English Gardens, and towards a small bridge that crosses a tributary of the Isar. Immediately, a shiver grabs hold of my spine. I feel an actual tingling, which functions like an electronic meeting reminder, though this one is hardwired. I'm aware that it was likely here, in the English Gardens, that in August of 1957 Michael and his girlfriend of the time Janine Blum met with his father, Karl—his father then a stranger to Michael, if Janine's memory captures it correctly—to have a picnic. Karl had carefully chosen his spot and brought along a blanket and a basket of strawberries, and even thought to bring sugar. It must have been a breathtaking meeting for Michael. Bittersweet. A moment of rare intimacy with his father, fraught with doubt and insecurity. Mixed feelings, shall we say.

The park attracts tourists and locals alike, and I'm already familiar with it from previous visits to Munich. But no visitor can step into the same English Gardens twice, and what is amazing to witness this time around is the tag team of surfers in wet suits from around the world. They are standing in queue, taking turns, boarding a standing wave. And they've gathered a crowd.

Joerg and I stop to watch. This is more like it, a display our generation can appreciate. I take video with my camera. It's the most happening thing in München, this standing wave. A fluke of nature more alive than the House of Art.

"And now you are making a book about Eva's son." Joerg states the fact, while we stand watching the surfers. It's the fucking German way not to beat around the bush. "Your father knew him. Isn't that right?"

"They were cousins."

"What happened to Michael?"

"He died of an overdose. He was an actor."

"Aha."

"He was in the movie *The Great Escape*."

"Can you show me?"

My private War on Michael began thousands of miles from this European city park with a purchase at FUTURE SHOP, but now is not the time to tell Joerg about that adventure.[9]

"I have the disc right here," I tell him, and pat the side of my shoulder bag. "We can watch it tonight."

"Not tonight."

Tonight Germany take on Turkey in a European Championship Qualifying Match at Allianz Arena in north Munich.

---

9   There is a War on Drugs and a War on Terror. No one has heard of the War on Michael, I realize, but the internal logic and outcome is the same. The War on Drugs means we have never been more surrounded by drugs and pharmaceuticals. The War on Terror has translated into more terror for people of all creeds. The War on Michael (WoM) is fabricated to give us all more Michael. The WoM has been prosecuted to increase his stature. Not to eliminate him. Not to cluster bomb his reputation. But to bring more of him around more often. At least to partially rehabilitate his IMDb STARmeter ranking, which as of this writing stands at an abysmal 3,802,520.

INT. BRAIN COMPARTMENT—Flashback to FUTURE SHOP. I was living then in Northern Ontario, a twelve hour drive around the rim of Lake Superior from Michael's Sault Ste. Marie. Excited, after I had found the 2-disc DVD collector's set special edition of *The Great Escape* at Future Shop, I kneeled before the television to watch. Then, I did not have Karl Paryla's letters from 1967, nor had I discovered Michael's Tagebuch from 1949. I had not collected oral history. I had the odd photograph of him, and the likelihood of a trip to Germany to visit his grave (I did not know where it was) and the movie studios (I was clueless about the film history) was about as strong as my chances would be years later of wrangling James Garner into an interview to speak about his role in the movie, and, while at it, perhaps rummage around in foggy memory for his lost impressions of a German actor named Michael Paryla. This interview with James Garner, which presented itself in time as a very sensible direction for my research to take, easily could have been Skyped—then blogged about and hyped—but Nein, Garner's manager had declined. Had said, No. The kind of 'relationship' I proposed was of no interest to his client. So yes, back then, the WoM had been a simple ground war, launched without a sensible exit strategy. I had not hired a celebrity wrangler to entice James Garner's manager. All I had to go on was Michael's sixty seconds in the movie.

So I sat down in the TV chair and picked up the remote and spent the next week obsessively reviewing the evidence. Delusion: I could deduce a lot from sixty seconds of face time if I watched closely. This way I may learn EVERYTHING about Michael there is to know: more than Master Wikipedia keeps on tap, more than can be gained from the collective memory. I was convinced that I could deduce and create something more true from the experience of watching the movie than I ever could from these pseudo-factual present tense set pieces that I

manufacture, from memory, to stage the book in a more imme-
diate manner.

Conclusion: in any case, watching the film and recording
my reactions, for a full week, a month, wouldn't that be an
interesting experiment? Yes. Yes, it would be. Real quality time.
Face time with Michael. And it was. It was a very 'interesting'
time. So intense that I had to back away from it. The results of
that experiment have been saved under the provisionary title
Stop Pause Play. Maybe that's what I'll call this book.

Germany 2—Turkey 1. It helps that Mesut Özil, the best
player on the pitch of Turkish heritage, plays for Merkel's boys.

The game takes us close to midnight. Afterwards Joerg con-
nects the laptop to his sound system and treats me to some
YouTube magic. Austrian hip hop is on the menu. White clowns
in sweats at a pool shed party. *Kabinenparty*. Joerg turns up the
volume and makes his big gangster moves, dancing black in the
kitchen. He betrays a genuine sympathy for the music, which
is quite good it's that bad. We party late and drink a lot of beer,
but there are no further questions about 'my project', no interest at all in watching *The Great Escape*. No Steve McQueen. No
Elmer Bernstein. Austrian hip hop.

The next day we drive to Haar, south-east of Munich, to visit
Joerg's mother Hannah. Hannah belongs to Michael's cohort
of the cousins. For decades, Joerg's mother Hannah has dealt
with having multiple sclerosis, and now she has been recently
diagnosed with a type of blood cancer. In the parking lot of the
long-term care hospital we meet Gerhardt, her husband. Joerg's
father. He shows us inside.

I sit level with Hannah in a chair at the bedside. Gerhardt
hovers at the far end of the room near the open window. Joerg
takes the wall. Birdsong filters into the room from the outside
gardens. From her supine position, Hannah asks about the

health of my family and manages a weak smile when I respond that everyone is well, including my parents.

"I met him." Hannah says.

"Do you remember his house, where it was in Munich?"

"No." She has no recollection. Again she smiles, more generously now. It is from Hannah that Joerg gets his red hair. She is light skinned, and freckled. Her eyes are kind. Hannah is a weaver. She makes tapestries, allegorical narratives spun in colored wool. Several of her artworks are hung in her temporary room here at the hospital. They have biblical themes for the most part.

"That was a long time ago," Gerhardt interjects. "He lived with a woman. Margaret, yes? And she died soon after him."

"That's right." I say. "Margaret. He lived with Margaret." But really, that's about it for knowledge about her. *Margaret Jahnen. Swindling, magniloquent and yarn-spinning Margaret.* Michael shared a house in Munich with Margaret. She had a teenage son when they met. Besides these facts not much is known about Michael's Margaret.

Eva demonized Margaret. But Eva's sister Irene had the generosity of mind to request a fair trial. Michael's aunt Irene is the only member of the family who sounds a forgiving note about Margaret. It was Irene who wrote to Eva on 30 January, 1967, the day she returned from attending Michael's funeral in Waldfriedhof. *My poor dear Eva. I went to the cemetery in your stead. How deeply the whole thing has affected me, I need not tell you.* The last time Irene had spoken with *him* was on Christmas Eve.

He was very tired and was here for only a day. He had been quite busy for some time and had finally made his way to the top. One can only speculate about how the incident happened. It was probably a combination of many unfortunate circumstances. He had apparently been complaining a lot about insomnia for some time; this was in addition to financial worries and friction with colleagues. On top of that, there was all his work and the insane theatre life—sorry, but I really find that he could not cope with that kind of life, neither physically or psychologically, and to mix alcohol and sleeping tablets is certainly dangerous for anyone. So, he probably didn't feel much.

Karl arranged for Michael's body to be transferred to Munich, for burial, in his own grave. But I knew so few of the people who attended. I felt like a stranger, amidst the vast forest. Karl did not attend: he could not bring himself to do this. He called and told me to write to you. I wanted to wait until the funeral was over—for a long time, I just couldn't believe it.

Eva received the letter in January. I remember reading it for first time thirty years after the fact; remember how I was struck by its gentleness and sanity, and at the same time I pictured Eva in Sault Ste. Marie, alone in the kitchen, reading the letter which I held in my hands. The paper and envelope had a thick black border.

What can I say to comfort you? I know that your sorrow is too great. Michi's life is behind him—he had a good heart and that is probably what's most important. He will not be forgotten, and we all will go the same route in the end. *Es geht so schnell vorbei dieses Dasein.* Life goes by so fast. Much too fast to gain even a slight understanding of what it actually is.

There is a two month break, before Irene writes again from Munich.

Meine liebe Eva! I received your letter dated April 6. I can definitely understand that you don't feel like writing back and forth all the time. No one expects you to. I know how deep your pain is and how hard it is to have to bear it. But please don't make the mistake of so harshly blaming exclusively Michi's entourage here.

Liebe Eva—Karl, Margaret and Jerry are pretty much strangers to me and I've never had anything other than a very casual connection with them through Michi. So I can really only talk about what I've seen and heard over the years—which is very little. In any case, Michi told me time and again that he got along wonderfully with Margaret, and once when I asked him—in the very beginning—what she was like, he said, *"Ganz wie Eva! Ich habe meine Mutter geheiratet!"*: "Just like Eva! I married my mother!" He was laughing at the time. I can still see and hear him; it was in Pasing, around 1959 or 1960.

In any case Michi loved Margaret, and Margaret undoubtedly helped him a lot. He had something to do with choosing her, too—why do you blame only her for that?

We all have our limits. We all move within our boundaries. We need to learn not to always expect or demand <u>more</u> from others than what they are capable of giving.

I went to Michi's grave last week. It's decorated with spring flowers. You have to try to understand Margaret's pain and stop blaming her—you will be more serene if you do. Life goes by so fast. It won't be long before we can no longer right our wrongs. We shouldn't always make new mistakes, but instead try to mend the old ones as best we can. We all act within our limits, but can show good faith in doing so.

Liebe Eva, from the bottom of my heart, I wish you much quiet time to reflect and much strength, I kiss you fondly. *Deine Irene.*

Once she wore light coloured blouses. Now black. Eva had not seen her sister Irene in a long while, not since she and Karl left Darmstadt for Vienna immediately following the Reichstag fire in 1935. Eva's family in Germany didn't *know her* now, anymore than they could fathom the desolation of Lake Superior in January. The windswept white of the lake, a barrenness the size of Bavaria. After the spring thaw she could drop Munich into the lake and not hear a thing more from her fair-minded sister.

Gerhardt winces.

"I met him just once." He doesn't want to partake in the story of Michael, I grasp that, but is far too entrenched in The FGW to refrain from stating his opinion. "It was in the lobby of the Münchner Kammerspiele. The late 1950s. I remember a handsome boy. But, I think, he was always unhappy because he could not be like his father."

Gerhardt is most likely remembering the 1959 Munich production of Bertolt Brecht's *Life of Galileo,* directed by Hans Schweikart, in which Michael played Cosimo de Medici opposite Friedrich Domin, who played Galileo. The set was designed by Caspar Neher, the man who designed the original set for *The Threepenny Opera* at Berlin's Schiffbauerdamm Theatre in 1928.

Michael, I would have said, could not have been more like his father. What a strange thing for Gerhardt to say. *He was always unhappy because he could not be like his father.* Michael went into acting because of his father, even returned to Germany to play in the same theatre houses where Karl made his name. He was not the success his father was. He didn't have the reputation Karl Paryla made for himself. That's what Gerhardt meant to say, I think.

The comparison between father and son leaves Michael's side of the equation wanting. Michael might have played Cosimo de Medici opposite Friedrich Domin in 1959 in Munich, but Karl already years before starred in the 1943 World Premier of *Leben des Galilei* in Zurich. And unbeknownst to Michael, his half–brother Stephan would later appear in the same play.

What is it about *The Life of Galileo* that the Paryla clan revolve around it, like the earth around the sun, like sons around their father? Maybe it's not just *Galileo* but Brecht who is pulling the strings. Eva likely crossed paths with Casper Neher in Breslau, when the touring production of *The Threepenny Opera* came to town. An interesting coincidence. But what does it all mean to Michael?

Enough questions for a tourist day.

After visiting with Hannah, we return to Munich, park the car, and descend to the S-Bahn at Rosenheimer-Platz, where we take it two stops to Marienplatz. We could have walked but we're late for the Anti-Atomdemo. Large crowds are expected to take part in the protest against Chancellor Angela Merkel's National nuclear energy policy. Merkel is angling to extend the term of several nuclear plants which are due to close. Eight plants in Bavaria will be effected. In reaction, forty thousand are forming a human chain ten kilometres in length between the offices of the atomic lobby.

"Between the headquarters of E.ON Energy and those shits at Siemens and the CSU." Joerg names the main players.

We make slow progress, inching past human links on the chain, towards the final demo which is set for 15:00 at the Odeonsplatz. I'm familiar with these streets and alleys and many of the landmarks. So would Michael have been: any visitor to Munich actually.

As we come upon the platz, Joerg stops me in my tracks. He reaches his arm across my chest and bars the way. There is no way forward without a history lesson first. Munich was the birthplace of the Nazi party. *Hauptstadt der Bewegung*, capital of the movement. Bavaria is sometimes regarded as 'the nursery' where the child-monster learned to crawl, eventually to squawk.

"Do you know this place?" Joerg asks.

He means the *Feldherrnhalle*. 'The Field Marshall's Hall' was built in the 1840s to honour the Bavarian army. Its roof shelters the statues of military leaders from The Thirty-Year War and The Franco-Prussian War. We're talking low-on-the-list generals like Johann Tilly and Karl Philipp von Wrede, who continue to fight for a place in the national memory. Things around here changed in 1923. Here I'll stop cutting from Wikipedia and paste a full sketch.

> On Friday morning, 9 November 1923, the Feldherrnhalle was the scene of a confrontation between the Bavarian State Police and an illegally organized march by the followers of Adolf Hitler. When ordered to stop the marchers continued; the State Police felt threatened and opened fire. Four policemen and sixteen marchers were killed and a number were wounded, including Hermann Göring. As a result, Hitler was arrested and sentenced to a prison term. This was one of the efforts by the Nazis to take over the Bavarian State, commonly referred to as the Beer Hall Putsch.

The Nazis erected a memorial to the fallen putschists on the east side of the *Feldherrnhalle,* opposite where Joerg and I are now standing in the street.

"Some nut put himself on fire here in the 90s."

"In protest?"

"For sure." Joerg refers to Reinhold Elstner, a World War II veteran who committed suicide on this exact spot in his seventy-fifth year. A Wehrmacht veteran, Reinhold Elstner decided he could no longer stomach what he considered to be the ongoing and blank demonization of the German people and army. A martyr, then, was Elstner. He chose the spot for obvious reasons. The same Odeonsplatz which is today packed with a rainbow coalition of citizens, old and young and male and female and rich and poor, served the Nazis for the midnight swearing in of SS men. During the war years, the memorial on the side of the *Feldherrnhalle* was guarded around the clock by SS henchmen. When passing the memorial, party members would give the Nazi salute. Giving the Nazi salute was not everybody's idea of a good time, but it was conspicuous not to stop. To avoid having to salute, a passerby would walk down a path behind the monument and take an alternate route to the Odeonsplatz. The route along *Viscardigasse* quickly became known as Shirkers Alley.

Joerg asks, "Shall we go around?"

It does not seem relevant. We go straight on through. There's a difference between history and superstition, which shall haunt us forever if we bow to magical thinking. The gathered forty thousand are evidence of that, proof the fucking German way is not locked in time, forever.

Michael Paryla as Cosimo de Medici opposite Friedrich Domin in *Life of Galileo* (1959).

THE GREAT ESCAPE ...
FOR THOSE WHO MISSED IT

THIS IS A MANHUNT. Roll camera, roll away Sturges. The motorcade swings into Neustadt Station. Nazis à la mode arrive in swank gangster cars. That's him in the lead car. I need to pause here. Is it a Mercedes Benz 260D or the popular Mercedes 540K cabriolet? Reich Marshall Hermann Goering, the Luftwaffe chief, was vigorously fond of the 540K. The armoured sedan limousine pretty much served as the moveable clubhouse of the Third Reich.

I point the remote. A sea of darkness. A bit of history.

STALAG LUFT III

Stalag Luft III was no ordinary prisoner of war camp. The POWs called it Goering's luxury camp. The Luftwaffe chief betrayed a chivalrous kinship with the Allied Air Force. Goering believed that captured enemy flyers deserved escape-proof comfort.

Completed in April 1943, the camp was situated in a forested region of Silesia, an eastern part of Germany, as far as possible from the Western Front. Locally it was positioned a half-mile south of Sagan, at the juncture of eight rail lines. At its peak, 10,000 men were billeted in six compounds: air force personnel given to superior education, aggressive behaviour, and self-reliance.

Extra precaution was taken in planning for its construction. In addition to equidistant watchtowers and two nine-foot-high perimeter fences, rolls of barbed wire wreathed atop and tumbleweeds between, an eight foot ditch, search lights, machine gun nests and guard dogs and patrolling sentries, the earth was implanted with seismographs and microphones. Day and night the underground was monitored for sound vibrations.[10]

KRIEGIES & GOONS

Kriegie (sing.). POW slang. Kriegie is the shortened form of the German word for prisoner of war, *Kriegsgefangener*. The Allied POWs named themselves Kriegies. Kriegies of The Third Reich referred to their captors as Goons. Goons paraded in jackboots and carried tommy guns.

FERRETS

Ferrets were the camp animals who specialized in escape detection. A half-dozen ferrets patrolled the compound at all times with probes and torches. Chief German ferret in Stalag Luft III was Oberfeldweber Glemnitz. Fieldweasel Glemnitz was incorruptible, but allegedly only tepidly clever. His second in command, Unterofficier Griese, was more dangerous. Nicknamed Rubberneck, Unterofficier Griese was zealous. Fortunately, ferrets could be bribed with black market goods. This means they could be tamed.

COOLER

A concrete block house with barred windows, a punishing destination for prisoners placed in isolation. The cooler at Stalag Luft III was situated in the Vorlager, a forecamp outside the main compound.

---

10   I like to imagine the tower guards, in winter, dressed in great coats, pacing the observation platforms, while over in the warmth of the commandant's office, their administrative counterparts—comfortably seated and wearing air-tight headphones: straining like hard-of-hearing war criminals—listened through nightlong shifts to the latest underground recording, the esoteric distortions of some segmented worm licking its way inside the shell of a seismograph. Talk about Lo-Fi. Talk 'bout avant-garde.

GEHEIME STAATSPOLIZEI

Secret state police. The evil formerly known as the Gestapo. Uniform consisted primarily of the trench coat and fedora. Plain clothes, yet dressed to kill.

GOONSKIN

A false German uniform. POWs manufactured these out of RAF uniforms.

TRAP & TRAPFUEHRER

Not what you expect. In POW camp parlance, a trap is the term for the opening of an escape tunnel. Sometimes it is the material used to conceal the tunnel opening, e.g. a concrete slab. The POW who would watch for ferrets and replace the trap at the tunnel opening held the rank of Trapfuehrer.

HUNDFUEHRER

The dog leader. A type of sentry who prowled outside the perimeter fence or inside the camp with a dog trained to go for a factual mistake.[11]

WIRE-HAPPY

A psychological condition related to cabin fever. A prisoner behind the wires for three or four years could develop eccentricities and entertain symptoms like visual and oral hallucinations. Wire-happy prisoners were prone to delusions and making brazen escape attempts in broad daylight. In the movie, Steve McQueen's fast friend, Flying Officer Archibald Ives, has the crazed-eyes of an emotionally distraught jockey. Ives is wire-happy. But, we sense, not for long.

---

11   Spoiler. To limit mistakes and errors where the movie and movie-making is concerned, I have enlisted the services of a professor of film studies, whom I shall henceforth refer to by his moniker, 'The Filmfuehrer', in honour of the vigilant Trapfuehrers of Stalag Luft III.

CODE OF CONDUCT

During the Second World War, it was an officer's duty to escape should he be taken prisoner. Attempting escape was an obligation imposed on Canadian and British and American POWs by their country's military code of conduct. Efforts were coordinated from inside by an escape committee composed of senior ranking officers. The escape committee comprised a legal and moral authority in a non-place where free will would find limited expression. Near the end of the war, escape attempts continued to be a vital part of the Allied strategy, intended to divert scarce military resources. Even unsuccessful breakouts upset law and order behind enemy lines. The collective effort of POWs in this pursuit was regarded as an example of 'carrying on the war by other means.'

THE ESCAPE COMMITTEE

Luft III's escape committee was headed by RAF Squadron Leader Roger J Bushell, known in the movie as Big X or Bartlett and played by Richard Attenborough. Roger Bushell was the mastermind of the plan to put as many as 250 men outside the wire. He planned for three tunnels, at least thirty feet deep, each with an underground railway and ventilation system. To execute the plan, Bushell set up secret factories and workshops comprised of forgers, tailors, manufacturers, scroungers, tunnelers, engineers and surveillance experts.

Meanwhile, as the plan unfolded, Roger Bushell became an active participant in the camp theatre. In the months leading up to the March 1944 breakout, he was busy with rehearsals, learning the part of Professor Higgins in a production of *Pygmalion*.

CHIVALRY

Several months after Stalag Luft III opened for business, Canadian Ken Toft and American William 'Red' Nichols

discovered a blind spot between two sentry boxes. After bringing their discovery to the escape committee, Toft and Nichols
were given the green light. Equipped with wire-cutters, and
employing high-school styled diversionary tactics in the main
compound, Toft and Nichols made their break in broad daylight. They made it as far as Frankfurt before being recaptured
and returned to Stalag Luft III, whereupon Colonel von
Lindeimer, the camp Kommandant, invited Toft and Nichols
into his office for a chat. The Kommandant was impressed
by the duo's brazenness and presented them with a bottle of
whiskey before dispatching them to their punishment. *Cooler.*
Two weeks.

In the movie, Steve McQueen and Angus Lennie re-enact
the Toft and Nichols' escape. They too end up in the cooler. In
fact, 'The Cooler King' and Hollywood Monarch, McQueen,
spends a good chunk of the movie in the cold room, tossing a
baseball against the wall, big leather mitt and all, to the considerable irritation of the wire-happy Lennie, who is refrigerated
in the next cell.

TOM, DICK AND HARRY

The escape committee baptized the network of tunnels, Tom,
Dick, and Harry. The logic to digging three tunnels simultaneously was simple: if the Goons discovered one, they might
suppose that's it for the shenanigans of these notorious POWs.
If they found a second tunnel, surely then Kommandant von
Lindeimer and his band of ferrets would conclude the game was
up, definitely.

MOLES, CREEPERS, AND TUNNEL KINGS

To be a digger you needed stamina and steady nerves. Sneeze and
a load of sand could collapse on your back and pin you. Moles
like the New Zealander Henry W. 'Piglet' Lamond burrowed

into the blind. Moles flew solo. The creepers were a separate breed. The creepers and over-ground crawlers cut through the wire and inch-wormed their baggy segmented-selves into the forest cover beyond the perimeter fence. The Tunnel Kings, a collective who played patiently at the long game, planned for the big show of a massive breakout. Kings like Crump Ker-Ramsay, Johnny Marshall, and Johnny Bull, and the original Stalag Luft III Tunnel King, Wally Floody, who was head of the Tunnel Committee. The Tunnel Kings worked closely with sand-dispersal chief George 'Hornblower' Fanshawe, and with tunnel-security chief George Harsh.

WORK

Work on the tunnels began in spring 1943. Harry and Tom were thirty feet down after two weeks. At this depth there was some house cleaning to do. Three chambers were excavated. Chamber One was five feet long and used to store gear. Chamber Two was used to store sand. Chamber Three was six feet wide and housed the air pump. The tunnel shaft along the horizontal was tight. There was no room to turn around, the men had to lie head to foot, and inch backwards to find the light. The morning shift used homemade spirit levels to check the floors. The night shift used the Wehrmacht's own prismatic compasses to check the final orientation. When Harry reached twenty feet, the tunnel men began to lay an underground railway, used for hauling sand. The trolley was made of beechwood bed boards and the wooden bearings were greased with margarine (not butter). A pipe line for oxygen was buried below the railway and attached to a pump, with an air vent opening near the head. Ah, praise the air pumps and the pumper: the first pump was made of an old accordion, the second from a kitbag and boot leather. Don't ask me what a kitbag is. The pumper was rags and flesh and blood.

THE YELLOW SAND

Whilst digging the first tunnel, Wally Floody discovered the yellow sand. Stalag Luft's infamously yellow-tinged subsoil was hidden beneath a layer of gray dirt. To construct Tom, Dick, and Harry, there was an estimated one hundred tons of sand to disperse without the camp ferrets sticking their nose in it. Note: Dug sand fills out more space in its loose form.

TROUSERBAGS & PENGUINS

Made from long woollen underwear, the original Stalag Luft III Trouserbags were designed by sand dispersal-chief Peter 'Hornblower' Fanshawe. The trouserbags were used for the hauling and dispersing of Luft III's bright yellow subsoil, which (the ingenuity of the aforementioned Kriegies withstanding), was a definite bitch to get rid of. Back in the days of 1943, trouserbags were a hit with camp Penguins. Penguins were the poor sods in charge of carrying out sand dispersal. Penguins were so-named because they shuffled as they strolled back and forth, through the compound (wearing the God-awful and itchy aforementioned trouserbags looped around the neck), searching for a safe spot to drop their load, under the constant watchful eyes of camp Ferrets like Rubberneck.

FAINT CRACK

When the Germans suspected an escape tunnel was being dug, the guards drove heavy wagons around the compound, trying to collapse them. The strategy was effective. Even if the sand was solidly shored up the whole way using bed boards, the tunnels often caved in. In fact, they frequently caved in spontaneously. Underground the tunnelers heard a faint crack before the sand collapsed; ominously (I'm taking an educated guess) the sound seemed to originate from within their own being. It was hardly enough warning to get clear before the yellow stuff buried them alive. Many a tunnel-man had to be hauled out by the ankles.

ESCAPE CONSTRUCTION: BREAKDOWN

A breakdown of the materials used in the construction of Tom, Dick and Harry: 4,000 bed boards; 1,370 beading battens; 1,699 blankets; 161 pillow cases; 34 chairs; 52 20-man tables; 90 double tier bunks; 1,219 knives; 478 spoons; 30 shovels; 1,000 feet of electric wire; 600 feet of rope; 192 bed covers; 3,424 towels; 1,212 bed bolsters; 10 single tables; 76 benches; 246 water cans; 582 forks; 69 lamps.

TOM & DICK

Tom measured 260 feet in the summer of 1943 when a ferret detected the entrance under the chimney in Hut 123. Thereafter, for security, Roger Bushell put Dick to sleep. Though it was not used in the actual escape, Dick's underground sleeve was handy for the storage of construction materials. Dick's trap, under the shower drain in Hut 122, was never discovered.

GOOD OLD HARRY

That left Harry. Good old 'Arry. The entrance to Harry was under the stove in Hut 104. The POWs had cut through a brick and concrete plinth and then dropped 30 feet before leveling off. This was the safe depth calculated by the escape committee so as not to upset the camp's sound-sensitive topsoil. Harry would run under the cooler to the northern wire and beyond a second boundary fence into the woods. The tunnel-men burrowed another 350 feet and laid out their trolley track for hauling sand, with its two station stops, Piccadilly Circus and Leicester Square. Oh yes, down in the claustrophobic dark, working by the glow of forehead-fastened fat lamps and under the constant threat of an overhead collapse, the incorrigible escapees got high on the fumes of success. Nobody lost (his sense of) humour. Harry took a full year to dig.

DEAN AND DAWSON

The forgery factory was headed by Tim Walenn. It's code name was Dean and Dawson, after the British travel agency. Walenn's merry group turned out over 400 different phony documents, reproduced hundred of maps and passbooks, and copied the whorled lines of banknotes, all with fanatical care. Favourite forgeries included the *Ausweis* for being on Reich property; gate passes; several types of *Urlaubschein* for crossing frontiers; the French worker's identity card; and the ordinary soldier's *Soldbuch*, a combination of paybook and identification card.

STOOGES AND DIVERSIONISTS

Prisoners not chosen for work in the factories or tunnels were taken by the security detail and performed as either a stooge or a diversionist. Stooges kept watch over the movement of Ferrets. In the diversionist category of persons, there was a range of roles to pick from, including becoming a member of The Sagan Serenaders. The camp choir toured the compound, keeping to a hectic schedule, and generally made enough noise to hide the sound of a hammer blow or scraping shovel. The elaborate security system set up by Roger Bushell and George Harsh was highly successful. The prisoners were able to protect the secrecy of the factories by tracking the movement of Ferrets within the compound, and could account for the location of every Goon in the system.

A MEMOIR

Most of this is found in *The Great Escape*, Paul Brickhill's wartime prison camp memoir. An Australian pilot, Brickhill was shot down over Tunisia in 1943. Upon capture, Brickhill was sent to Stalag Luft III, where he remained a POW until the end of the war. Brickhill was a trusted piece of Roger Bushell's escape machine and was involved in the construction of all three tunnels, including the infamous Harry. He was put in charge of arrangements to protect the document forgers, who worked, exposed, in front of windows. At the last moment, Bushell barred Brickhill from joining the escape party when he learned the latter suffered from claustrophobia. 'A correct, if infuriating decision,' writes Brickhill in his memoir.

*

THE GREAT ESCAPE

STEVE MCQUEEN JAMES GARNER RICHARD ATTENBOROUGH IN
'*THE GREAT ESCAPE*'
CO-STARRING JAMES DONALD CHARLES BRONSON
DONALD PLEASANCE JAMES COBURN
PRODUCED AND/DIRECTED BY JOHN STURGES SCREENPLAY
BY JAMES CLAVELL & W.R. BURNETT BASED UPON/THE BOOK
BY PAUL BRICKHILL
MUSIC/ELMER BERNSTEIN COLOR/BY DELUXE PANAVISION
A MIRISCH-ALPHA PICTURE

APPROX. FEATURE RUN TIME 2 HOURS 52 MINUTES COLOR 1963

DISCLAIMER
Although the characters are composites of real men, and time and place have been compressed, every detail of the escape is the way it really happened.[12]

---

12   Dreadfully quaint disclaimers like this one, which follows the opening credits of the movie, are a thing of the past.

ESCAPE STORY?

The American director John Sturges cut his directorial teeth making combat films with the US Army. His fascination with the escape story began in 1950, after reading a serialization of Paul Brickhill's memoir in *Reader's Digest*. Sturges tried to hook MGM, but studio boss Louis B Mayer was unimpressed. 'What the hell kind of great escape is this?' he asked. 'No one escapes!' The picture would be too depressing (fifty men are recaptured and murdered) and, besides, it would not appeal to women (there were no female characters). Mayer had a point. And Sturges wouldn't make his film until twelve years later. Meanwhile there was *Gunfight At The O.K. Corral* (1957), *The Old Man and The Sea* (1958), and *Never So Few* (1959). Sturges left MGM and signed with Mirisch Company in 1959. His first film with Mirisch was *The Magnificent Seven* (1960). It starred Steve McQueen, James Coburn, and Charles Bronson. That same year, Sturges was fronted money to buy the rights to *The Great Escape*. He immediately contacted Paul Brickhill in Australia, who signed on as a partner in the deal.

SCREENPLAY

Up to five screenwriters worked on the film adaptation of Brickhill's memoir. In the original screen treatment, William Roberts was given the task of establishing the technical flow of the film. Forget characterization, make the complicated linear. Walter Newman was hired to flesh out the original treatment by Roberts, but Newman, irritatingly, followed Paul Brickhill's memoir too closely into sidetracking subplots and was dismissed before a polished script was in hand. Next up, a constructionist: W.R. Burnett. Burnett ripped the thing apart and found a new narrative line which focused on the ins and outs of the tunnel operation. This pleased Sturges immensely. James Clavell worked on location and during production and is spotlighted alongside Burnett in the opening credits. When things got slow, Ivan Moffat was hired to enhance the action sequences.

PRISONERS OF THE TRUTH

The first truth in acting is circumstance. This is an old Stanislavski trick. But the cast of *The Great Escape* were not method actors in the usual sense. The character roles in the movie were composites, created from historical persons, actual POWS, and in addition many of the actors, from both the Allied and Axis contingent, had their own wartime prison camp experiences to draw upon.

Donald Pleasance, who plays Flt Lt Colin Blythe or 'The Forger,' based on the map-maker Desmond Plunkett and forger Tim Walenn, served as a radio operator aboard an RAF Lancaster bomber. Pleasance was a POW of Stalag Luft I in Pomerania. Richard Attenborough, who portrays Squn Ldr Roger Bartlett, the Roger Bushell character 'Big X,' also served in the RAF. James Garner of the American contingent served in the Korean War and worked as an actual scrounger like Hendley, his resourceful character in the movie. Steve McQueen was a former marine. McQueen's character, 'The Cooler King', was partly inspired by Eric Foster, a seven-time British escapee from German camps. James Coburn, who plays Sedgwick 'Manufacturer' (with a crap Australian accent), served in the US Armed Forces as a public information officer. Sedgwick is a creation of screenwriter James Clavell and an amalgam of compass-maker Al Hake and Johnny Travis, the actual camp Manufacturer. Charles Bronson was a B-29 tail-gunner in the Pacific. His character, Flt Lt Danny Velinski, is a smorgasbord based on Wally Floody, F/Lt Ernst Valenta, F/O Danny Kroll, and F/O Wlodzimiez. Wally Floody was the Canadian mining engineer and an original member of Luft III's escape committee, who later served as a technical advisor on the film set.

Among the Goons, Richard Graff, who plays Werner 'The Ferret', was an army sergeant at the Russian Front. Hannes

Messemer, 'The Kommandant', was a former POW in a Russian camp. Hans Reiser, who plays Kuhn, was a prisoner of the Americans. So was Til Kiwe, Frick the Ferret; Kiwe spent a good part of the war in Arizona. And Harry Riebauer, Sergeant Strachwitz, served six years in the German Army at the Russian front, seeing action in Stalingrad.

EVEN BERNSTEIN AND JAMES CLAVELL
Even Elmer Bernstein, responsible for the film score, composer of pastoral strains, orchestrator of pluck and circumstance, whose cocky melody of rattling snares and competing fifes and piccolos speaks to perky defiance—this Bernstein (not Leonard: unrelated) was enlisted in the US Army and served in the radio unit in NYC during WWII. And the screenwriter and novelist James Clavell—of *Shogun* and *King Rat* fame—had joined the British Royal Artillery at age seventeen. Clavell spent three-and-a-half years in Changi Prison, in Singapore, a POW of the Japanese.

IMPROVISATION
Many scenes in the movie were improvised. Good. Herein lies strength. Genius is struck left-handed. There was no 'final' screenplay. No such thing. By the last week of filming at least eleven versions of the script were in circulation. Nonetheless the actors believed firmly that with fictionalizing real life came a great responsibility. Who might have felt this more than Charles Bronson, himself the son of a coal miner, whose character Tunnel King was a composite of no less than four former POWs of Stalag Luft III?

PROMOTION DEPARTMENT & BLOND BIMBOS
From day one, United Artists was hot on the tail of John Sturges, hounding the director to slip some women into the story. One

idea put to Sturges by the promotion department was having the American Scrounger—James Garner's character—blackmail his way out of Goering's homoerotic compound early on, and then shack up with a German Mädchen beyond the wire. This Mädchen could be quite something! Like, an American bombshell! Or an Aryan Ode to Joy! Sturges didn't bite. Even after shooting began, the letters from United Artists kept coming: could Dispersal, the David McCallum character—after he is shot near the end—be cradled in the lap of a leggy bystander? McCallum could speak his last words across the bow of leggy bystander's low-cut blouse. United Artists went as far to suggest Sturges and crew find their gal by organizing a Miss Prison Camp Beauty Contest in nearby Munich. Claptrap. Sturges would have no part of the publicity department nonsense. Go figure, a nuts and bolts director, not a tits and ass man after all.

DRAMA MCQUEEN

Sturges began shooting in early June, and by July he had a bigger problem on his hands than quenching the promotion department's thirst for a femme fatale. Steve McQueen. McQueen had decided his part was too small. His character Hilts was confusing. In the original screenplay, Hilts appears in the barracks but then disappears from the film for a good thirty minutes. To McQueen, a star on the rise, who'd done *The Magnificent Seven* with Sturges alongside fellow Great Escapists James Coburn and Charles Bronson, a little character development was a modest request. After walking off the set in protest, rumours spread that McQueen had been fired. This wasn't true. Nonetheless, Mirisch and United Artists grew alarmed. The corporate heavyweights fretted about losing McQueen's star power. Even if no Americans participated in the actual breakout, Hollywood stars like McQueen, Garner and Bronson were deemed invaluable and necessary for drawing audiences into movie theatres and putting bums in seats. Additional sums were forthcoming if money was needed to hire a new writer ... McQueen returned to the set after six weeks, only after Sturges hired the writer Ivan Moffat. Moffat created the scene inside the camp where McQueen breaks out though a blind spot in the perimeter fence, and he also amped up McQueen's cooler gig, for which the All-American is given a baseball mitt and ball to throw against the cement wall.

HISTORICIZED
The name Michael Paryla does not appear in the film's final credits. Initially cast as an extra, my distant cousin was eclipsed by the star power on set. Indeed, it is impossible to identify my relative unless you have access to family photographs. Even so, speaking from experience, Paryla was hard to find. Imagine that moment when I pinned him down, my mixed emotions and über surprise. There he was for all the world to see: dressed in plain clothes, ravishing, and up to no good. Of a slight build and boyish yet. Flaxen hair. Positively plagued by his blond hair. Cousin Michael was convincing.

*

FACTORS OF SUCCESS
Stalag Luft's escape committee articulated four factors of success: 1) No moon; 2) A moderate wind to cover up noises; 3) Reasonable weather; 4) No Ferret snooping outside Hut 104.

THE ESCAPE PARTY
The escape committee estimated that, out of the 600 or more that had been involved in the operation, approximately 220 men might be able to get through the tunnel. To start off, 70 prisoners were selected. Each of them had already learned a fake identity. German speakers were given priority and rewarded

with train tickets. The rest of the lot would hard-ass across the country on foot.

OPENING NIGHT
24 March 1944. The theatre is in dress rehearsal for *Pygmalion*. The faint rumble of bombs dropping on Berlin sixty miles away can be heard in camp. Sirens and air raid alarms. The power switches off. The boundary lights and searchlights go out. So far so good, but then it begins to snow. *For the hard arsers the going would be slow. They would be easy to track down.*

1ˢᵗ MAN OUT
Johnny Bull struggled to loosen the boards of the exit trap. He used his little shovel to scrape through. Alas, the tunnel surveyors had blundered. Harry was short. The exit hole was twenty feet shy of the treeline. But there was no turning back—the meticulously forged papers were stamped. Time to improvise.

2ᴺᴰ MAN OUT
Roger Bushell decides to make a go of it and drops the part of Professor Higgins on his understudy. Bushell is the second man out at approximately 9:45 PM. He is wearing a black overcoat (an RAF coat dyed with boot polish) and a dark felt hat and carrying the papers of a French businessman inside his attaché case. He heads directly for Sagan railway station.

FUDGE
Let's hear it for the hard arsers. The hard arsers, wearing petit berets and carrying blanket rolls and cans of fudge, heading into enemy territory on foot. Hitler is about to call for the largest manhunt of the war and without a doubt the hard arsers don't stand a chance. They might as well get seated in the

snow right now and lean back against the base of a pine tree and gobble down their concentrated escape food (made from goods contained in Red Cross parcels—a hefty compound of sugar, cocoa, Bemax, condensed milk, raisins, oats, margarine, chocolate and ground biscuits), if they can stomach it, in one go.

ALARM

Out of the two hundred and seventy airmen with tickets for the escape, seventy-six make it beyond the treeline and disappear into the soulless Silesian night before the camp escape alarm sounds. The next three coming are captured by sentries at Harry's mouth. The remaining prisoners en route hurry back, past Piccadilly Station and Leicester Square—no time to chat—and reappear, hands-raised, under the stove in Hut 104.

MOVIE TIME

2:06:37
Exterior Shot. Morning. Neustadt Rail Station. A handful of escapees in civilian clothes reach the station. These include Big X, the Roger Bushell character played by Richard Attenborough, and his partner Intelligence, played by Gordon Jackson. Big X and Intelligence ignore Dispersal, who is loitering by a lamp post further along the concrete platform. Dispersal is a loner. When the camera turns on him, he buries his face in the newspaper, *Die Völkischer Beobachter*. But it's obvious to a movie audience who Dispersal is: David McCallum.

The train is late. Big X and Intelligence betray anxious expressions. Momentarily, Hendley the Scrounger and Blythe the Forger, played by James Garner and Donald Pleasance, respectively, approach from the opposite side of the tracks. Hendley leads Blythe like an old woman by the arm. By this stage, Blythe has gone blind from his painstaking work—five hours a day for a year—in the forgery factory. He can see no evil. Hendley the Scrounger looks around, aghast. Two-thirds of the people waiting for the train to Breslau are escapees. Already many have missed their connection.

On the eve of 24 March 1944, Berlin was hit hard by an air raid. This fact explains the train's delay. However the air raid is not in the movie. The actors waiting on the platform have been instructed to behave accordingly: like escapees who wouldn't have known there was an air raid over Berlin the previous evening. Thus here the actors are the real prisoners of the truth.

2:07:54

Exterior Shot. The motorcade swings into Neustadt Station. Nazis à la mode, Michael included, arrive in time to catch the train.

Neustadt's historical antecedent, Sagan, was part of the Breslau Gestapo and Kriminalpolizei area. Accordingly, the motorcade personnel would have been hand-picked by Oberregierungsrat Max Wielen, area chief of the Kriminalpolizei. Which makes the actor Michael Paryla, what? Gestapo or Kriminalpolizei? One or the other.[13]

---

13   Nota bene. The fact that Michael's mother, Eva, born in Breslau, learned of her *Mischling* status in 1935, after the invention of Nuremberg Laws, and fled by train to Vienna, quite possibly along the very rail lines represented in the movie, puts him, Michael, the conscientious Gestapo man, in the stranger-than-fiction bin. There is no evidence BTW that Attenborough and Jackson—fine products of the Mirisch Brothers forgery factory— knew anything about this, i.e. Michael's family history and how often it runs parallel but never nicks the illusion of historical accuracy.

Big X and Intelligence are first to board the train when it arrives. They fear nothing so much as John Sturges' directorial wrath. Ensuite, the remaining POWs—Scrounger, Forger, Dispersal, to name several—climb aboard, according to plan, setting the foundation for a series of clever set pieces later on.

We get our first full body shot of the aching chimera Michael Paryla when he strolls past the station house in his unbuttoned tan trench coat and brown fedora at 2:08:14. Four seconds of flesh here, flanked by two extras. The accompanying figures are members of the local Landswehr; they are not Gestapo or SS or even Subliminalpolizei. Brown haired, not blond, they blow. Woollen jackets cinched at the waist. Fabulous billowing pants tucked into knee-high polished leather. They are clowns. Jodhpurs-clad, local yokels. There's no disguising their lumpen follow-the-Fuhrerness.

Michael Paryla confidently climbs aboard at 2:08:37. He turns on his right and we see his back after another nine seconds.

Next frame: Train no. 78185 cranks its way forward, breaking off from the station platform like a long ship out of harbour.

2:08:58
Interior Shot. Train. We see commuters on a busy run taking their daily travels along the Berlin-Breslau line. Big X and Intelligence enter the crowded coach. Facing camera is a fresh-faced Nazi youth. Seated beside him is an elderly woman: stern, stout, and tight-lipped she is, evidently humourless and yet pleased to bits with her provincial self. So, these are ordinary citizens, commuting for the Third Reich. *Alles in Ordnung.* All

is in order, and in its place, youth and old age. Sharing the inverse side of the bench is a pair of off-duty SS officers.

Big X steps forward. He stops before the sluggish SS officers. The officer in the aisle seat is dozing and has his feet up on the seat.

Big X clears his throat. The sleeping SS man comes to and drops his feet to the floor. Big X and Intelligence take their seats.

2:09:35

Exterior Shot. Nameless Village Square. This sequence was filmed in Füssen, an hour's drive south of Munich, a town with a distinct Alpine quality. James Coburn enters the square on foot, carrying a brown leather suitcase. He must be one of the hard arsers. He looks about like a boy scout, then approaches a stand of bicycles to his right. He selects one and inserts his suitcase under the jaws of the back-wheel trap. Nonchalantly, he pulls a pair of metal cutters from his breast pocket. The cutters are rudimentary. They resemble a harsh pair of toenail clippers. Nonetheless Coburn snips chain and lock and then leads the bicycle by its front handlebar out of captivity. He plays it very cool: Coburn is chic, a casual bicycle thief, dressed in Henri-Cartier Bresson era brown tweed and cap.[14] Indeed, Coburn is The Manufacturer.[15] Sturges, the director, gave Coburn free-

14 What does this reveal? Henri-Cartier Bresson served in a photo unit of the French Army until he was captured by the Germans during the Battle of France (1940). After two unsuccessful attempts, Bresson escaped on his third try from a prisoner-of-war camp inside Germany. He found his way back to France and served in the French Resistance, joining a group that helped escaped POWs until the end of the war.

15 Voila, Brickhill's fine description of how Johnny Travis, the real manufacturer and camp smithy, made the aforementioned wire clippers from tie bars ripped off the huts "...in a home-made forge he heated the clippers till they were red hot, poured a few grains of sugar on the metal around cutting notches, and heated it up again so the carbon in the sugar baked into the metal. Then he plunged it into cold water, and steel came out hard enough to cut wire." The ingenuity never ceases.

dom, and Coburn designed the character (his own) himself. What does this reveal?[16]

At last, The Manufacturer takes the stolen bicycle out for a slow, meandering ride, accompanied by the pastoral strains of Elmer Bernstein's soundtrack.

2:10:25
Exterior Shot. Paved Road. Day. Meadowlands and pastures. This scene was filmed on a stretch of open highway outside Füssen.

The hyperactive Hilts character played by Steve McQueen climbs out of the ditch and ties a wire to the barrier post. He scoots across the road and strings the wire, fastening it to the far post.

Here the soundtrack grows noticeably more menacing. Hilts hides in the ditch. The idea to stretch piano wire across the road to decapitate the enemy came from the French Underground, who used the technique during the war. The Underground had observed that motorcycle guards travelled front and rear of high brass cars. They would stretch piano wire at a 45 degree angle and lie it slack across the road. Once the car had passed, they raised it taut and knocked off the back rider. This seems to be what Hilts is up to here.[17]

---

16 A counter-intuitive chestnut: the actor is never so vulnerable (never more revealed) as when pulling an alien self over his or her own. Acting is a mask that eats away at the face.

17 Trust me, I got this from a reliable source and made copious notes from which I am cribbing quasi-verbatim. Seems I might be suffering from some researcher's over-my-head-in-this-gunk incipient blindness regarding copyright infringement; this malady coupled with a growing sense of impotence versus the compelling veracity of the primary material.

McQueen was an experienced rider and liked to do his own stunts—hell anybody's stunt—but insurance rates for the rising star were hugantic. The director John Sturges gave McQueen the green to buy all the bikes he needed and to hire stuntmen of his choice. McQueen hired his friend Bud Ekins, who flew over with several pals from north Hollywood, where Ekins owned a bike shop.

Meanwhile, a rider comes whipping around the curve. An Australian stuntman by the name of Tom Gibbs plays the German tripped by Hilt's wire at 2:11:13. Ekins had tried the stunt several times with no success. Tom Gibbs the Australian landed the stunt on his first try, but had to perform it three times before the camera caught it. The shot was done with a simple cut—a switch from the skid to a shot showing the bike hitting the ditch. Look closely at the thrown rider's carcass: McQueen's stunt double, Bud Ekins, is substituted for Gibbs in the second half of the shot.[18]

2:11:20
Exterior Shot. River's Edge. Dawn is breaking. The watery sham before our eyes represents the Bobr, a tributary of the Oder; but the scene was filmed on a stretch of the Rhine between Wiesbaden and Koblenz.

Here fugitives Charles Bronson and John Leyton, aka The Tunnel Kings, have made it—surprisingly by sauntering lethargically through the brush—to the river's edge.[19]

---

18   Trust me on this, too, stuntmen can pretty well do what they want since nobody else wants to do what it is they do.

19   'The Tunnel Kings' has a rockabilly ring. John Leyton, one of the Kings, had a Number 1 hit on the UK Singles Chart with "Johnny Remember Me" in 1961. Leyton did teen idol pop with a Wild West feel.

Cut. The camera switches angle and The Tunnel Kings open their eyes wide and see: there is a small wood dock along the shore, and a skiff bobbing in the water. The escapees register a doubletake. Who can believe their eyes? [20]

2:11:38
Exterior Shot. Country Road. Day. Fields. Herbivores grazing. Unidentified escapee thumbing a ride. He must be another hard arser. Back in the day, German-speaking prisoners were gifted train tickets and travel passes by the escape committee, while the arsers were sent out in the waist deep snow wearing great coats and carrying blankets, without so much as a false identity. But the movie was filmed during summertime. No great coat for this unidentified escapee. He is wearing a long black leather coat and carrying a package of some kind. It can't be fudge, can it?

Momentarily, a covered truck comes to a stop. The arser exchanges words with the driver and tips his hat before going around the front of the truck. He hops inside the cabin beside the driver, shifts his weight, and the truck is in gear.

2:12:01
Exterior Shot. River's Edge. Day. The Tunnel Kings hop off the dock into the boat. Leyton steadies the rudder, while Bronson manhandles the oars. Their skiff is a rowboat, after all. [21]

---

20 Unlike James Garner who rejected my appeal for an interview after his manager did or did not have cocktails with my 'hired' celebrity wrangler in Toronto at a TIFF event in 2010, John Leyton, a perfect gentleman, responded positively to an interview request in 2011. I'll be releasing excerpts from this exclusive interview in the following pages.

21 Then *what is a skiff?* My question, exactly.

The soundtrack is almost Handelesque, a harpsichord lapping and flowing as the escapees glide downriver to the Baltic Sea.

The river scenes are based on the Per Bergsland and Jens Muller escape story. Bergsland and Muller reached neutral Sweden by boat via Stettin. The only other successful escapee from the March 1944 breakout was a Dutchman by the name of Bram van der Stok. Van der Stok was the 18th man out of the tunnel. The night of the escape, he'd taken the train to Breslau and counted ten other escapees on the station platform. His next stop was Dresden. At Halle, he changed again for a train to Holland. This part of the journey took thirteen hours. Throughout, the Gestapo walked through the train car checking the papers of every passenger. Bram van der Stok made it to Gibraltar via Belgium, France and Spain. In total it took him four months to get to England.

2:12:23
Exterior Shot. Roadside. Day. Hilts wheels his motorbike out of the ditch dressed in full Wehrmacht drag. Obviously McQueen harvested his outfit straight off the stuntman's back. Without much ado, he speeds off down the road on his brand new ride.

2:12:50
Exterior Shot. Day. Out in the country. The train zips along like a theme to the soundtrack. The plot in a capsule slips through Silesia, chugging on stealth. Suspense and smooth sailing to the box office.

Nature's passivity, its spectatorship, is criminal. The sunshine is maddeningly neutral. That's naturalism for you.

2:12:54

Interior Shot. Train compartment. Day. The ticket collector enters the coach and strides past James Garner and Donald Pleasance and the McCallum character Dispersal. Garner shoots up, lights a cigarette, and follows the ticket collector through the doors of the coach ahead. Garner will explore. He is The Scrounger. In the next coach, he encounters the rosy-hued Nazi youth, the grey-faced witch, and the sleepy SS men (as for the latter: it must be their higher functioning evil which makes them so drowsy). The camera also catches a glimpse of Big X and his sidekick, Intelligence.

Cut to a close-up of James Garner at 2:13:23. Garner hauls on his cigarette and stares coldly ahead. Michael Paryla is coming from the opposite end of the car. Paryla yanks the sliding door. Garner retreats the way he came; presumably having seen enough. On his way, Garner whispers *tally-ho* to the McCallum character. *Tally-ho* is a codeword (obviously). Garner moves on. He nudges The Forger on the shoulder (by this point Blythe is flying blind and on the surface of things he cannot tell an American from a German) and escorts the Donald Pleasance character towards the exit.

McCallum is nonplussed. He sits back firmly. *Tally-ho* must mean nothing to him. Has he not studied the script?

McCallum replaces his wire-rim spectacles and adjusts his newspaper. He reads what every passenger on the train is reading. *Die Völkischer Beobachter*. The paper of the National Socialist German Worker's Party, The People's Observer. The headline is visible: *Tag für Tag hohe blutige Verluste der Sowjets*.

'Day After Day More Bloody Losses by the Soviets'. The war is not going well. The *Ostfront* is a bitch. Remember, this is March, 1944.

2:14:07

Interior Shot. Train. Day. The Gestapo man Michael Paryla continues his rounds. He glances at the identity cards offered by the pair of SS officers. He stops at Big X and Intelligence. There is something about *them*. Here at last the camera has our man Paryla speaking his first lines.

   Gestapo: Ihre Pässe bitte. *Your pass, please.*

   (He takes their passbooks.)

   Gestapo (after a pause): Vous êtes Français?

   Big X: Oui.

   Intelligence : Moi aussi.

   Gestapo: Merci.

   Big X: Merci bien.

2:14:24

Interior Shot. Train. Day. The Scrounger and The Forger continue to retreat, cars ahead of our Gestapo friend, sprinkling *Tally-ho*. They are making for an escape, by jumping from the train.

2:14:34

Interior Shot. Train. Gestapo Michael (standing) flips through the pages of Dispersal's passbook.

Gestapo: Sie reisen für Ihre Firma?

Dispersal: Ja. Für mein Gescheft.

Are you travelling for your company? Yes, for my business. Gestapo Michael studies Dispersal's passport, then the live specimen before him, before uttering a lacklustre *Danke.* Mind, Michael barely permits 'Thank You' to exit his lips. It is a hesitant, trapdoor-of-a-*Dan-ke*; you could say even, a begrudging 'you are lying to me and we both know it' kind of Thank You.

He exits the coach and the door slides shut behind him and that's the last an English audience sees of this actor alive. The running time is 2:14:56.

AFTERMATH

26

Hitler received the first full Gestapo report at his mountain residence Berghof, in the Bavarian Alps, on Sunday morning, _____ hours after the breakout.

Incensed. Humiliated. The Fuhrer ordered a nationwide manhunt—*eine Großfahndung*—the largest of wartime.

100,000
Oberregierungsrat Max Wielen, Breslau area chief of the Kriminalpolizei, sets the trap.

The nationwide search order is broadcast on German radio. More than _____ German troops join the hunt. Gestapo and Sicherheitspolizei work through trains checking papers. Local police and regular troops and the home guard watch over the fields and country lanes, while Hansel and Gretel sweep the forest.

5,000,000
An estimated _____ German citizens spend time looking for the escaped prisoners.

Holy gross gangs of dung!

73
_____ of the seventy-six POWS are tracked down, the majority in the days following the break.

8
Meanwhile, by the electromechanical typewriter, Gestapo chiefs in ____ cities receive unprecedented and top secret orders.

Hitler wants the lot shot, Geneva Convention or not. He wants them dead. But. Hitler's top darlings, Himmler and Goering, are against this.

'To shoot them all would make it obvious that it was murder,' Goering sputters.

50

This number, symbolic of the utmost reserve and fair play, is calculated not to do irreparable damage to relations with neutral nations.

The Sagan Order was commissioned by Himmler and penned by his second in command, Obergruppenführer Ernst Kaltenbrunner: "The increase of escapes by officer prisoners of war is a menace to internal security. After interrogation the officers are to be taken in the direction of their original camp and shot en route. The shooting will be explained by the fact that the recaptured officers were shot while trying to escape, or because they offered resistance, so that nothing can be proved later. The Gestapo will report the shootings to the Kriminalpolizei giving this reason."

So:____. ____ British bunny rabbits will be shot.

3

Neutral nations. Sweden, with whom Nazi Germany traded for iron ore, is one. Portugal, with its wolfram, is a second. Doing irreparable damage to relations with Switzerland, on whom the Nazis depended for their looted gold transactions, seems, in perfect hindsight, to have been an utter impossibility.

Name ____ neutral nations during the Second World War?

1

It is left to ____ man in Berlin to compose the wish list. The Gestapo and SS for their part will happily carry out the killings.

> Kriminalpolizei Chief Arthur Nebe
> (Reviewing the records of the recaptured prisoners and marking names with a red cross):

> *Der muss dran glauben.* He gets it.[22]

?

The same clever set piece is repeated, in separate locations, throughout Germany, from Saarbrucken to Munich.

At dusk, the recaptured POWs are herded into a covered truck. After several hours on the Autobahn the vehicle stops and the prisoners are entreated to watch the sunrise. Since it is such a long journey to camp, why not therefore jump from the cargo deck and stretch your legs? Cigarette? Also for your friend. Take this opportunity to relieve yourself.

According to courtroom testimonies, handcuffs were removed and the majority of men were shot from behind, in a relaxed posture: in a field, flies open, smoking while urinating and watching the morning stars, the fading lights, but probably scheming, already dreaming of their next escape attempt.

On examination the exit holes were found at the skull base.

---

22   The same Arthur Nebe was implicated as a conspirator in the Hitler bomb plot of July 1944, and hanged, wikipediately, by piano wire.

2

Because fifty is a statistic and _____ is a tragedy.

On the night of the escape, S/L Roger Bushell and Sous-Lt Bernard Scheidhauer found their way to the Sagan railway station and caught a train to Breslau. Then east to Saarbrucken. Waiting on platform for a train to Alsace, Bushell and Scheidhauer were questioned by a uniformed German in French. Posing as French businessmen, both Bushell and Scheidhauer conversed admirably. But the German used an old trick: he shot a question at Bernard Scheidhauer in English, *and Scheidhauer answers in English*. The game is up. [23]

In Saarbrucken, Roger Bushell and Bernard Scheidhauer were interrogated by the chief of the local Kriminalpolizei, Emil Schultz. Schultz, along with Oberlieutenant Dr. Leopol Spann, Gestapo Chief at Saarbrucken, and driver Walter Breithaupt, murdered Bushell and Scheidhauer by the side of the autobahn on the way to Kaiserslautern.

'Bushell crumpled slowly onto his right side.' Eerily precise descriptions likes this one, in Paul Brickhill's memoir, were lifted from courtroom testimonies.

Their bodies were taken to Nene Bremm concentration camp near Saarbrucken for cremation. The urns containing the

---

23   When I begin to tell acquaintants the Michael Paryla story, give the outlines, say, at a dinner party, people inevitably think of the representative scene in the movie and of the Gestapo man who intercepts Richard Attenborough and Gordon Jackson as they are about to board a bus in a nondescript Germany city. This Gestapo man and the smug little trick he plays on the disguised escapees is a crowd pleaser. When I confess that my relative is not *this* Gestapo but another, 'he's the guy who ... ' , the reaction is not good. Curiosity crumples into disappointment. *If only your Michael was that other guy, then you'd have a real story on your hands.*

ashes were then returned to Sagan for burial. Bushell was thirty-three and Scheidhauer twenty-two. [24]

23

Of the remaining ＿＿＿ recaptured POWs, seventeen are sent back to Sagan, four to Sachsenhausen, and two are locked away in the high security Colditz Castle.

3

Only ＿＿＿ escapees—one Dutchman, two Norwegians—make it to freedom. It must taste great.

1/3

A new Kommandant, Oberst Braune, arrives at Stalag Luft III to replace Von Lindeiner.

Kommandant Braune outlaws Red Cross parcels and installs a strict regimen of three mandatory appells per day. Braune also shuts the camp theatre.

The POWs grow wary when only about a ＿＿＿ of the escapees have been returned to camp. They knew many more had been recaptured.

1944

"It was cold-blooded butchery and we are resolved that the foul criminals shall be tracked down."

---

24   In case you want to know, and so you don't begin your own manhunt: Leopol Span was killed in April 1945 during an air raid on Linz. Emil Schulz was found under a false identity in Saarbrucken and was hanged at Hamelin 27 February 1948. The driver Breithaupt was 'given life' on 3 September 1947.

Anthony Eden, House of Commons. London, May _____.

250,000
Wings Commander Wilfred Bowes and Flight Lieutenant
Francis McKenna of the R.A.F. Special Investigation Branch
depart for Germany in August of 1946.

Six interrogation teams are established in Hamburg, and
over _____ German citizens are questioned.

18
On July 1, 1947, before a War Crimes Court in Hamburg,
begins the trial of _____ Gestapo men held in custody.

Paul Brickhill attends the trial, which is held in the Curio-
Haus, inside "an old-fashioned gray courtroom."

14
By day fifteen of the trial, all eighteen are convicted and found
guilty. Four are given prison terms. _____ are hung at Hamelin
Gaol on February 26, 1948.

1962
Meanwhile. 2:15:03. THE MIRISCH COMPANY INC.
PRESENTS. Ext—Day. Stunt doubles for James Garner and
the blinkin' Forger-gone-blind Donald Pleasance, leap from
the hind caboose and tumble down the embankment and roll
behind piled hay for cover. Cut to a shot of James Coburn,
the chic manufacturer, all wobbly, riding stolen goods to the

strains of Elmer Bernstein's soundtrack. Cut to Charles Bronson and John Leyton rowing into the sunset, down the narrow Bobr, and never to appear on the same decorated set again. The soundtrack is poignantly aimless now until such a point as Steve McQueen—astride his ride—resurfaces at the frontier. The Alps loom ahead. The snowy peaks are lit. Switzerland, McQueen mutters under his breath (obviously Switzerland is a swear word). McQueen gives 'er juice and speeds off right smack into a checkpoint. Bad luck. Here the hyperactive American must idle. At the roundabout McQueen is spotted by stuntman Roy Jensen, playing a German guard. McQueen lacks proper identification. He straight-legs Jensen to the gut, then heads for the hills on his modified Triumph. This audacious action by the American kicks off the finale. The chase is on. McQueen is closely followed by a flock of German stuntmen and a sidecar manned by Bud Ekins and Chuck Hayward. But no one can quite keep up. The German stunt riders hired in Munich are useless off-road. And, cut!

Solution: McQueen rides off a secure distance—the action is stopped—he turns his Triumph around and comes riding back, changes bike, changes clothes, puts on the German uniform. Roll camera, action: McQueen rides again, over the same ground, in pursuit of himself.

Steve McQueen is the centerpiece from here on. He speeds away from the Germans (who follow in silly numbers), eventually losing them when he changes places with his stunt double, Bud Ekins, who jumps the six-foot-wide wood and barbed wire frontier fence with great panache. The iconic fence jump was one of last scenes of the movie to be shot, in September 1962. Most of the actors by now had been sent home. The extras, many of them students from Munich or Heidelberg, had returned to the classroom. Allegedly it was McQueen's idea that his character would steal a German motorcycle and attempt escape by jumping the boundary fence between Germany and Switzerland, although motorcycles were not used in the March 1944 escape. The director John Sturges climbed aboard and United Artists leapt at the suggestion (in place of the female touch, macho deliverance would do nicely: a rising star in flight is a sexy and dangerous sight).

But first, the crew reconstructed the wartime border between Germany and neutral Switzerland. The able Sturges contracted five local farmers to build a mile long double barrier. Insurance fees kept McQueen from even attempting the jump, which nonetheless, launched him to international stardom. For many years, it was accredited to the actor, not his stunt buddy Ekins, who was paid 750 USD to do the deed.

1963-2009-1944

The film is released. Michael Paryla advances through the train compartment to compartment, swaying side to side, and I watch him as the camera does; through the director's eyes. The shot is well established. It is *Germany, March 1944, the 11ᵗʰ anniversary of Hitler's rise to power as Supreme Ruler.* Sturges the American is working magic with history. Stalag Luft III is the stuff of legend. *Ja, Ja. Das ist Deutschland* and Michael Paryla is the blond bimbo on the train. My cousin moves through the cars, no fuss, single-mindedly, with the casual swagger of a superior race. Swaying not much, not much at all because by this point, after a full day of shooting, running up and down the Munich-Hamburg line, he's got his sea legs.

Whenever I watch this scene, I'm irked by the knowledge that John Sturges, who planned the shoot, didn't see half of it. Sturges shot plot and his actors with methods. He shot the superficial. Sturges had his own technique of lining up the camera and his actors on the set. Yet for all his alleged experience at teasing out the idiosyncrasies of secondary characters, Sturges let Michael Paryla go easy. Michael Paryla as a Nazi, on the map, not thirty years after his parents fled by train through the same neck of the woods: who catches this on film?

I see Michael Paryla making his career move, juxtaposed with more innocents than it makes sense to count, aboard a modified train, like the one rented by the film crew from the German Rail Bureau, riding the death fugue.

Deutsche Bahn ice 164

TRAVEL BY TRAIN IS AN EXCUSE FOR BEING. Thirty travel writers agree. Between stations the self reports to nobody in particular. Ask Paul Theroux, whose dreamed truths are as good as Freud's. 'Tourists don't know where they've been, travelers don't know where they're going.' Sounds very quaint, somewhat pat, but you know what he meant, and even if I don't know where I am going with this now, it doesn't matter because the real tripping happens horizontally, out the side window of the train.

Welcome aboard Deutsche Bahn ice 164, leaving München Hauptbahnhof for Hamburg Bahnhof with stops in: Ingolstadt: Nürnberg: Würzburg: Fulda: Kassel-Wilhemlshöhe: Göttingen: Hannover: Uelzen: Lüneberg, Hamburg.

Michael's scenes in *The Great Escape* were filmed on this rail line between Munich and Hamburg, an active route in the summer of 1962. The German Railroad Bureau collaborated kindly with the film crew, finding Sturges a passenger coach from the era. A railroad engine was rented and two condemned cars were modified to house the camera equipment. The passenger coach was fitted with platforms to support arc lamps, which illuminated the train interiors with its precious cargo of Attenborough, Pleasance, Jackson, Garner et al. On the flat car, Sturges mounted his Chapman crane, which was designed to swing out over the passenger coach. It would be used to film the scene where stunt doubles for James Garner and Donald Pleasance jump from the train. This happens after Gestapo great, Michael Paryla, and his lumpen sidekicks, drive them to desperation. Especially James Garner: more than any other on the train he reacts strongly to the sight of Michael Paryla. More reason to Skype *him* and not someone like the blind and deceased Donald Pleasance.

The second to last car was reserved for Wardrobe. Here, Bert Hendrikson's crew languished. What they got up to is anyone's guess. Maybe an S&M-themed Nazi-regalia dress party. These things were very rock n' roll back in the day. Very outlaw, very *Easy Rider*. What we know they did not get up to is finding cousin Michael a properly fitting trench coat. His sleeves are very short.

The Filmfuehrer, my go-to film studies advisor, offers this angle on the origin of Michael's ill-fitting costume: "What we seem to be dealing with is an actor who did not look good in the rushes or didn't sound right to the director being bumped for your relative, and then the director just winged it, not hard since the lines are short. These things are done in a minute, especially at the end of the day if the light is changing."

A workable hypothesis. Michael was fluent in German, and had functional French. He knew the historical background material like the back of his hand. He could have improvised, no problem. And the informality of process, the spur of the moment change in plans, would explain why he'd been stuck with a kid's-size jacket, with sleeves that exposed plenty of forearm and wrist. Bert Hendrickson had done the costumes for *The Magnificent Seven* (1960) and *West Side Story* (1961). So, he had run his measuring tape a long distance over the stars. Why then so drastically short-sleeve the Gestapo on the train? Because Hendrickson had sized the coat for a different actor. That must be it. In a flash, Michael graduated from extra to bit player. He was in the right place at the right time. His lines do not match James Clavell's draft screenplay of 26 April 1962, because Michael was winging it.

My mind is racing. Meanwhile, The Filmfuehrer has not stopped feeding me the insider angle:

> If an actor feels good to the director on the set, or they look good in rushes, they will get bumped up. Or, if the director improvises, they may just bubble up through the baseline energy of the scene. In none of these cases do they have lines written for them, so they are not involved in the casting for 'parts' which is based on the shooting script, and from which actors and/or their agents negotiate contracts. This includes credits.

Michael had no agent as far as I know. But is that likely?

The shooting was squeezed between actual runs. Inside the radio car, the rail bureau operator received signals from further down the line. When the radio operator alerted the engineer and crew to traffic on the main line, Sturges et al. retreated to a siding, where they could watch passenger cars like the one I'm riding today sail by at eighty miles per hour.

The youthful DB ticket collector is wearing a black cap and a blue short-sleeved shirt under a navy vest. He is unshaven. His red necktie hangs limply, a casual formality.

"*Bitte, ein Frage?*" I bring him to attention.

"*Ja, Natürlich...*" He can be of help, naturally. An official of the state rail bureau, dressed in the drag of the Dairy Queen or Burger King.

"Where will I find the restaurant?"

"Closed today—unfortunately for you. There was a power failure. But, shortly, we will serve hot pretzels."

I frown and at the same time ask myself WWJD? What Would Joerg Do in a situation like this. A power failure on Deutsche Bahn ICE? This is not The FGW, or is it now?

The train goes through Ingolstadt, birthplace of Frankenstein's monster and also where Audis are polished and made precise, and Würzburg, destroyed more thoroughly than Dresden and, wikipediately, in just seventeen minutes by 225 British Lancaster bombers. And Nuremberg, who can forget Nuremberg, where the Nazis partied under Albert Speer's architecture of light. It is nothing spectacular on a Sunday morning. Nuremberg. Nothing special. BMW dealer, placards for the SPD, radio towers, tiled rooftops, football pitches, nondescript industries, Autobahn entry ramp, sparse woods, fields and then forest.

Alles Normal. Nothing out of the ordinary.

"Pretzel?"

Nuremberg is where Rudolf Steiner, founder of anthroposophy and spiritual father of the Waldorf School, gave his February 1918 lecture 'The Dead Are With Us'. The Waldorf School that Michael attended during the war was in Switzerland. In Germany, the Nazis shut them down. Too radical for The FGW. Hitler was hostile to Steiner's mystical philosophy, which he associated with the Jewish frame of mind.

"Nein, danke."

No pretzel now. I have no appetite. I'm busy scrawling notes. Giddy with an experience tied to its own documentation, which is not what it ought to be, pure experience, but something electrifying nonetheless. So what if you cannot observe yourself in the moment without changing yourself in the moment. At least there is movement and, however minor, metamorphosis. It must be why actors so often find themselves in front of the mirror. Here I am. No, it's not me. Catch him if you can.

The living are not always with it, but according to Rudolf Steiner the dead are with us. Correction. The 'so-called dead'. Once they pass through the gate of death, Steiner's so-called dead bide time awaiting karmic resolution and rebirth. Steiner believed without an iota of doubt in reincarnation. But notice, again according to Steiner, that reincarnation takes its own sweet time. In the meantime Steiner strongly recommended reading to the dead in order to help them develop their soul, between death and rebirth.[25] In the lecture 'The Living and the Dead', given in Berlin in February 1918, during what must have been Steiner's Germany-wide Clairvoyant Consciousness Tour, he outlines the correct method for reading to the dead. This is handy because reading to the dead is not first nature, and to this day among the so-called living there remains confusion concerning The Freaky Steiner Way. Listen to what Dr. Ernst Katz had to say in 2004 during his address given at the American Anthroposophy Society's General Meeting:

> I have been asked whether one should read aloud or silently. What matters to the departed soul is what goes on in your conscious mind. He or she picks up the thoughts and feelings of what is being read. Many people can only hold a thought clearly in their mind when they read aloud slowly. So that is what they should do. When such people read silently they skip through the pages and do not dwell with sufficient intensity on the thoughts they are reading. Other people do not know what they are reading when they read aloud. All their energy goes into pronouncing the words. For them it is better to read silently and try to understand every sentence. At first one should read in the language that was closest to the departed soul in life, usually the mother tongue. After a few years, one can read in any language, as long as one understands the thoughts and meaning of the words one is reading. Rudolf Steiner speaks here of five years.

---

25 *Read to the dead*: Here is a growing market publishers ought to explore within the shrinking marketplace for books, and a fresh angle for booksellers. Even a so-called writer like myself can see the potential: the in-store table piled high with volumes and the neat sign 'Especially for the Dead: Rudolf's Picks'. Or maybe the idea has already been taken to town by clairvoyant retailers and national radio hosts.

> A second bridge between the living and the dead is based on the
> possibility of asking questions of a departed soul and receiving
> answers. The questions must be of a soul-spiritual nature, not
> of a materialistic kind. It is best to entertain the question when
> one goes to sleep, but it can also be done during the day...

Steiner is quite precise about scheduling any communication with the so-called dead at dusk or at twilight. It appears that in these hours, in a drowsy and liminal state, both the living and the dead are at their most gullible. I'm inclined to ponder this in relation to prose fiction, and in particular in relation to the social contract between so-called writers and so-called readers, in which the latter group conveniently agrees to play dead and suspend disbelief at the title page. Curiously this arrangement does not motivate in the writer ambivalence toward truth, nor does it render the reader more easy to fool, which is surprising. And counter-intuitive. Which leads me back to the early days of the War on Michael. Sometime ago it occurred to me that what pushes people to falsify and invent lies is precisely the pressure to tell the truth.

In addition to being read to, the dead have work to do. It's not all Facebook and Tumblr.[26] According to Rudolf Steiner 'after the death of the physical body, the human spirit recapitulates the past life, perceiving events as they were experienced by the objects of its actions.' I personally like this idea of a formal and systematic review of each our actions from the point of view of the other, as part of the prerequisite to receiving your karmic benefit package for the next life. It is something the so-called living should practise as well: treating others as we ourselves expect to be treated. This part of spiritual rehabilitation makes good sense and forms a major part of The FSW.

---

26   I wonder what Steiner would have done with Skype. It's not my cup of tea, Skype, but then I'm not nearly the social networker Steiner seems to have been.

Michael attended a Rudolf Steiner school in Zurich during the war, but now I'm thinking it's possible he was sent from Berlin to boarding school in Habkern, through the years 1946-48. His letter to 'Georg' implies something of the kind. Whichever years it was, going to a Steiner school does seem to have made a lasting impression on him. And why not? Steiner's way regards thinking as an organ of perception through which the direct experience of a spiritual world can be reached. Anthroposophy privileges the faculties of perceptive imagination, inspiration, and intuition—in combination, these faculties cultivate a form of thinking independent of our senses. Steiner's spiritual philosophy potentially has a lot to offer someone with an artistic temperament.

Steiner's writings are bewitching. Even if the mystic is a quack, I can tolerate bonkers better than Das Boring. Anthroposophy gives me something to ponder on the train, and I wonder now if Steiner's brand of mysticism had any influence on Michael's 'development'. And yet, what can you say about these things? Hindsight is a trap. There is the tendency to read too much into the so-called lives of the dead. In any case, the WoM is something that started long ago and long before I had even heard about Rudolf Steiner and his impossible anthroposophy. In other words, I started talking to the so-called dead Michael before I knew it ever might be fashionable to do so. It was Michael's ex-girlfriend Janine who put me on the Steiner trail originally, referencing him during a conversation we had about Eva and Antoine, and about Michael's schooling.

The speed of this train is magnificent. I feel it may have mystical healing powers. Excuse me, but this is more like The Fucking German Way, surely. Engineering.

Under a cloudless sky, Deutschland drifts by like a silent movie. The giant canvas lit by heroic sun, the scenery generated by successive wind farms outstretched on the far hilltops—the garden of steel stamens and bright blades work precisely to rotate my panoramic view from rolling country and gentle, sloping pastures to the urban exteriors and the frozen frame of the next station.

It is much faster than the train the film crew leased from DB for several weeks in the summer of 1962, and considerably faster than the original trains from 1944. Nobody in their right mind—not a Hollywood stuntman, not even an escapee—would jump from this train. You'd be sucked underneath, sliced into ribbons and spat out. The ICE is top-notch.

STATELESS PERSON OF
UNDETERMINED NATIONALITY
A Review of the Evidence

** Important—Avis—Wichtig **
Spoiler and Plot Summary Alert

AUSTRIA (1935 to 1938)

Ages one to three are spent in Vienna.

Status: Refugee.

Activities: Birth, breastfeeding and potty training.

Physical Characteristics and Identifying Features: The boy is blond.

Emotions: Experiences feelings of loss (during weaning) and tingling of the power of the will (anal retentiveness).

Accomplishments: Michael quits his oral and anal phase reluctantly, and cuts his teeth early, learning to walk and talk. Object permanence.

Reason for departure: The post-Anschluss party in Austria that tore the skin off Vienna.

Method of departure: Hide and seek over and across the Alps.

Things Michael hates: Too early to tell.

Michael needs: Mother.

Favourite question: 'Why?'

SWITZERLAND (1938 to 1946)

Ages four to eleven are spent in Zurich.

Status: Displaced person.

Activities: Waldorf School. Michael learns a bit of French and about The FSW.

Physical Characteristics and Identifying Features: Pudgy.

Emotions: Experiences (more) feelings of loss (parents separate, his father leaves).

Accomplishments: Michael locates his erogenous zone.

Reason for departure: The end of the Second World War.

Method of departure: Train.

Things Michael Hates: Travelling.

Michael needs: His father.

Favourite question: 'Am I good or bad?'

GERMANY (Part I: 1946 to 1949)

Ages 11-14 spent in the Russian sector of post-war Berlin.

Status: Stateless.

Activities: Black Market. Spying.

Physical Characteristics and Identifying Features: Still blond, still a round face.

Emotions: Hidden.

Accomplishments: Survival.

Reason for departure: Failure to thrive.

Method of departure: Airlift.

Things Michael Needs: Siblings or Friends.

Michael loves: Romeo (German Shepherd).

Favourite question: 'Where am I going?'

CANADA (1949 to 1956)

Ages 14-21 spent in Sault Ste. Marie, Ontario and in Montréal, Québec.

Status: Undetermined Nationality.

Activities: Immigration to Canada, Clarinet, Basketball, Theatre.

Physical Characteristics and Identifying Features: Tall and handsome.

Emotions: Insecurity.

Accomplishments: Attends Sault Ste. Marie Collegiate Institute and McGill University. Tonsillectomy. Falling in love.

Reason for Departure: Debatable. He wants a career in acting (absolutely). He misses Germany (perhaps). He seeks reunion with father (likely).

Method of Departure: Airplane.

Things Michael Needs: Self-confidence.

Michael loves: Practical Jokes.

Favourite questions: Questions of Self.

GERMANY (Part II: 1957-1967)

Ages 21 to 32 are spent in Germany, primarily in Munich, Berlin, Bremen, and Hamburg.

Status: Actor.

Activities: Insomnia, narcotic yearning, and death.

Physical Characteristics and Identifying Features: His emptiness. An outline without core.

Emotions: Doubt, self-doubt, despair.

Accomplishments: The ability to fool himself. Falling in love (again).

Reason for departure: Debatable. Difficulty of being. Complications of childhood. Untenable father–son dyadic syndrome. Pure exhaustion.

Method of departure: Also debatable. Untenable lifestyle. Accidental overdose. Suicide. A misaligned heart and scars to myocardium.

Things Michael Hates: Himself, and reviews of himself.
Michael Needs: Spiritual rehabilitation.
Favourite question: 'How shall I live?'

THE WAR ON MICHAEL

THROUGH THE MANY YEARS of the War on Michael, when all had gone suddenly quiet on the front and you could hear a pen drop, I followed the same strategy and launched emails to members of the family, to acquaintances and ex-classmates of his. I asked for reinforcements, for extra help. And usually I got it. From abroad and from within Canada, no postage and at no charge.

These days my emails are more frequently addressed to scholars and librarians and historians and archivists, though sometimes I hit on casual aides, like my friend The Filmfuehrer. The Filmfuehrer does come up with the most amazing things. For example, to clear up the common misconception spread by commentators that the bike Steve McQueen used in the movie became the Fonz's in *Happy Days*, the Filmfuehrer writes:

> Though Fonzie drove many bikes, he settled on a 1953 Thunderbird. This is obvious from the lack of rear shocks and huge springs on the saddle of his bike. Triumph went to swing-arm rear suspension in 1954. Rear suspension is a must for stunts like the jump in GE and the bike's rear shocks are visible. The seats on these bikes had no springs. So Fonzie's bike was not McQueen's.

I feel there is a 'sit on it' joke in here, somewhere, regarding The King of Cool, but The Filmfuehrer is not onto it. Instead there is the matter of his own credentials: "I speak from experience of owning four Triumphs, a 1953 21 (350cc), a 1958 TR6 (650cc), a 1966 T120 (650cc) and, in Kathmandhu, a 1972 Tiger Cub (250cc)."

Once I asked him to recommend a film studies reference text. The rapid turnaround email incorporated the following definition of filmmaking.

> A film is made three times, and each version is different. First version is a script, and this is a compromise with regards to the original story. It's the document that gets people onside—a sort of prayer. Second version is what is shot by the camera and recorded by the sound engineer of the actor's efforts on a decorated set—something that may or may not follow the script. Third version is the assembly of what was actually recorded with the camera and sound devices by an editor into the final story— which may or may not be what the director had in mind.

But I like it. And I like this on film production:

> In his or her mind, a camera operator is seeing, through the eyepiece, the images projected onto a screen in the theatre. The director is seeing, or looking for, an emotional sequence that completes itself within the context of all the other pieces, including both variables of acting technique and constants in script structure, needed to assemble the story. He or she also wants the actor to go to the limits of their powers. Shooting is to a degree an act of harvesting.

While he often gets his wheels stuck in arcane matter, The Filmfuehrer does occasionally traffic in the unexpectedly poignant aside. Here he is, dishing on border guards and actors, with Michael's role in the movie forefront in mind:

> You could mention that the power of the border guard is total, within their extremely limited zone of authority. This spatial context is identical to that of a film actor on a set.

And here he is, on the question of suicide:

> My intuition tells me suicide is important. I have the benefit of an interesting insight into suicide. A psychiatrist told me that in his experience people never committed suicide at the nadir point... it was always when the solution to a long standing problem appeared. i.e. A man tries for years to get the bank to give him money to start a business. He gets it approved, and kills himself. So this fits with Michael.

Lastly, here he comments on an early draft of the Michael book; apparently The Filmfuehrer is a bit of a literary critic:

> At present, there is far too much light and not enough darkness. And the darkness required is not the thin, easy darkness of the forest at night. It is a dense, difficult-to-traverse darkness thick with the spoor of wandering human souls. Thoughts and ideas are light, details are dark because they must be dug from deep within the story's soil. Thus I feel a deep need for some detail from Michael's childhood and/or some detail or idea about the woman he loves.

The point is that, as well being as a fount of information, The Filmfuehrer can be a tonic when the going gets tough. Frankly, I would not have gotten this far without him. I owe him a great deal. But there are times when even The Filmfuehrer will not do. Times when I need to return to the original battleground and bring the fight back to the making of the movie. Thus when I feel very up for it, I open communication with agents and management groups, the hired representatives of members of the original cast; for example, John Leyton's management group, JRM Partner, in the UK.

Subject: Great Escape - Michael Paryla

Dear Sir or Madam,

I would like to contact your client John Leyton.

I am a Canadian writer currently working on a book about Michael Paryla, a family relative and refugee from Nazism who had the part of a Gestapo agent in *The Great Escape*.

Michael Paryla was an extra and not credited in the movie, though he had several lines.[27] He appears in the movie at 'Neustadt' and is in the train scene.

It is my hope that Mr. Leyton might agree to a brief interview with me regarding his memory of Michael Paryla and his own part in the movie.

I realize Mr. Leyton may not remember Michael Paryla, but Mr. Leyton might be interested in the fascinating story of Mr. Paryla's own escape and return to Germany. [28]

---

27   He was a bit player, actually, and there is a difference, but at the time I didn't properly know a rush from a synch, a bit player from a walk-on from a non-speaking role from a principal. I didn't know a whole lot. Re-enter The Filmfuehrer: "There is probably a very specific union definition but I would say that normally, you have crowd scene extras etc, who get no credit, and this would include interiors, up to say a restaurant size. Smaller than that, a few people in a room, you are no longer an extra but have a bit part. If the person's face is alone in the frame, or they are in the frame with a principal character, they are no longer an extra but a minor member of the cast. If they speak, then they can be sure of a higher rank ... about as high as you can get before having a 'part'."

28   Like he might. Like he cares. Witness the incontinent egonomics in action.

Thank you for your time and patience. I hope Mr. Paryla's story is of interest to Mr. Leyton. An email or telephone conversation about these matters would be of immeasurable value to me, both professionally and personally.

Sincerely,
Andrew Steinmetz
Ottawa, Canada

And the swift reply:

Hello Andrew,
John thanks you for your interest. John never met Michael or was present when the train scene was shot. At that time he was in Munich waiting for the 'lake' shot to be filmed. However if you want to send me a couple of questions that you would like John to answer he will be happy to send you a reply.
Best regards. Steve

Wow! How do you like that, Garner? Some primary research material at last, which my therapist and a fictional list of publishers have been begging me for! For ages! This potentially is Book-Deal-clinching. Considering the value of the information I stand to gain, it is surprising how 'unprofessional' my response is to Leyton's agent Steve, which I've thrown off in the wind-tunnel of compulsive hen-peck finger-typing:

Hello Steve, and Hello Mr. Leyton

Thank you for your very generous reply. And thank you for your time. Before getting to my questions, BLA BLA BLA BLA BLA BLA tell you a little more biographical BLA BLA BLA.

Michael Paryla was also in Munich at the film studio, and I know for certain he met Charles Bronson. Mr. Paryla had a house in Munich near the film studios. There are many eerie coincidences that link his private life to the film. For instance, BLA BLA BLA BLA BLA BLA BLA BLA BLA BLA BLA BLA BLA BLA BLA BLA BLA BLA BLA BLA BLA Michael's father BLA BLA BLA Bertolt BLA BLA BLA BLA BLA the same city where the British tried the war criminals responsible for murdering the 50 escaped prisoners BLA BLA BLA buried BLA BLA BLA BLA BLA BLA BLA BLA BLA Waldfriedhof Cemetery, very close to the Bavariafilmstadt. Hamburg and Munich are important BLA BLA BLA BLA BLA BLA BLA BLA BLA BLA BLA BLA.

While I have had some good luck tracking down biographical details, I am considerably less experienced at digging up documents related to the film. For example, I'm told Mr. Paryla's contract and casting audition files should rest with Stalmaster-Lister & Co. I've not been able to contact to Stalmaster-Lister & Co.

Here now are my questions . . .

I have precisely eight, which I formulate on the spot. I list them and send my overwrought and long-winded reply to his first reply away. And then the long wait. There are no more emails for quite awhile. I have asked for too much. Obviously, I've been overexuberant. Obviously, they must have caught my scent or the spoor of my wandering human soul and were scared off. There's nothing coming my way from across the big pond. One day, months later, I compose a third, more restrained, email. I ping Mr. Leyton's agent and immediately get a response. Here are my questions to Mr. Leyton, followed by his answers.

Q1. From my reading I was able to find out that many of the fictional characters in the film were based on historical people. Was your character—Willie, Tunneller—based on a historical character, and if so, as an actor, how did this influence your performance?

A1: We all knew that *The Great Escape* was a true story and I knew that the character I was portraying was based on a real person who was in Stalag Luft III. I don't know exactly who it was as there were several tunnellers. We did not meet any of the original POW's during filming but the fact I was portraying a real character in a film that was a true story involved research and understanding of what the POW's went through.

Q2. Could you share with me any details about your experience on set filming the lake or river scene with Charles Bronson?

A2. The river scene was the very last scene to be shot. Saying goodbye was quite emotional as Charles Bronson and I had worked together on the film for six months. Sadly we never met up again.

Q3. Looking back, what is particularly very difficult about 'becoming an actor'? Becoming an actor when you are the son of an actor?

A3. Acting is a very precarious profession, which is the first thing that any aspiring young actor must realise and accept. Being in the right place at the right time plays a huge role in an actor's career and finding the right representation is crucial. Following in the footsteps of a famous father makes it very difficult, as there are bound to be comparisons and criticisms. Frank Sinatra, who I appeared with in *Von Ryan's Express*, is a prime example. His son was a fine singer but was never going to escape from his father's shadow. He even had to cope with the same name, Frank Sinatra Jr.

Q4. Many of the actors in the movie had wartime experience and were former prisoners of war. Some of the German actors were prisoners of the Americans, for example. Was this kind of thing — an actor's previous wartime experience — discussed on the set?

A4. To my knowledge no previous wartime experiences by either Americans, Germans or British were ever discussed on the set.

Q5. Can you describe the mood and relationship between the German actors and the rest of the crew (from USA and England) on set?

A5. Everybody got on well. Hannes Messemer (who was a POW in Russia) and Robert Graf were very friendly. Unfortunately I never had the pleasure of meeting Michael Paryla as he was not involved in any of my scenes.

Q6. Do you remember how the film was received in England when it was released? Do you have an idea about how it was 'received' in Germany, whenever it was released there?

A6. It was received very well in England and the USA. There were a few ex-service men who complained about the American involvement, particularly as it was billed as 'A Glorious Saga of the RAF'. I have no idea how it was received in Germany. [29]

---

29 *Prädikat wertvoll!* It got a yellow star from *die Deutsche Film-und Medienbewertung Wiesbaden* remember. Personally, I don't think the FBW should be going around handing out 'yellow stars' to Second World War movies, but that's their internal business.

Q7. Americans were not involved in the actual escape, and yet the movie included the heroic acts of the All-American Steve McQueen. Was this kind of thing ever discussed on set? Historical inaccuracies?

A7. Historical accuracies were never discussed on the set. There were a few elements of the film that didn't adhere to the facts, such as the American involvement. However at the end of the day we were making a commercial movie and I think it was inevitable and acceptable that a bit of 'Hollywood' should be allowed to creep in. After all, what is the first thing that every-body remembers from the film—Steve McQueen on the motor bike and the jump over the barbed wire. That's Hollywood!

Q8. Are you still in contact with anyone professionally related to the making of the movie who might remember Mr. Paryla, and be willing to answer some questions I have?

A8. I am no longer in contact with anyone professionally related to the movie. Sadly most of the actors and crew are now dead. You could try contacting Tom Adams through Equity or Spotlight in the UK. Adams played 'Nimmo' and was, I believe, in the train scene with Michael Payala (*sic*).[30]

I hope this is some use to you. It was all a very long time ago—50 years next year![31]

Good luck with your book.

---

30   I tried contacting Tom Adams. No response from Spotlight or Equity. There were no further emails.

31   Look out for Blu-Ray! 2013 is the 50th anniversary of the movie's release. By then the War on Michael should be gone with the wind.

EXTRA HATER

Jonathan F. Vance, PhD, Professor and J.B. Smallman Chair, Department of History, The University of Western Ontario, is the author of *A Gallant Company: The True Story of 'The Great Escape'*. After reading his book, I sent Professor Vance an exploratory Mr. Paryla BLA-BLA-BLA-BLA email in the hopes that he might know a little more about

> … the reaction IN WEST GERMANY (at the time and later) to the making and release of this Hollywood blockbuster. In other words, the movie was a hit in the USA and UK, but how was it received in Germany ?

Vance replied with the kind of *I'm afraid I can't tell you anything about that* letter that I had grown familiar with and frequently received from experts out there in the field.

> The only thing I know about the movie in Germany is that a lot of the extras were students from the University of Heidelberg. One of them was a former professor of mine, but his part ended up on the cutting room floor!

And so it was this Professor Vance who led me to Michael Kater, Distinguished Research Professor Emeritus of History and a Fellow of the Royal Society of Canada (FRSC), at the Canadian Centre for German and European Studies, York University. Kater was an exciting find. He'd been an extra in the movie, and therefore more or less had the same experience on the decorated set as Michael must have had. In other words, I could extrapolate from Kater's experience. Not only that, I soon found out that Michael Hans Kater was born in Germany and like my Michael had moved to Canada as a teenager. What were the chances I'd find an extra Michael right here in my Canadian backyard? Professor Emeritus at The Canadian Centre for German and European Studies, no less.

Immediately I fired off an email to Professor Kater, who responded:

> Dear Mr. Steinmetz, thanks for the mail. The very successful Jonathan Vance is a former PhD student of mine. He has advised you right. But I was not a PhD student at Hidelberg [sic] at the time (that came later); I was playing modern jazz in Munich night clubs then (for a year, 1959-60), and hanging around with musicians, young actors (actresses!), painters, artists, writers. It was a marvellous time. The young man who asked me to be an extra along with himself, an artist...

> Hence I remember fondly my days as an extra in the film. I was five feet away from Steve McQ. [sic] and trying to catch a baseball he threw me, several times. I did this, but they cut out the scene when editing. Otherwise, he was racing around on that motorcycle they gave him in his spare time, destroying all the farmers' meadows. You may quote me on that.[32]

> I would love to talk to you but I am very busy meeting a book deadline.

> Unfortunately, I do not remember Mr. Paryla.

It was a good-natured response from a busy academic with a book deadline to boot, but it was not what I had in mind, and it would not suffice, since I too had a book deadline, if not a real or definite one.[33] Kater may well have played pitch with 'Steve

---

32 Done.

33 Obviously my so-called book deadline is self-imposed and not legally binding or whatever.

McQ' but he hadn't yet engaged in a game of email dodgeball with *der kanadische Schriftsteller Andrew Steinmetz.* I responded to the busy ex-extra Kater without delay—and again as with my correspondence with John Leyton's manager, I acted from inside the ADHD wind tunnel, addressing him as, Professor Emeritus at The Canadian Centre for German and European Studies, "Dear Professor Hater".

Of course, I realize my error as soon as it slips my outbox, making a blip as regret slides down my throat.

The tone of Hater's response confirms Kater caught my dirty little Freudian trick and sublimated it.

> I cannot set up a call because I am in and out of town. I shall answer a few questions by e-mail but only if you refer to me by name in the book, should you use the information. [34]

> Why Canada? Are you not in the States?

No, I'm not in the States. I'm right here in little-big-town Ottawa. What I presume just happened is the following. Upon receiving my hate mail, Kater plugged my name in a search engine, and the first Andrew Steinmetz to surface was the historian and author of *The Gaming Table: Its Votaries and Victims.* This is not the right Andrew Steinmetz. But who cares. In the end, I send him pretty much what I sent Leyton. His answers are to the point.

> Q1. Did you sign a 'contract'?

> A1. Nothing. I don't even recall there was a casting audition. I was given a Northern Rhodesian pilot's uniform to wear.

---

34   Done.

Q2. I'm interested in knowing what the atmosphere was like on set, especially in regards to the different nationalities collected in Germany to film a war movie 'not long' after the end of the war—Germans, Americans, Englishmen; was there any self-consciousness about this? I'm told by John Leyton that the atmosphere was very friendly. I don't doubt this but I am interested in knowing your experience, your feelings related to this collection of nationalities.

A2. I am sure it was friendly, we had a good time. I don't remember any particular feelings or experiences.

Q3. Did you meet and do you have any memories of the better known German actors in the movie, like Robert Graf, Hannes Messemer, Til Kiwe, ect [sic] ?

A3. No to all questions.

Q4. I am assuming you were born in Germany, though this might not be correct. As someone who is German-born, how did you feel acting in this movie which was set during the Third Reich? Did you feel self-conscious about this in any way?

A4. No. I enjoyed the experience and needed the money.

Q5. Do you remember how the film was received in Germany when it came out? (It was a hit elsewhere.) I'm interested to know what reaction there was in Germany to the film and its past?

A5. By the time the film came out in Germany, I must have been back in Canada doing my MA at U of T. I have no idea how it was received there.

Q6. Many of the actors involved in the movie had wartime and/or prisoner of war experiences—for example, Messemer was a prisoner of the Russians. Were you aware of this during the filming? Was it spoken of?

A6. I don't even remember those actors. I think I told you all I know. I was doing many crazy things at that time and this was one of them.

There were no more emails.

'Shot In The Never Get Bored'

DAS GOOGLE IS MY ESCORT. It knows all my secrets. Knows what I want. My history. So it takes me directly to www.cinema.de, where I hope to get a feeling for the present vibes surrounding *Gesprengte Ketten*. Forget the tame yellow star rating it received from the very stolid FBW—hear nothing more from the film bureau ensconced in Castle Biebrich on the Rhine—the movie receives full marks for 'voltage' and the editor's 'thumbs up' verdict at multiple online sites. In no time I pick up the trail of *Ein obercooler Steve McQueen und weitere Stars im legendären Fluchtdrama von 63*. This sounds more like it. I'm feeling lucky, so I Translate This Page:

> War 1944: The Germans have a warehouse built specifically for pris-
> oners who have escaped many times. What Major Bartlett (Richard
> Attenborough) and his fellow prisoners does not prevent another
> outbreak plan. Great effort, digging Hilts (Steve McQueen),
> Velinski (Charles Bronson) and other prisoners (James Garner,
> Donald Pleasance among others) three tunnels...The thrilling
> escape movie classic by John Sturges (*The Magnificent Seven*) was a
> hit movie of the 60s, and the stars brought in his own experience:
> Bronson toiled as a teenager in the coal mine, his claustrophobia in
> the tunnel was not played! Pleasance was shot down a bomber pilot
> and was in a German camp. Motorcycle Freak McQueen makes a
> self-assembly chase: He also plays one of the Nazis who persecute
> him by motorcycle.

You get the idea. Warehouse for a camp. Claustrophobia not played, but real. Motorcycle Freak Steve McQueen pulling off wheelies and illusions:

> His character gets the correct type a thrilling motorcycle chase donated. On the run from the captors, he graduated with his bike, even after today's conditions still mad stunts. And the motorsport enthusiast and mime it did not take itself very neatly to give rubber.

A 'mime' must be a stuntman. Machine-translating 'stuntman' as 'mime' is one hell of a counter-intuitive stroke of brilliance, I feel. But I wonder what would Bud Ekins have to say about it, him the Marcel Marceau of Motorbikes? Did Bud Ekins not very neatly give rubber? He did. He who jumped the barrier fence on a Triumph TR6 Trophy 650cc. He did neatly give rubber in the motorcycle chases he donated.

Rich stuff from Google Translate. Rich stuff. And much fun to have this mass of febrile and fertile gunk to mess through, as the train I am on speeds to Hamburg. Whatever is working away beneath the white interface, the resulting ambiguity is pleasing. There is accuracy, yes, you may want to consider that, but sometimes I prefer to be lucky. Who doesn't. To this end, the Online-Filmdatenbank is an *ausgezeichnete* site for online reviews. So too is Filmstarts.de.

More please. Here an anonymous film kritik introduces John Sturges to a German-speaking audience. The oracle speaks:

> The name John Sturges is perhaps not anyone an idea. The director is an undeserved dimension behind the recognition of other contemporaries left behind. His greatest success—the *Magnificent Seven* aside—was *The Great Escape*, a war film about a prison breakout that boasts high-profile actors and the audience prepares a thieving pleasure.

A thieving pleasure, *genau*, you could not contribute a more redolent profile of John Sturges. There is the suggestion of an enigma in representing the director Sturges as an 'undeserved dimension behind the recognition.' I don't know what this means, but I like the sound of it.

The movie's historical background:

> Southern Germany in 1944: The Second World War is in its heyday. Many officers find themselves Allied prisoners of war. The problem: Germans, looking for the escapees can not fight on the front, and broken off, which again could not be captured again intervene in the war.

Let me translate, I feel lucky: *The many Germans who join the hunt to recapture the escapees cannot contribute to the war effort on the front line. The unrecaptured escapees get a second chance to wreak havoc.* Trust me. This relates to an idea mentioned earlier and one held by the Allies, that it was each prisoner's duty to attempt escape and that even unsuccessful events upset order and diverted attention from the front lines. You have to understand that what belies the cold white interface is algorithmic maturity: the warm intelligence which produces machine-translation which is as reckless and imperfect as any human being. Instantaneous, intuitive, and inspired.

One criticism that emerges from multiple reviewers is that the movie portrays the atmosphere inside Stalag Luft III in too light a manner. Like a summer camp:

> The prisoners in the movie get on surprisingly well. One gets the impression that the outbreak has just sporting reasons, the nasty camp life, he is not owed. This is underscored by the stirring music. And that's the only thing the film is guilty of: the war described as an adventure playground, the big boys doing exciting things. Injured soldiers can not be seen, all doing splendidly.

Another reviewer wrote:

The prisoners would have preferred to spend the rest of the war in the camp, instead, they behave as if all a game. Because war is not funny, it's only the average rating …

War is a game and escaping is a sport played by public school educated officers. Goering's Stalag Luft III is a strict boarding school.

Another:

Class film, shot in the never get bored, despite the length. Even top performances by the actors. As a teenager, I liked the film really happy, but when I look at it today, I find the humor very inappropriate, especially the cheerful music theme.

This observation about the music is bang on. Elmer Bernstein's plucky score—the parade snare hijinks, the "much quoted merry whistle along"—smacks of post-war propaganda.

I'm still very interested to know what Germans nowadays feel about the movie's characterization of Second World War Goons. You would think there would be a dissertation available on this from which I could crib. Several German Studies scholars whom I contacted conscientiously agreed that German reaction to Sturges' movie would be an excellent dissertation topic. They advised that I search for reviews in *FAZ* and *Filmkritik* and even *Der Spiegel*. German print periodicals. But I'm impatient and much prefer the unauthorized views expressed at the Online-Filmdatenbank.

"The Germans are depicted as not only the evil, despicable beasts," writes one reviewer.

"Also encouraging is that not all Germans are depicted in the film as the usual flat bang batches. There are people, not dull thugs," opines another.

I take it that 'flat bang batches' is a reference to Hitler's juvenile bowl cut. But I'm not really sure, and that's the fun thing about doing business with Google and its friend Babelfish: not everything is so boring and exact or precise.

> In particular, the figure of the camp director by Luger (Hannes Messemer) revealed an unusual image of the Nazi officer. He is a man who likes it quiet. He has no interest to spoon-feed the prisoners, but is cultivated. When he meets the most senior British officer at the first meeting serving beverages, he does not condescendingly, due to mutual respect. He does his job, and he with the nationalist ideology has not care much, it shows ... The same goes for the guard Werner (Robert Graf), who in the credits is given "man with a heart". The other characters were filled with German native speakers, which gives the film added authenticity.

Michael, for example, is a native speaker who adds much authenticity to the film. But for all his value-addedness, he gets no simple 'man with a heart' credit.

I found this note on historical accuracy to be especially poetic:

> Ultimately, the film pays homage to its historical origins insofar as he [Sturges] remains with the number of the fugitives, and how it came about that so few of them arrived at the truth.

Here I understand the phrase about so few fugitives arriving 'at the truth' to mean so few of the escapees—only three—made it to freedom. To equate freedom with truth is brilliant. You could not get an opium-addled English Romantic poet to come up with this stuff. You might get something very close, but not exactly this.

Despite some minor grumbles then, there appears to be consensus that in *Gesprengte Ketten* the Goons were fairly treated by their American movie masters.

Meanwhile the entertainment value of the movie itself is never in doubt. "Without exaggeration simply great." Online you find comments like these:

> Great Escape means more than three and a half hours of excitement and thrills!

And!

> Sturges filmed this authentic story that pulls the audience right from the start in their wake.

And!

> Be it the bold and incredibly handsome Steve McQueen, James Garner, the heroic, to the particular firm Charles Bronson and Richard Attenborough as Major Bartlett—here is the big Hollywood stars in the hand. Terrific actors, who manage to captivate the audience for nearly four hours—what can you expect from a good movie more? [35]

Though I fear that I might be wearing thin Das Google's welcome, I cannot resist this one final postscript:

> PS Watch the movie in English, as a German it can be very amusing about how Richard Attenborough in the SS as a German accent goes through!

Listen to it. Sir Attenborough's German accent is crap.

---

35   Nothing. You can expect nothing more from a movie than to hold the particular firm Charles Bronson in the hand. All that squatting in the coalmines as a child and now inside the soundstage tunnels must have made for especially firm hindquarters.

Hangin' in Hamburg

BEFORE LEAVING MUNICH, cousin Joerg put a bug in my ear. *Be careful of Hamburg women. They can be very aggressive.* He laughed, raised his eyebrows.

Joerg had in mind the Reeperbahn, Hamburg's mile of sin. The district in St Pauli infamous for its hard-core sex clubs is where The Beatles earned their stripes, playing gigs at the Indra, The Top-Ten, and The Kaiserkeller. This was 1961, 1962. But forget the charms of the Reeperbahn, the women are also uber-aggressive in the borough of St Georg, where I have booked a very affordable room, and where the tired streets by the Hauptbahnhof reek of urine and are splashed with vomit. The cousins of St Pauli and St Georg share much. Drug abuse, prostitution, a high crime rate. I read that the Senate of Hamburg has enacted a law to ban weapons in the Hansaplatz, a 'meeting place' around the corner from my hotel. Taking a stroll outside, after checking in, I am comforted by the knowledge that hand guns and even knifes are verboten. Hopefully the street crews are law-abiding.

St Georg is home to the Taiba Mosque, formerly the Al-Quds Mosque, where the Hamburg cell of the 9/11 terrorist plot gathered to worship. This is news to me, a bit of trivia that I didn't know before arriving. Really, there is something intriguingly unappealing about the neighbourhood. Even before Michael's father came to Hamburg to see for himself Michael's apartment on Mühlendamm Strasse and to review the autopsy with the pathologist, he described the neighbourhood in which Michael lived as very dangerous. After establishing the seedy nature of the borough, he wrote to Eva that the last twenty-four hours of their son's life still remained a mystery. He parroted acquaintances, all of whom noted that Michael was a social extrovert, *it was simply impossible for him not to go out at night*. The theatre staff who had met with Karl acknowledged that Michael adored the nightlife. If this really was so, then Hamburg was his kind of town. The Beatles returned in 1966 and perhaps Michael went to see them play one of two shows at Ernst-Merck-Halle. In hindsight I find it interesting how Michael had gently admonished his young friend Ken Taylor, years before, in Sault Ste. Marie, one day when they were listening together to contemporary music. Ken had disparaged the new sound. "Listen to it," Michael told his friend. "It is what is being written now. It is what people are playing these days."

Karl theorized that Michael may have gone out to a neighbourhood bar, where someone slipped poison into his drink and followed him back to his apartment. He believed that the police's conduct—they did not investigate the possibility of a conspiracy—was negligent *to say the least*. Because the police were not of suspicious minds. They saw pills and whiskey and a man living alone. They took the comatose actor at face value. They checked for vital signs but not for sediment in the glass, not for clues, the taste of a plot.

Karl was wary of foul play. He was in shock. Having lost Michael at the precise time when, allegedly, the two were bridging a period of estrangement, *he had begun to imagine things*. At least this is what I thought when I first read his letters years ago. *Karl is excited. He's exaggerating. Karl is looking to lay the blame on someone, in who-done-it fashion.* But now that I am here, in St Georg, in my compact room and staring myself in the mirror, my own mind is firing. I'm spooked and on guard against the unspecified but pervasive psychological menace of the place. Sordid Hamburg has put me on edge. The entire project has. The WoM is getting to me.

I look out the window on ugly Steindamn Strasse. From here it is an easy walk to Mühlendamm Strasse, and not far to Asklepios Klinik St. Georg, where the poor boy was pronounced dead.

I say 'boy', but he was thirty-two. Not a boy but a young man. I was thirty-nine when the war started seven years ago.

Not a room in which to get quiet work done, after a day out. It is the type of room you bring a prostitute back to, a room of such trompe l'oeil micro-proportions that it turns its own tricks. What comes to mind is the following scene:

> The lights come up. There is a metal-framed bed with a sheet over it. The landlady stands at the door with a hanky over her mouth. A detective stands in the middle of the room but slightly stage right. He is wearing an overcoat and a hat which is tilted back. He looks around. During the scene he picks things up rather casually and looks at them as if they might be clues. He takes some notes but only occasionally.
>
> The Detective: What did you say his name was?
>
> Landlady: I didn't. He was a quiet tenant.

A room like this cordially invites night-long bouts of self-loathing and self-doubt. Its very existence writes prescriptions for sleeping aids and bottles of whiskey.

Hamburg is where I feel closest to Michael, and where I feel most troubled. It is here where he came to end his life, or that is one way of reconstructing things. Tragedy (is) fraught by the rigid illusion of inevitability. And in coming to Hamburg myself, if I am in fact reconstructing things with a measure of accuracy, I feel I have arrived at the same threshold Michael came to, where predestination and free will meet and greet and you justly shake under a shower of cold terror. I'm shivering now, watching myself in the mirror. The mirror reflects the flat present, while in behind, silvery, it hints at infinite waters, infinite opportunity, and fascinates me with the notion that we the so-called living are improvised as of this and any moment.

Once the War on Michael started years ago, I understood in the pit of my stomach that coming to Hamburg was unavoidable. It was expected and predictable, but it was something I put off doing because of a very basic element of distrust I have in myself, at least partly owing to my susceptibility in any situation to mimic the most desperate man in the room. Whether because of empathy or insecurity or sub-zero self-esteem, I do not quite understand it. But I *know* it. I know it in my bones. So forgive the melodrama, and I'll have to be careful now, especially here, so close to Michael's ground zero apartment.

Already I can feel myself slipping, losing equilibrium, falling out of me, into him. Liebe Michael. My emotional twin.

After unpacking, I repack and carry my luggage to the reception.

"I'd like to check out, please."

"Room number?" The hospitality agent is dressed like a flight attendant, in a navy blazer with a gold pin on her lapel.

"42."

After squinting at the screen: "Sir, you only checked in less than two hours ago."

Yes, in fact, the young gentleman at the opposite counter swiped my credit card. He turns around and she explains to him in German that I must be crazy. I want to cancel my room after checking in.

"Sir, how can I help you?"

I would like to get out before the nightmares. "I would like to leave this hotel, please."

"What *is* wrong with this hotel?"

"It's not my... my kind of place."

"What is?" I've been screwing around, I'm trying to rip them off, having had my thrill. That's what he thinks. Or is he teasing me? "If you leave suddenly at this time, you will lose your money."

But not my life. "That's fine."

"One moment, until I print a receipt. You must sign."

I must and I will.

*

Night time. A different hotel and I'm on my way out to get something to eat. The restaurant was a tip from the gentleman working the front desk. La Famiglia on Böckmann Strasse. Only just around the corner. *Familiäre Ambiente.*

Perfect. I'm here on family business, so why not. Why not rest the head on the ample bosom of an Italian family restaurant. It's what I need right now.

Before leaving the hotel, I peek inside the lounge. It's also a possibility. Bar snacks, grill, beer, and I could stay in. I wouldn't need to merge into the Hamburg night, when already I feel fragile. There is a scrum bar-side, sports jackets and cleavage, nylons and neon. No. Not tonight. *Eine familiäre Atmosphäre ist besser für das kanadische Goldlöckchen Andrew Steinmetz.*

La Famiglia is just around the corner and set at street level, a cavernous setting of white stucco walls and decorated with regional maps of Tuscany. I'm shown to a table. Menu arrives promptly. Then the host. I choose something from the chalkboard. *Taglietelle mit frischem Lachs und Broccoli und Rahmnsoße.* With a half-bottle of Montelpulciano. Yes. Things are looking up, so I get to work, riding a wave of optimism, riding my surging appetite, making room for sudoku beside the warm bread basket. Sudoku, I don't mind occupying myself with a game of numbers and trial and error, nothing is nearly as non-judgemental and satisfying as math, nor as magical when it all works out. I'm thinking about this—is math non-judgemental? What does that even mean?—when the door behind me opens, letting in a draft of night air, and, in train, nails on ceramic tile, a dog, it must be.

I turn and, abruptly, but right on time, two young men and a well-behaved mutt, stand table-side.

The host welcomes them. Must be regulars. The mutt as well, for as soon as they are seated at the adjacent table the host disappears to fetch a blanket for 'Lucas'. Because it is October, and the tiles must be frigid. He spreads it out on the floor.

Next I hear barking, merely minor grumbles, and not from Lucas, no, from beneath undisclosed tables inside the restaurant. Nothing loud, only the appropriate canine greeting, creatures making their presence felt. Not a human head turns. *Alles Normal.* I had no idea that I was in such esteemed company. But now that I know it, my comfort level is rising, and Goldilocks begins to truly relax for the first time since his arrival in Hamburg.

The host has the mutt lick his hand and then takes the order. He leaves and now the dog is looking at me, a bit wild-eyed. His masters are deep in conversation, ignoring poor Lucas. The old man returns with wine and gestures to indicate that he will return with bread for Lucas, if that is permitted. Of course, they signal to the old man. Let Lucas eat cake for all they care. The host turns and is heading for the kitchen when I see my chance. I wave my bread basket in his face. *Bitte schön!* He takes the basket from my hand and flips all three slices of baguette to Lucas.

Despite stereotypes, Germany remains peculiar. Uptight and strict, rule-bound and organized, yet liberal in social policy and plain pragmatic about keeping restaurants dog-friendly. There is no evidence that Michael kept a dog upon his return to Germany. Romeo, the shepherd, was his last. Romeo joined the family in Berlin by 1948. I am more sure of this date than much about Michael. That's because I wear Romeo's tag around my neck for good luck. The aluminum is neatly engraved '1948 Berlin'. The profile of a dog is etched on its flat face. Registration no. 48500. It fell to me, after Eva died—inheritance is too grand a word— and it has taken me years to recognize the oddity that in post-war Berlin, when so little was up and running, the city got at it and registered domestic pets.

You could understand that dog in a lot of different ways. Michael's good friend from Sault Ste. Marie, Ken Taylor, is right. *You couldn't call Romeo an ordinary animal.* He represented that part of their past they could love, openly.

A different hotel and I'm well fed on salmon, broccoli and tagliatelle in a cream sauce. And a second half-bottle of Montelpulciano. I have a very full stomach and a wine buzz. It is the friendly Italian way.

I sit on the bed and switch on the TV as I unpack. I have a marathon day planned for tomorrow.

Brazil versus Ukraine. Kaka and Shevchenko. I'm set for the night.

*

Here I am bright and early in a café on Alstertor Strasse, across the way from the impressive Thalia Theatre. What we have here is a temple of the arts: fluted Doric columns, the sparkling white marble façade. Michael's last stage. I plan to get inside for a tour this afternoon courtesy of Fräulein Asche. But my first appointment of the day is with Dr. Michaela Giesing at the Hamburger Theatersammlung, a special library at the University of Hamburg. The Theatersammlung collects literature and information on National German theatre events, with an eye for the theatre history of Hamburg. The collection comprises countless volumes and more than 380,000 newspaper clippings, systematically collected since the end of the Second World War.

Dr. Giesing and I have exchanged emails over the past months, and she has been helpful and efficient, gathering together archival material. It was Giesing who wrote on my behalf to Sandra Asche, asking if she would please check in the *Personalunterlagen* for Michael Paryla's address. I'd already queried the *Staatsarchiv* twice with no success. The office of the *Sterberegister* did not respond. In Germany, at least in Hamburg, information about the so-called dead is not easy to come by.

The S-Bahn leaves me at Dammptor. I exit the busy terminal in the direction of the university, following the crush of students. Outside, I verify the campus address. Von-Melle-Park 3. At last I'll meet this Dr. Giesing, someone for whom Michael is the subject of objective study. As director of the archives, she holds the key to material that might unlock Michael's story. A corner piece of the floor puzzle. Well, I don't actually believe it—it isn't likely that I'll find that something– but then I've come this far and under what pretext if not because I hold out hope. Why put on a method writer's lumbering show if you can't suspend disbelief for a measly hour?

I keep returning to Karl's rationale and as he put it:

Establishing full clarity about all the unsettled details of his
death has no value whatsoever for our poor boy, and yet it is a
part of his short life, and we owe it to him to follow every trail
to the end.

Allegedly then, the WoM has no value whatsoever for his
life, and yet *we owe it to him to follow every trail to the end*. The
puzzle might just be the WoM, launched without a sensible
exit strategy, and without any clear goal. In other words, the
motivation for this trip might have been—might be now that
I'm here—to find out why I have come to Hamburg. Might
Dr. Giesing tell me? I don't expect she will be as playful as all
that.

Within blocks of the station, I stumble upon the site of
a monument. The stone is set on a triangular patch of grass,
squeezed between dissecting roads. I step onto the grass to read
the black commemorative billboard:

In the year 1933, 24,000 Jews lived in Hamburg. Here began
the way, which, for thousands of Jewish citizens of Hamburg,
ended in the extermination camps of the Nazi regime.

So I find myself at Hamburg's Jewish Deportation Square—
and surprised to be here. 'Here began the way' doesn't quite
capture it. But what does? Across the road, the blackened sar-
cophagus of Dammptor Station looms above the canopy of
trees. Students on the way to morning classes and lectures—
in hoodies as advertised: thin white wires indicating some
mass intra-iPod music therapy experiment—take no notice of
PLATZ DER JÜDISCHEN DEPORTIERTEN. Why would
they? The platz emits no ambient sound.

I take a photograph and then, in case it doesn't turn out, transcribe the text into a notebook. I also scribble a note to self: *Everywhere I look for Michael, it's the same thing. You cannot have Michael or The Great Escape without the Nazi past and the Holocaust. You cannot have the film without tripping over family history. You cannot have us without them.* This isn't entirely true or accurate but it captures the essence of my journey.

The archives are on the third floor of the Carl von Ossietzky Library. I stop at the ground level security office for directions. The man tells me the way in simple *links und rechts*; still, I manage to fall through, and find myself at the shipping and receiving dock. Turning around, I retrace my steps to security and he tells me again in grim Hansel and Gretel the obvious way to the Theatersammlung. I *danke schön* him and I'm off, but, taking after my mentor, what leaves my lips is hesitant, a trapdoor-of-a-*Dan-ke*; you could say, even, a begrudging 'you lied to me and we both know it' type of Thank You. Poor fellow, he must get it all the time.

Upstairs at the Theatersammlung, I find three women of tired-age toiling at separate workstations in the front office. No one moves a whisker. They have more important things to do than greet a visitor. I cannot compete with the morning newspaper, data entry spreadsheets, database interfaces, nor the window overlooking the grey campus. I know how it goes, sometimes. Whatever it is you do it can get very quiet and one can get consumed by negative thoughts about absent people, and it becomes then very difficult to put yourself at the service of a live patron. At the archives, anyway, I suspect live beings rank exceedingly low, and are of meagre interest in comparison to the aggregation of the primary materials.

Battle Axe Einz, stationed near the door, asks if I have an appointment.

"Ja," I say, "um 10.00 mit Dr. Giesing." I pronounce ten o'clock—'zen hure'—forcefully, something I learned to do in my intermediate German class years before the war. 'Hure' comes out 'oo-wah'. Almost 'oooh-awe'. My accent does not ruffle Einz. Her temperament is fixed. Her thermostat is centrally controlled. However, I'm a bother to her, since I haven't followed procedure. There must be some procedure, there always is. Yet I have come in cold. Whatever is eating her, my mood lightens after speaking that phrase 'am zen hure'. Instantly I remember a whole batch of the stock phrases I learned once upon ago. *Gehst du ins Kino heute Abend?* Are you going to the movies tonight? *Oder das Theater?* Or the theater? *Nein.* No. *Warum? Haben Sie Kopfschmerzen?* Why? Have you a headache? *Ja, habe ich.* Yes, I have one. *Ich habe Aspirin. Hier nehmen Sie eins.* I have Aspirin. Here take one.

Perhaps I have been too harsh on Einz. This early, she may have a Kopfschmerz or better yet a Kephalgie, which sounds more impressive. If so, I have just the remedy. *Aspirin. Hier nehmen Sie ein!*

I exit to go find Giesing's office, which is around the corner and down the hall. The doctor is not in her office either. So I return to the Theatersammlung, where life goes on as normal and I am not worthy.

Then, a woman strays in.

"Herr Steinmetz, Hello." Dr. Giesing greets me with a neat, forensic grimace, dressed in a powerfully-odd pantsuit. "Your coat you cannot bring inside. Leave it you must on a hanger." Yoda is spoken here by the chief archivist.

Dr. Giesing directs me to a table inside, where I can sit and review the materials. The rules are simple. I may use my camera to copy archival photographs but am not permitted to use a flash. Newspaper clippings should be photocopied.

"This is wonderful, thank you for all the work you did." I'm greatly indebted to Dr. Giesing and would like to express my gratitude, formally, before sitting down to my meal of Michael.

"Oh, no." Horrified, she is. Nothing personal will do. No gratitude accepted by the archivist.

"You've done a lot of work."

Her features cloud over. Again with the tight grimace, like she is passing a foreign emotion. Dr. Giesing inches sideways on the carpet and clasps her hands, a gesture that seems to indicate she is pleased, also, with the results of the research she has done on my behalf, even if such requests are routine and the results are nothing out of the ordinary.

"I never would have found all this without your help." She flinches visibly at the word 'help'. I realize my mistake. *Professional you are.*

I fully expect the frigid Dr. Giesing to exit stacks left, unassumingly, and leave me to it, when she defies my powers of intuition and observation and pronounces something very personal about Michael.

"It's difficult for the son of an actor to become an actor. And his father, Karl Paryla, was such a strong actor."

Dr. Giesing has been giving Michael more than routine thought.

JUNKER VON BLEICHENWANG

In his penultimate role, Michael played the part of Junker von Bleichenwang, a young country squire, in Thalia Theatre's 1966 production of Shakespeare's *Twelfth Night, or What You Will.* The German adaptation is called *Was Ihr Wollt.* The press photographs and newspaper clippings retrieved by Dr. Giesing are primarily from this production, which evidently was well-received by the critics.

The first clipping is dated 23 September 1966. *Hamburger Anzeigen und Nachrichten*. Under the heading "Eine turbulente Komödie (A turbulent comedy)", Walter Gattke writes:

> Das eigentlich nebensächliche Trio der komischen Gestalten, das mit Herbert Steinmetz (Junker Tobias), dem blendenden Michael Paryla (Christoph von Bleichenwang) und dem einmaligen Hubert v. Meyerick (Malvolio) glänzend besetz war, liess das Haus in Lachstürmen erbeben.

It's stirring to find his name in German newsprint. Michael Paryla. Right there. Digital representation is nice, but this is the real thing. *Dem blendenden Michael Paryla*. I have you at last. The Dazzling Michael Paryla. I have you on your soil, a theatre in Germany. But there is something else. You are not alone. At once I am off to find Dr. Giesing, who has found sanctuary at a table in a clearing located deep in the stacks.

"Did you see this?" I point, handling the giant scrapbook awkwardly. "Herbert Steinmetz. One of the other actors was 'Steinmetz'." Dr. Giesing is nonplussed. "No relation, but..." But still.

"Yes." Giesing relents. "Herbert Steinmetz." She peers sceptically at the scrapbook, anchored at my hip. "An actor from Stuttgart, I believe."

Well, yes. An actor from Stuttgart or from Hobart or Nairobi. It does not matter. That's not what I meant. By coincidence, opposite Michael on stage was a Steinmetz, though not of his mother's clan. What are the odds? Dr. Giesing isn't a betting woman. Fair enough, if disappointing. In contrast, I'm inclined to generate pseudo-scientific hypotheses on the back of my hand. I'm all for jumping in with two feet and getting it wrong the first time. What did it mean for Michael to find himself on stage opposite an actor who shared his name—his mother's maiden name? The Steinmetz name. Did he identify with Steinmetz?

I return to my table of Michael without an answer. There is a lot to digest. I have my laptop but no WI-FI, and hence there shall be no real-time flirting with Babelfish, or, for that matter, with any other quick and loose online translator. My initial reading of this material is therefore captive to my own rickety algorithms, assimilated from two years of university-level study at Michael's alma mater, McGill. Hence the blizzard of elliptical dots:

> The trio of…actually incidental…odd comic characters…Herbert Steinmetz………the dazzling Michael Paryla (Christoph von Bleichenwang)…..and the unique Hubert v. Meyerick…brilliantly presented…left the house in gales of laughter.

Translation: His part was unimportant ('actually incidental') and yet Michael was dazzling in his own, essentially non-speaking way. Bravo. My excitement now is tempered by the realization that, as in the movie, his part is minor. *He was a gifted actor. But he didn't have major roles. He had minor parts. He didn't live long enough to have more.*

Alas, there is something uncanny about his Junker von Bleichenwang. I find more fragments of the same:

> Michael Paryla gave his Bleichenwang outlines but no core.

> —Friedrich Hartau. Boy Goberts Regie—Sieg im Thalia mit Was ihr wollt. *Hamburger Morgenpast.* 24 September 1966.

Empty of personality, charmingly silly, the living plaything, Bleichenwang (Michael Paryla).

—Jochen Oldach. Fang an mit Shakespeare. Boy Gobert inszenierte "Was ihr wollt" in neuer Bearbeitung am Thalia-Theater. Berzallorfen (?) Zeitung. 24 September 1966.

Michael Paryla et al, mercilessly exaggerate these peculiar characters.

—*Wien*. 30 December 1966.

The anonymous reviewer in *Wien* uses the word *'Outrieren'* to describe Michael's performance, one month before his death. Outrieren is Austrian slang for laying it on thick. The review was printed in Vienna and it's plausible that Michael's father took notice of it. If so, I'm convinced that *he'd* have remarked on the name Herbert Steinmetz. The name Steinmetz would have had meaning for Karl, surely. And what would he have made of Michael's carrying on as Junker Bleichenwang?

The jokers present themselves in so shallow and pleasant a manner, Michael Paryla's needy Bleichenwang … They really do carry on.

—Christian Ferber (*Die Welt*. 24 September 1966).

They bravely play above the conventional … Steinmetz only a bit, but Michael Paryla clearly goes above and beyond (goes to excess).[36]

---

36   Michael with method for brains goes above and beyond to great excess. Meanwhile, Herbert from Stuttgart—like a good Steinmetz—goes 'only a bit' beyond the conventional.

—Walter Schroder. *Bild*. 24 September 1966. Under the heading: 'Manchmal ist es zu lustig' (Sometimes Too Funny).

Michael Paryla's hesitant, inhibited and dumb Bleichenwang has a bizarre attraction.

—H. A. Trauthig. *Stacker Tageblatt*. 27 September 1966. *Ein Fest für Augen und Ohren*. Hamburger Thalia-Theater *trumpfte auf mit 'Was ihr wollt'* ('A Feast for Eyes and Ears: Hamburg's Thalia Theatre Triumphs with "What You Will"').

Translation for deaf ears: Michael seems out of his mind. Restrained and blocked, his Bleichenwang is quirky and absurd. Scanty. A scurrile attraction.

It's unanimous then: bizarre and bewitching, outlines but no core, excessive. Michael is dazzling. Out of his mind?

'DER KAISER VON AMERIKA'

After a half-hour break which I spend strolling through the campus, keeping my distance from the deportation platz, I return to the archives where I don't find a scrap—not one newspaper clipping that mentions Michael in the role of Sempronius in Thalia Theatre's January 1967 production of Shaw's *The Apple Cart, Der Kaiser von Amerika*.

"Why do you think this is?" I take my grievance to Dr. Giesing.

"I don't know."

"It makes no sense."

Dr. Giesing sighs. She won't comment on that. On the other hand, Dr. Giesing is modestly excited to present me with an olive green workbook. She was literally on her way to bring it to me. *Soufflerbuch* is handwritten in the top right corner. *Herr Michael Paryla* is crossed-out.[37]

I am holding Michael's prompt book for the play, the same he used during rehearsals and for performances of *Der Kaiser von Amerika*. Together, Dr. Giesing and I look inside. The typescript is edited in pencil. Passages of text are underlined, notes scribbled in the margins. Whole lines from the play have been erased, others modified. Shaw goes under the knife. Even him.

"Could this be his handwriting?" I ask Dr. Giesing.

"Maybe," she answers. "But, probably not. This was the job of the *soufleur*."

Turning the pages, I scan the German. I'm only superficially acquainted with the play itself, a political satire about the fictional English King Magnus and his elected Prime Minister, who argues for the end of the monarchy. Act 1 opens wwith Sempronius and Pamphilius, young political secretaries of the king, seated at desks and facing each other, in an office of the royal palace.

To begin the play, Pamphilius asks Sempronius: "What was your father?"

Sempronius is startled.

---

37   This is very interesting to me, the sight of his name with a line in pencil drawn through it, his identity negated but not erased. It brings to mind immediately—uncannily—an artefact contained in the letter my grandfather (Michael's uncle) composed in 1935, when he and my grandmother were for a while held up in Vienna, and looking to emigrate to the UK where he could practice, untroubled by the Nuremberg Laws, as a doctor. In a draft copy of his letter addressed to foreign hospital boards, unsure as to how to describe his present predicament, my grandfather, Herman Hans Steinmetz, stumbles over the sensitive issue of his Jewish background. One has a window into his mind: in order to avoid becoming a target, you process any request—internal or external—to define yourself through the wobbly mirror of ambivalence and indeterminacy. So my grandfather, stranded in Vienna, goes ahead and explains that he has worked as a medical assistant in Germany but was "dismissed from my hospital because ~~of my Jewish origins~~ I had not the Approbation." The strike-through is his. Is this the psychological precursor, that which prompted the cancellation of Michael's name on the cover of the Souffleurbuch? No—there is no logical, no rational connection—but then, instantly, upon sight of ~~Michael Paryla~~, the two events are emotionally fused. Within my own thinking, that is. Is it really as magical as all that?

So am I. Startled that the question of fathers is established in the first act of Michael's last play.

> Sempronius: My father?
> Pamphilius: Yes. What was he?
> Sempronius: A Ritualist.
> Pamphilius: I don't mean his religion. I mean his profession. And his politics.
> Sempronius: He was a Ritualist by profession, a Ritualist in politics, a Ritualist in religion: a raging emotional Die Hard Ritualist right down to his boots.
> Pamphilius: Do you mean that he was a parson?
> Sempronius: Not at all. He was a sort of spectacular artist.

There are many critical reviews of the production but not one mentions Michael's turn as Sempronius. None that I find. Which is odd, if you consider his portrayal of Junker Bleichenwang—an equally small part, in a play produced by the same theatre house only months before—was noted in a handful of newspapers. Why not Sempronius? One line of thinking might be that the bizarre and bewitching Bleichenwang had bizarrely bewitched and undone Junker Michael. That's not very cogent though. Alliterative, okay, but not reality-based. Not germane. Another hypothesis might be that Michael was going through a crisis of some sort—with Margaret?—and the wear and tear was beginning to show in his work. It's possible. His last plays were presented in repertory. The Shaw opened in January, after Michael had been home to Munich, briefly, at Christmas. His aunt Irene and grandfather Emil Steinmetz had seen him then, and for the last time, over the holidays. Irene's letter to Eva several weeks later provides a glimpse of the condition he was in. *He was very tired … He had apparently been complaining a lot about insomnia for some time; this was*

*in addition to financial worries and friction with colleagues. On
top of that, there was all his work and the insane theatre life ... he
could not cope with that kind of life, neither physically nor psychologically.* No such corroborating evidence is forthcoming from
Hamburg's ensemble of theatre critics. His Sempronius—tired
or terrific—is ignored. Frozen out. Equally noticeable is the
matter that the Hamburg newspapers make no mention of
his tragic passing, which occurred on the evening of the 12th
performance of the play.

The Vorstellungbuch—Dr. Giesing has dug it up: Thalia
Theatre's Yearbook—does describe in straightforward language
the theatre's staff's efficient management of the events behind
stage, and onstage, the eve of Michael's death. But even here
there is nothing in the way of commemoration. No addendum
to the entry of 21 January 1967, which records that the actor
Michael Paryla was a no-show at curtain time.

So, no public word of Michael's passing, no mention of
Sempronius in the press, and no eulogy in the Vorstellungbuch.
He goes out with his whispering myocardium, without leav-
ing a note. I don't understand it. Nothing in *Bild* or *Zeitung*.
Nothing in *Hamburger Morgenpost*.

"Isn't it strange?"

I have opened the scrapbook, and turned over page after
page. I am asking Dr. Giesing, keeper of the Theatersammlung,
for a second opinion.

"Yes, it is *strange*," Dr. Giesing eases her way into the sub-
jective realm. I sense her reluctance to wade in deeper, but continue to push my case.

"The critics mention Bleichenwang, but nobody touches
Sempronius. What's going on?"

Dr. Giesing is not a betting woman. She's already made
that abundantly clear. She's an archivist, not a polemicist. Her
role is to preserve the past. Interpretations cost extra. They are

personal, and may incur emotional wounds. In every direction, people may get hurt. For her it's all no-fun and no-games until, for a second time over the course of the day, Dr. Giesing cracks. Yoda is back.

"I to you said, it's difficult for the son of an actor to become an actor." She pauses. Yes, I remember. "And his father, Karl Paryla was such a strong actor, too." Long rest here. Several beats. "But this is not a story about acting. Your story is about a son and a father, a father and his son."

Dr. Giesing has opened a door and, promptly, she leaves for her cubicle in the stacks. What kind of work is it, I wonder. I'm inclined to think Giesing takes full advantage of the library's peace and quiet to rehearse and prepare for moments like these. For the meticulous delivery of, *But this is not a story about acting.* Of course not. Who said it was? No fucking way. *Your story is about a son and a father, a father and his son.* A father and his son. There you go. Yoda and uncle Gerhardt (Gerhardt of the thesis "I think he was sad because he could not be like his father.") and John Leyton (the Leyton of "Following in the footsteps of a famous father makes it very difficult.") appear to be on the same track here and weaving the same reductive Oediplot. Giesing and her gang are pushing the limits. Giesing's gone and nudged Michael's story from the private to public realm, pursuing the universal and potentially more appealing story about the larger forces at play: Sons and Fathers, and about the archetypes and myths that amuse the unconscious and in hindsight seem to make a mockery of free will. Facile? To me it is. Which is one reason why I must keep telling this story until I have it half-right.

I carry on—making copies of the press photos, newspaper clippings, and theatre programs, careful that I capture the sad essence of the olive Souffleurbuch, with Michael Paryla in the top right corner, touchingly crossed-out. I scan a bunch of articles, and as I do all this I read superficially about Ingrid Andree and O.E. Hasse and 'Die Charmante Paula Denk'—lead actors in *Der Kaiser von Amerika*—who have done splendidly in the roles of Orinthia, King Magnus, and Lysistrata, respectively. I've been three hours but I don't want to leave here until I find something that might explain Michael's ghost turn in *Der Kaiser von Amerika*. Sure enough, after another thirty minutes, I find what must be exactly what I am looking for: some kind of reward for perseverance, an answer to my faith in the complete omniscience of the archives.

The headline reads "Thalia-Theater gastiert in der Wiener 'Burg'". A single paragraph in the 18 January 1967 edition of *Hamburger Abendblatt*. 'Wiener' catches my eye. The ensemble is taking its production abroad for a guest appearance at the Burgtheater, February 2-8.

Michael's unheralded Sempronius was headed for Vienna. Was this the trigger? Three days after, Michael was dead.

"Where next are you travelling to?" Dr. Giesing inquires. "Your next stop?"

"Curio-Haus."

"Oh yes, so close. Five minutes."

Before leaving, I ask Dr. Giesing if can take her photograph, standing outside the doors to the Theatersammlung. Initially flustered by the request, her face conforms to utter neutrality. She passes a hand across her forehead, brushes aside non-existent bangs: and I've got her, a memento to take back home for my own archives, the better that I can remember her.

*

Michael Paryla counts lives on his fingers. Junker von Bleichenwang in Boy Gobert's Thalia Theatre production of *Was Ihr Wolt.*

The Curio-Haus. Rothenbaumchaussee 11. The building is named after Johann Carl Daniel Curio, the founder of Hamburg's first teacher's association. Once a meeting point for unionists and artists, today the building houses private enterprises. On the sidewalk, I scan the commercial billboard: Jura One *individuelle Examensvorbereitung.* STYLE HOUSE *personal artist management.* Axel J. Nolte RECHTSANWALTKANZLEI (Solicitor). Appeased, I walk through the archway and into the courtyard and look through the windows into the historic ballroom. Was it in here? No telling. I return to the building front, where I find the plaque:

This building was established in 1911 for the society of the friends ... named after Johann Carl Daniel Curio ... In 1946-48 the trial by the British military court against SS-members who were responsible for crimes in the KZ Neuengamme took place here.

Curious. The Michael archives, Hamburg's Jewish deportation Square, and the Curio-Haus are in close proximity. KZ stands for *Konzentrationslager,* meaning Concentration Camp. So the SS officers from the Neuengamme Concentration Camp were put on trial in the courtroom at the Curio-Haus, as were the Gestapo men involved in the murder of the 50 recaptured prisoners from Stalag Luft III. The plaque does not mention it but it was here that Paul Brickhill came to witness the trial proceedings. Meaning, more fearful symmetry. More tyger, tyger burning bright, in the forests of the night. Meaning I cannot put aside the idea that Michael's fate is framed by his character in the movie, the Michael who kindly assists a band of Nazi assassins, the very specific strain who were tried here in a War Crimes Court in 1948 and afterwards hung at Hamelin Gaol. In 1967, twenty years enigmatically *später,* Michael died, alone in his apartment on Mühlendamm Strasse, in close proximity to the Curio-Haus, where his movie-mentors—i.e. the thugs who murdered 50 British bunny rabbits—were found guilty of War Crimes. Coincidence? The jury is out. For my money, it looks like Michael may have arrived in Hamburg, in late 1966, *on the surface of things* to play the light and dazzling Junker Bleichenwang and also the sorely forgotten Sempronius. When in actuality Michael was summoned to Hamburg. He was summoned to stand trial, and was found guilty, but—seriously—of what crime?

Leaving the university neighbourhood, I cut across town to the Asklepios Klinik St Georg. From the botanical gardens,

I walk south and cross the Kennedybrücke and continue along An der Alster, skirting the Aussenalster, the large artificial lake at the heart of Hamburg.

I have been a bit of a blabbermouth, over the years, when it comes to Michael's story, as you might imagine. It has gotten to the point where I have this little routine and I follow a script just as casually as I can, while listing specific dates of interest and facts, as though they were second nature. Once when I was at a party and started telling Michael's story, taking the time to set the scene and invoking a number of themes like Germany, war, acting, exile, overdose, my highly-educated captive speared his elusive martini olive and tossed out the name Klaus Mann, son of Thomas, and in no time had launched a counteroffensive involving the story of the actor Gustav Gründgens. No, my captive on this occasion was not The Filmfuehrer. He was a professor of Modern Languages. In his mind my Michael blended with Gustav Gründgens. In fact, I'm surprised Dr. Sigmund Giesing had not thought of Klaus Mann and Gründgens. So allow me the digression. Klaus Mann had a *sehr* complicated relationship with his Nobel Prize-winning father, Thomas, author of *Buddenbrooks, Death in Venice*, and *The Magic Mountain*. In his diaries, Thomas Mann wrote heatedly of his infant son's beauty. Raised in Munich, Klaus and sister Erika spent a theatrical childhood nestled like peas in an Oedipod. However short, any introduction to Klaus Mann is an invitation to explore the great family Mann traditions of incest, homosexuality, suicide, creative genius, and depression.

Asklepios Klinik St Georg is a good thirty minute walk. Time enough to marry a few lines about Klaus Mann to a brief history of barbiturates, a detour which will get me where I want to be, finally, in regards to setting the scene of Michael's last exit.

Klaus Mann's novel *Mephisto* is about the rise of Hendrik Höfgen, an ambitious actor in Nazi Germany, who sells his soul to the party to further his career. Mephisto was first published in Amsterdam in 1936. The openly gay Mann, stripped of German citizenship, had been living in exile since 1934. Mann's *Mephisto* is a roman-à-clef based on the life of Gustaf Gründgens, Klaus' brother-in-law, with whom Klaus had a brief affair. Following? Here is where it gets confusing and makes the most sense to let Wikipedia do some of the legwork:

> In 1924, Klaus Mann, his sister Erika, Gründgens, and Pamela Wedekind had all worked together on a stage production of Mann's *Anja und Esther* and had toured through Germany. Gründgens and Erika Mann got engaged while Klaus Mann similarly got engaged to Wedekind. The first two got married in 1926 but divorced in 1929 ... Gründgens became a renowned theater and movie director. While Mann never called Gründgens an adversary, he admitted "moved antipathy". Although he attacked Gründgens in newspaper articles, Mann hesitated to use homosexuality as a theme in the novel and decided to use "negroid masochism" as the main character's sexual preference.

Mephisto's protagonist Hendrik Höfgen is an alliterative allusion to Gustav Gründgens. Gründgens was best known for his interpretation of Mephistopheles in a 1956 production of Goethe's *Faust* at the Deutsches Schauspielhaus in Hamburg. The *Schauspielhaus* stands by the exit of the Hauptbahnhof, not far from the Hansaplatz and my hotel, and not too far from Michael's former address on Mühlendamm Strasse.

Gründgens is buried in Hamburg at the Ohlsdorf Cemetery. He died in 1963 by an overdose of sleeping pills while travelling in the Philippines. Wikipediately, Gründgens' last written words were: "I believe I have taken too many sleeping pills; I feel funny, let me sleep it off."

Klaus Mann died of an overdose of barbiturates, too. His suicide is uncontested. In Cannes, in 1949, a reclusive and depressed Mann had called for a wave of suicides among Europe's intellectuals to protest the Cold War. After the Nazis, after years in exile, Klaus Mann had called it quits.

The path to oblivion found in barbiturates and alcohol is well trodden. Michael's death in Hamburg followed on the heels of a half-century of scientific research and development. Emil Fischer and Josef von Mering published their paper on Barbital, the first hypnotic, in 1903. Von Mering had recently returned from a trip to Verona, Italy, and Barbital was given its brand name 'Veronal', for the city's glassy beauty. Veronal was manufactured by Merck in Darmstadt, Germany, the city where Michael's father Karl Paryla earned the first engagement of his career with the Reinhardt Theatre, and where Michael's parents settled into an apartment shortly after getting married in 1929.

With Veronal, the barbiturate era had begun. Next born was Phenobarbital (Luminal) in 1919. Pentobarbitone (Nembutal) joined the family in 1923. Hexobarbitone (Evipan) in 1932 was one of the first short-acting agents. Thipentone (Pentothal) in 1934 is ultra-short acting. Barbiturates are classified according to their duration of action –long, intermediate, short and ultra-short—but the gratification offered by all these drugs is the same, oblivion. They endow sleep to insomniacs and for anyone in need relieve the intolerable anxiety of everyday living. But there's a downside. Barbiturates are physiologically addicting and the abstinence syndrome can trigger life-threatening symptoms. The development of tolerance means that, over time of use, increased dosages are required to do the trick. With barbiturates there is not much difference between the dose required for sedation and the dose that can cause coma or the sleep of the dead. Barbiturates have what is called a narrow therapeutic index. Pair a propensity for tolerance with a narrow therapeutic index, and the real danger kicks in. Overdose deaths occur most often when barbiturates are paired with other depressants such as alcohol. Then accidental deaths follow the familiar pattern: they occur when a user takes one dose, falls asleep, and then awakes confused and unintentionally takes another pill. To err is human, we all know that; however, human error combined with a narrow therapeutic index turns out to be lethal.

Michael had found a doctor who continued to prescribe him pills after his breakdown in Bremen. His father was sufficiently familiar with the ways of actors, and he was cynical of the ways of doctors. According to Karl, Michael had 'unfortunately fallen under the supervision of a doctor whom I wouldn't necessarily trust'. Doctors are treacherous, is the message. They are most helpful after death, as in the case of a pathologist like Dr. Franz.

Asklepios Klinik St Georg. Here at last. The hospital is the oldest in Hamburg. There are several low-level buildings—yellow stucco, Georgian style—joined by modern abridgements. I wander through the car park searching for the emergency department entrance and notice a sign indicating the helicopter landing pad. Methods may have changed, but here Michael was rushed by ambulance the night of his January 1967 escape; here, inside one of these buildings, the attending physician Dr. Wuehl performed cardiopulmonary resuscitation on an unresponsive Sempronius; here, in the pathology lab, in the basement no doubt, Dr. Franz located scars in Michael's myocardium and noted other key findings; and here, months later, by invitation, Michael's father came to 'receive' the autopsy report.

I had a long talk with Professor Franz, and it turns out that Michi effectively was not healthy and that scars in his myocardium

decisively contributed to his unfortunate passing. He also asked
me about his childhood illnesses, among other things, whether
he had had jaundice…In his opinion, the scars or damage in
his myocardium could have stemmed from an infection following an operation to the tonsils. Aside from that, there were no
other critical findings. …The report as you will see for yourself
is thorough and well done.

No other critical findings. In fact, the report disclosed that one
of Michael's testicles was smaller than the other. Dr. Franz had
also discovered an active gland in the pituitary region, which,
according to him, 'should stop functioning after puberty and
may signify a continuing infantilism'. Karl Paryla mentions
neither finding in his letter to Eva. At the time they might
have seemed irrelevant to Karl, comprising an insensitive and
needless invasion of privacy. However as any properly trained
pathologist will demonstrate, there are no limits to a person's
privacy during the post-mortem examination.

In the same letter of April 1967, Karl writes: "Certainly,
a grown man is no longer a child that one can raise." It is a
curious comment, and especially curious for Karl to make. Karl
was absent for Michael's childhood; he was not around to raise
Michael into the grown man he infantilizes so many years later.
Perhaps his tone reflects the fact that when Karl and Eva separated, Michael was no more than four years old. It's maybe
this four-year-old Michael that Karl keeps alive in his heart—
and not the young man who returned to Germany to become
a theatre actor. Conceivably, the mature Michael—grown and
'no longer a child'—confronted Karl with an uncomfortable
reality. By then Michael's father had two sons by Hortense,
his second wife, Nicholas and Stephan, both of whom would
become actors. Whatever is at play, there is on Karl's part the
temptation, if not to infantilize, then to patronize. Even when

he speaks of Margaret—Michael's 'life partner'—one gets the impression that Karl believed Michael was in need of a caretaker. Margaret is merely a proxy for Karl and Eva. *We can't blame her for our child's death. She took great care of him.*

Asklepios Klinik St Georg was without a doubt a landmark I didn't want to miss. But whatever ambition I had when I set out has turned maudlin in flesh. I'm faced with making a decision like the one Dr. Wuehl faced: when should one stop CPR? When do our futile efforts become macabre? When should I stop beating his chest? I might be hurting him. Doing unintentional damage. What comes to mind is I am flogging a dead horse. Yet Karl's letters contained something else, a contrasting argument: *The unsettled details of his death has no value whatsoever for our poor boy, and yet it is a part of his short life, and we owe it to him to follow every trail to the end.* That's why I am here. To follow the trail to the end. I remember this now as I walk through the hospital courtyard, finding no trace of him, no Michael, here, no ghost.

Ahead, I see the street sign. Mühlendamm Strasse. I turn left and walk up from the corner of Hohenfelde. Without his address, I'm left to wander both sides of the street, links und rechts, Hansel and Gretel, warm and cold. Nothing special here, nothing to report. Brown brick four storey apartment buildings. After taking photographs, I decide it's time to leave. I've documented the experience, if not felt much—if not had the authentic experience, whatever that possibly could be. I have to keep moving if I want to make my appointment with Fräulein Asche at the Thalia Theatre.

Mühlendamm Strasse marks the boundary of an immigrant quarter, a rough warren of streets. I follow Steindamn, where family-owned shops stretch for blocks, in the direction of the Hauptbahnhof. Steindamn intersects with Mühlendamm and runs alongside the south limit of Asklepios Klinik St Georg.

The Taiba Mosque is at 103 Steindamn. I stop at a fruit store to buy a single banana and a pack of Camels. Then I continue along the street. Everywhere, I notice, are families. Children play outside on the sidewalk while parents work the cash and teenage sons and daughters stock the shelves. The immigrant quarter extends four or five blocks. Then St Georg's sex district comes alive, and Halal abuts peepshow. In the shadow of the Hauptbahnhof, the clash of civilizations is complete. The sex and drug trades have taken the street.

The Author is Dead

IN NOVEMBER OF 1989, on a night train to Berlin, the curtain split for an interrogation.

'Passkontrolle.' Your passport.

A week earlier, I had been in Budapest. There, I had heard the first reports about the Wall coming down.

Now, riding my Eurail Pass, I was headed for a party in the end zone of the Cold War. Except, the East German border police had not warmed to the Zeitgeist and would not let me go easily. Waking from an uneasy sleep, I handed my passport to this totalnightmarian, and waited on edge as he compared portrait to face, face to portrait.

What was amiable about the Eastern Bloc was the Black Market. You could change your money on the street without documentation. True, often you got taken and were scammed and lost everything. So you traded in your roll of dollars for a wad of Yugoslav Dinars or toilet paper (same thing). Whenever that happened, it didn't bother me too much. Losing money is a freedom. It counts for nothing compared to losing your sanity.

I noted that the border guard seemed to be staring an inordinately long time at my passport. My daughter learned to make her letters before the age of three. My own handwriting is unwilling. I only came to possess a proper signature a decade or so ago. Signing my name was always suspect, a bit surreal. The sensation was intriguing but worrying. When I was an English Literature major, I read John Keats' 1817 letter to his brothers, George and Thomas, and right away several things dovetailed in my mind:

> ... and at once it struck me what quality went to form a Man of Achievement, especially in Literature, and which Shakespeare possessed so enormously—I mean Negative Capability, that is, when a man is capable of being in uncertainties, mysteries, doubts, without any irritable reaching after fact and reason.

After my trip to Berlin, I took clerical work in a hospital. In the medical library, I found a set of identity disorders that fit perfectly my sense of a negated self. I don't mean to imply I had it as good or bad as Shakespeare, not even close. To my dismay, I found in the list of signs and symptoms 'evidence of the subject's inconsistent handwriting', and 'subject's want of a signature'.

No identity constant, no constant identity = trouble. Straightaway, I could imagine that one of the effects or affects or defects is the deep sensation that you are a slipping or spinning variable in a mathematic equation which balances algebraic terms on either side of a flashing equals sign. Yes, and just like a first-year medical student who will self-diagnose a minimum of three terminal illnesses per rotation, I did the math and forced the connection and ultimately concluded that my sloppy hand and oft-experienced inability to cash a traveller's cheque (Germany—1981, England, Germany—1989, Barbados—1995) due to the 'want' of a signature, as well my tendency to mumble, the inability to recall important personal information, and a dull conversational tone, that these things were … in some way … are proof … that the author is dead.

UNCERTAINTIES, MYSTERIES, DOUBTS

The day I learned to sign was an autumn day in Montréal. From the window of the library, I had a view of the McGill University campus, Michael's alma mater, mine as well. I had moved up, from clerk to librarian, and one of my tasks was to help patients find information in laymen terms about neurological syndromes and disorders. 'Informed decision-making' was the mantra for a better tomorrow.

On that glistening day, I was asked upstairs to witness the will of a terminally ill patient. I exited the elevator on the seventh by the nursing station. It was situated like a border house at a halfway point between the unit's east and west wings. Encased in glass, a clerk was sitting at the desk. Her pen dangled like a whistle on a string around her neck. In behind her, the floor nurses were doing their charting seated at a long table. I noticed them, their repose in relief, a row in white like swans, pouring themselves into handwriting, mugs of coffee set at the elbow.

Seven East housed the brain tumour unit. Neoplasm, Brain. I had been taught in library school to use a controlled vocabulary. Medical Subject Headings, the MESH language. Searching the literature in natural language increased the noise and distorted your results. Expand the tree, that was the way I'd been taught; expand the MESH tree and find the proper terminology on a lower branch—centipede-looking things like Subependymomas and Oligodendroglioma. Unpronounceable units of sound, and so alien, until you encountered the living host—a woman of twenty-eight or a man of forty-nine—up close in the office.

After they left the library, after *performing* a medical literature search, often I would pick through discarded photocop-
ies in the wastebasket. Given time I would read more closely
about certain clinical trials and about agonists and about cell
types studied in research laboratories around the world. I read
lots about linear accelerators and the gamma knife. About
novel approaches and methods used to breach the blood-brain
barrier. And the picture I gathered from all this was of a tidal
wave of groundbreaking research spreading through the hemi-
spheres. Reading the occasional case history—the most elegant
genre of narrative I have ever come across—I began to appreciate the patient grace with which medical science has taken
into its own hands the crash-test biology of all human beings.
Even so I recognized there are disaster cases where nature and
nurture collide with indifferent force, producing the private
consequences and results that defy description. Most of all
I sensed that scientific authors understood much more than
they ever let on.

The solicitor was waiting outside Room 707. Briefcase on
the floor, he grasped a Styrofoam cup of coffee. "Thank you for
coming," he said, explaining that he'd arrived from Toronto by
train in the morning and everything now was rush rush. "This is
very important for Judy," said the solicitor. "Your role is simple.
Ten to twenty minutes."

I was ushered into the room and introduced. "Hi," said
Judy, a plain hello. Hands tucked in her back pockets, shoulders
boosted and slightly turned in, Judy was stereotypical Judy, an
athletic figure in blue jeans.

While her lawyer readied the documents, Judy spoke to me,
directly, and ever so casually. "The doctors finally had a look
at my films. I got some pretty bad news." I knew not to stare
but caught the patch of stubble above Judy's left ear. A three
square inch area, a defined zone—the cordoned off area where

the surgeon went in. "I still have to wait for the radiologist's report. That's what they say. But the biopsy showed most of it."

Hands clasped behind my back, and submerged in the deep freeze of protocol and decorum, I found it difficult to breathe. What is appropriate? *Be here now nowhere else.* But I could not help but notice the sprinkler system, sprouting from the ceiling. Metal daisies hanging from irrigation pipes. The bedside table was another familiar hospital item, height adjustable, on wheels, four beige plastic paws concealing black rubber rollers. The table with a lift-up lid, like a school desk, had a mirror hinged on the underside for shaving or for making a mask.

The solicitor separated the papers into three piles, hesitated, and then retrieved a stamp and ink pad from his briefcase and set them on the high table at the bedside. *This is for the car.* He righted the stacks, each like a deck of playing cards. I watched him do this and patient Judy watched him. *This is for the house. This is for the car. And this is everything else.* The solicitor withdrew a couple of steps, and Judy stepped forward. Judy circled, pen ready, before landing the tip. She put her signature on paper and I felt faint as I watched the man who had prepared the will and testament twist a cufflink through the eyehole in his sleeve, winding it like a wristwatch, taken with it.

Then it was my turn. I signed my name twenty-plus times to the legal documents.

Years later, I remember every detail of that afternoon, who said what, who did what, though it was and is not much.

There was a centipede named Oligodendroglioma.

There was the clerk encased in glass and a row of swans in white making letters.

There was Judy in blue jeans and a white turtleneck in Room 707.

Thank you for coming.

The doctors finally had a look at my films. I got some pretty bad news.

The solicitor shuffled the papers and cut the deck.

This is for the house.

At one point, I turned to the window and touched the ventilation grid set in the window frame, poking my fingertips through. Seven floors up, cars parked bumper to bumper below on University Street.

This is for the car.

Two men in green overalls are seated on the curb by the hospital's west entrance.

This is everything else.

One of them drops his cigarette to the ground, the other man packs a ball of tinfoil into his fist.

An ambulance silently rides up the street.

Andrew, your turn.

The men stand. I watch them rise up, and then like synchronized swimmers, yawn, straighten their backs, reaching skywards.

The Actors' Entrance

I TAKE THE SIDE DOOR, the actor's entrance. Fräulein Asche, from the administrative office, greets me in the lobby.

"You have found it, alright?"

"No problem."

"Have you gone to his street?" In her middle twenties, Sandra Asche betrays a gentle and natural curiosity in the deceased.

"Yes."

She looks pleased with this answer.

"But you didn't have the address."

"No."

"Shame."

Yes, a shame. My attempts to find Michael's address have been foiled by a highly efficient German bureaucracy and my own suspended belief that knowing such a thing really matters in the end.

Fräulein Asche's tour begins at the entrance hall and with a look inside the box office.

"The theatre employs over two hundred workers," she informs me. These include the ensemble of actors and a team of artistic directors, and administrative and communications staff.

When I appear flabbergasted at the number of 'workers', she counters, "Yes. Why not?"

"It's a good number."

"Yes."

Onwards: she lead me inside the labyrinth of passageways that connect the dressing rooms and ateliers to machine and storage rooms. Behind stage the air is stale. But here with Fräulein Asche I feel cleverly tucked behind the bulwark, insulated from the inconsequential daily grind. The passageway curves and the passage bends and at last we come upon a dressmaker—finally, one of Thalia's two hundred employed souls.

She turns to face us, lips pursed, mouth stuffed with pins, when Sandra asks if we may enter.

"Of course."

I circle the room, a space stretched by floor-to-ceiling mirrors. The dressmaker bows to a piece of material in her lap. Fräulein Asche shows me the door. We exit and turn in the direction of the dressing rooms. I sit in the chair facing a mirror ringed with light bulbs. Here Herr Paryla contemplated his role before a performance? Here he waited before the stage manager called out his name? Was it 'Michael' or 'Junker von Bleichenwang'? Last, it was 'Sempronius'.

Fräulein Asche waits in the doorway. I snap another photograph and catch a glimmer of the lyricism which the place holds for me. *Behold, he is lost and never found. He leaves and never arrives. Behold, the very old story of the Prodigal Son. Behold, the legend of a young man who did not want to be loved for who he was; mostly,* I'm thinking, *because Michael Paryla did not love himself.* This sounds about right.

When he left Canada for Germany in 1956, he was twenty–one. Both of his parents had been actors, and both had been trouble for the times: Eva the Mischling and Karl the Communist. There was a curse upon his household, but there was method in blood. He left Canada a young man; empty as a promise he went abroad to become anew, and in the land of his ancestors erased Mike Paryla, line by line, and from city to city searched inside and outside for his new identity.

Behold, a refugee, displaced since birth, looking for a home in the heart of his father.

I'm not convinced.

After returning from Hamburg, I telephoned Michael's half-brother, Stephan Raky-Paryla. Like father, and like Michael, Stephan Paryla is a stage and movie actor. He lives in Vienna and I had wanted to pay him a visit while in Europe—make a side trip to Austria—but when I had called Stephan before leaving on my trip, he had been reluctant to talk to me.

I partly understood this reaction. I had called without warning, from Canada, to discuss events which had taken place more than thirty years ago and to ask questions about his father's first marriage and the death of Stephan's half-brother. Stephan in return inquired about me, my age, and what my relationship to Michael is, exactly. I chose the route of explanation that ran through Michael's mother, Eva; I was her grand-nephew; Eva's brother is my grandfather; my own father and Michael were cousins.

There was silence at his end. I sensed, however, that Stephan was relieved. He was now recalibrating. I knew that Karl Paryla had the reputation of a womanizer. Maybe Stephan's initial thought had been that I was an illegitimate child—and not the first to call without prior notice and claim Karl as their father. The very moment this scenario suggested itself I knew it was rooted in the truth. Perhaps there were illegitimate children throughout the land, and over the years, a pretty multiple number had come home to roost. Whatever, I got the feeling Stephan was worried, and that it was not a new worry but an old one, and part of an ongoing story. He thought I was after estate money, a piece of the Paryla pie, if such a sweet thing existed.

My second call caught Stephan in the bathtub, relaxing, before the night's performance. His voice bounced across the water and echoed against porcelain. Syntax notwithstanding, Stephan Paryla-Raky's accent is very English. His online bio promises that he speaks French, German (several dialects), Russian, and Spanish. English is tiddlywinks for him; probably he can quote Shakespeare longer than I would like to listen to it. He was less suspicious of my motives the second time around, and more philosophical. He was smoking a cigarette in the tub, and probably sweating, too. Stephan was a man of experience, someone not easily put off balance. He could play a part in this.

> Eva Steinmetz was my father's first wife. Michael was born to them in Vienna. Well, I remember a smart boy. Blond. He was a fine guy, a good-looking kid. Handsome and very clever. You know, I didn't see him very often. This year, I am sixty-one. In 1967, I was nineteen. I lived in Vienna with my father and then in the DDR, in the East. But we would sometimes go to Munich and there I met him several times. As I said, I remember a bright boy, a very likeable fellow. But all in all it was for a very short time that I knew him.

> His death was a bit of a mystery. In such cases, after so many years—what do you say—all tracks lost, the trail goes cold?

Someone called to him. He asked me to hold on one moment. Then he was back:

> I am sure you know the story. The theatre doctor had been serving him barbiturates. You know what happens, yes? Over

time the concentration in the blood increases. He suffered from insomnia and he always took sleeping pills and whiskey mixed with milk to fall asleep. This was his habit. I went with my father to Hamburg and entered his flat and we found it how he had left it. There was the bottle of pills and the glass with milk and whiskey in it. When the ambulance guys found him there in bed he was still alive, and they brought him to the hospital where he died. This apparently was good. If he had survived, he would have been then an idiot. It was better how it happened, that he was too exhausted to regain consciousness.

So Stephan had visited Michael's apartment in Hamburg, accompanying his father in 1967. The whiskey and barbiturate cocktail has been part of the story from the beginning, but until now I knew nothing about Michael's milk habit. I couldn't get over the image of Stephan, then nineteen, entering the apartment with his father, to inspect the scene, and finding the glass of whiskey and milk and half-bottle of pills, in the place of Michael. The half-glass of milk was a detail to ponder. My father, a retired physician, has an explanation for what happened to his cousin:

> I think that the milk in the whiskey was meant to reduce irritation of the stomach caused by the alcohol. The entire prescription is, really, malpractice, because it was, even then, well-known what happens: people who have taken barbiturates to sleep, wake up during the night—think they have not gone to sleep yet—and either take more barbiturates or more alcohol, and in this way overdose. This is what seems to have happened to Michael.

Sound reasoning, but it doesn't get to the bottom of the morbid fascination I felt growing for that half-glass—even as

I still had reclined-in-the-tub-Stephan warming to Michael. Michael's milk turned the stomach uneasily. It symbolized something else surely.

Milk is for children. Milk is the potion served at night to help little men sleep. Here we have Michael's father arriving at his son's deathbed and finding a glass of milk. Whiskey and barbiturates—adult fare, for sure—but the whiteness in the glass clouds the picture.

After he'd recounted all he could remember, I informed Stephan that in my possession I had three letters his father had written to Eva after Michael's death. I briefly described the contents. They were remarkable, I told him. Letters of pure expression and deep feeling. Would he like it if I made copies and sent them to him? "No," he replied. "I lost my father ten or so years ago. I loved my father. Those letters belong to his life. I don't want to see them or know about them. They belong to him. And to Eva. That was their life. It's not for me to know about it. I don't want to read them."

Alright. The letters are private. They do belong to his father. The contents and intellectual property, the emotional freight, belong to Karl Paryla. But the more important issue, for Stephan and for his family, is that Eva and Michael complicate the past, perhaps even the present. For me the letters shine a light, but the same words cast shadow in their corner. Fair enough. I could see my way around that. We talked a bit more and at one point I mentioned to Stephan Michael's part in *The Great Escape*. He wasn't aware Michael had been in the movie. Neither did he seem very interested. How could that be? I was astounded. But then I remembered that Michael was uncredited in the first place and, secondly, war films are not for everyone. Perhaps there is no great hunger among a generation as close to the war as Stephan's is to watch Second World War films. They likely suffer from considerable war fatigue, which is understandable. But, as is often said, they started it. My interest in the movie derives from Michael's involvement, otherwise I would never have taken an interest in Stalag Luft III. Had Michael been cast for a bit part in, say, *Cleopatra* instead, the top moneymaker from 1963, I'd be hard pressed trying to link Michael with Ancient Egypt, but to London and Rome I'd have gone, which is where Twentieth Century Fox filmed the movie that just about bankrupt them. I'm trying to say that it's merely a fluke I have spent so much time researching a Hollywood war movie as opposed to a love story, and that I have no special interest in Nazis and the evil they do. However, there is a problem with this view, which implies that Michael's involvement in *The Great Escape*—in *that* particular movie—was a matter of chance. I don't think it was chance or coincidence. Unless chance is more determined than it is usually given credit for. Unless chance is a stubborn player after all and bullies and schemes and tips the scales and rules from behind the scenes what should come to be.

Since events which might as well happen as not do not exist.

Not, anyway, when your pursuit of the truth falls under a deadline.

Meanwhile, time is running on and this call is getting expensive and since I know very well that it's bad manners not to ask an artist about his own work, I inquire innocently if Stephan was making any films these days in Vienna. His reply:

> Here are not so many American films being made, in Austria or Germany, not any more. In 1978, I was in this series *Holocaust*, with Meryl Streep and James Wood. I remember going to a restaurant where I talked to Streep for hours. In the film we did it the old way. We taped one-to-one. It was my original voice

that was used. I played an SS guy. Sgt. Foltz. This SS guy who shoots a bunch of Jews and leaves them in a ditch.

I smothered the mouthpiece to kill my gasp. SS. This SS guy. What are the chances? Michael in 1962. Stephan in 1978. What is it about the Paryla clan? They share a father. Anything else?

Michael Paryla as Don Cesar in a production of *Ein Bruderzwist in Habsburg* by Franz Grillparzer. The play is about a fratricidal quarrel. (Place and date unknown).

The stage is raked. Sandra Asche and I sit side-by-side in the upper reaches of seats. She takes a deep breath.

"Impressive," I say. From our vantage, high above, the stage has a ruthless quality. What is it? Ambition and promise and dreams put in honest perspective. The uphill battle of make-believe.

Three figures are at work down on the stage. They keep pointing up, at the lights hanging above them. It looks like they're discussing arrangements, preparing the set of an upcoming production. Theatre people, Michael's kind of people, the cult who are conserved in the Hamburg's Theatersammlung. Which reminds me of something: the page I scanned from Thalia's Vorstellungbuch, describing events the night of 20 January 1967. Sitting in a row, overlooking the stage, I pull up the image for Sandra Asche.

"Do you know what it says?" She asks, and places her hand on my arm.

"Yes."

"You've had it translated." I nod. Thank Dr. Giesing for that. "That's good."

Nonetheless Fräulein Asche begins her own translation, reading aloud. She narrates in a soft voice. "He didn't come to the theatre before the show, and it says here, the play begins late." I know about this. "In fact, he did not show up the entire time."

She sits back and stares forward for a long while, her profile illuminated by screenglow.

A complete translation reads as follows:

Play:	Report on the performance of
The Apple Cart (Der Kaiser von Amerika)	Friday, January 20, 1967
Start of performance: 8:15 PM	12th performance
Intermission from 9:38 PM. to 10:02 PM	I. Act 8:15—9:17 PM
End of performance: 10:48	II. Act 9:18—9:38 PM
Curtains: 27	III. Act 10:02—10:45 PM

Particulars:

On the last sign (7:55 PM), the stage manager and the evening stage director were informed by some actors that Mr. Paryla (role of Sempronius) had not yet arrived at the theatre. After consultation with Mr. Rappel, the play began 13 minutes late with the entrance of Mr. Kelevenows (Boanerges). Since Mr. Paryla did not show up for the entire performance, Mr. Genke took over his role. Neither the flow, nor the understanding of the play were compromised. Mr. Hasse requested that no announcement be made to the audience.

Fräulein Asche states, "The play was okay without him. Nothing was lost." Then she goes quiet. It doesn't sound right. No. *Neither the flow nor understanding of the play was compromised.* But what concision. What cruelty and what beauty in cruel concision. Neither the flow nor understanding. Michael's absence was handled with show-must-go-on professionalism. The actors waited—no announcement was made—and then they started with the second scene of the play. In subsequent performances, Dr. Giesing had remarked in an email, the role of Sempronius was played by the actor Fritz von Friedl.

Now tell me, what substance is there to the character Sempronius that his absence from the first act (rather disappearance from) has no impact on the rest of the play? What kind of lightweight was he? Michael allegedly suffered from performance anxiety—and from insomnia—but why worry so much when cast in the role of said unimpressive Sempronius?

I shut the laptop. The slope of a raked stage allows for an actor to stand 'upstage' or 'downstage'. The actor who stands further from the audience stands higher on the stage than the actor who is downstage. He might 'upstage' the actor below him, who must turn his back to the audience in order to address the more elevated actor. Upstaging another actor, by drawing attention to oneself, is the figurative offspring of the raked stage.

In reality, on the evening of 20 January 1967, the action ongoing behind the curtain, beyond the raked stage, was halting and less assured than the official report and description in the Vorstellungbuch. The events of that night followed a more ambiguous narrative. When Michael did not show up, there was some frantic calling around to find him. This continued even after the play commenced. Eventually a phone call was made to Michael's partner Margaret Jahnen in Munich. Instinct told Margaret that something was terribly wrong. The second act of the play had ended, and she instructed the theatre staff to race to his apartment on Mühlendamm Strasse and break down the door if he did not answer. Send the police and firemen. At once!

While lounging in the bathtub, Stephan Raky-Paryla gently insinuated that something was off, maybe even suspicious, in the manner Margaret had reacted that night:

> The night of his accident, when he had not shown up at the theatre, the stage manager had called Margaret in Munich and she had told them, Please go at once to his apartment and use violence, break down the door to his flat. In the end this was a bit strange, that she knew precisely what must have happened.

Well, I don't know, nothing too strange about this. I presume Margaret knew Michael's habits better than anyone. She *was* his life-partner, was she not? If anyone knew how he suffered, she must have.

Police and firemen were dispatched (unlike me, they at least had learned his address), but no doctor. Next Michael was lifted from his bed and taken by ambulance to Asklepios Klinik St Georg, where he received a firm heart massage, but never regained consciousness. And whatever you might say about that—that it was finally in everyone's best interest that he did not survive, because if he had he would have been reduced to some kind of intellectual vegetable (the opinion of his half-brother); that, in retrospect, neither the flow nor understanding of the play was comprised (according to the note in the Vorstellungbuch); that it was a big mistake that no doctor was sent with the police and firemen (the opinion of his father); that there is something odd in Margaret Jahnen's heartsick reaction, in that she seemed to know precisely what must have happened (again his half-brother)—whether or not you stand upstage or downstage, live in the past or come from the future, Michael was no more.

Behold, he died last night in the city of Hamburg.

In the sunlit and white stucco mezzanine, Sandra Asche and I intersect paths with the current artistic director of Thalia Theatre.

"This is a wonderful place," I tell him. Not a wonderful theatre, which it might be, but a wonderful, magical place, which it is for me.

"Aha." He steals a glance at Sandra, puts a finger to his cheek. And directly, without further ado, shares a memory of his about Michael's father. He did not know Michael Paryla. But once, long ago, he had the privilege of doing a show with Karl Paryla. Here in Hamburg. Which was terrific. Am I surprised?

Not at all. The sins of the father, or something like that.

"That's my only connection to your project," he tells me. "Good luck with your project."

With my little project, my schoolboy fascination. "Thank you."

Though in the press there is no evidence of it, Michael did in fact show up for eleven performances of *Der Kaiser von Amerika* before missing the twelfth. In Act One again, Pamphilius (played by Horst Gentzner) sits opposite Sempronius (Michael). Pamphilius probes Sempronius for more information about his father:

Pamphilius: By the way, is he alive? I should like to know him.

Sempronius answers, No, his father is not alive. His father, he says, died in 1962 "of solitude." Solitude is an odd thing to die of, but we are in a play. This is the fucking theatre. Where you can actually die from a lot of things like loneliness and solitude. Where you can go out of mind watching pretentious nonsense. Sempronius provides some context, which makes it all the more credible: shipwrecked, his father swam to an uninhabited island where he went "melancholy mad".

Pamphilius asks Sempronius to clarify.

> Sempronius: He couldn't bear to be alone for a moment: it was death to him. Somebody had to be with him always.

In the scheme of art influencing life and life reflecting art, seen through the conundrum of fathers and sons, the above sounds much more like a description of Michael's tendencies, such that we know of them, than of his father's. It was Michael who allegedly could not stand solitude. In the evenings he was pulled out the door of his apartment by the lure of company, and merged into the night. Michael we might imagine dying of solitude. But not in 1962, which by the way was his Gestapo year. And for the record Karl Paryla died in 1996.

Getting back to *Der Kaiser von Amerika*, when Sempronius describes his father's occupation, saying he was a "Ritualist," Pamphilius is confused:

> Pamphilius: Do you mean that he was a parson?

> Sempronius: Not at all. He was a sort of spectacular artist. He got up pageants and Lord Mayors' Shows and military tattoos

and big public ceremonies and things like that. He arranged the last two coronations. That was how I got my job here in the palace. All our royal people knew him quite well: he was behind the scenes with them.

All our royal people knew him. He was behind the scenes. That was how I got my job here at the palace. Was Michael granted his place in this palace of make-believe called a theatre through the reputation of his father, the celebrated Karl Paryla? Thalia Theatre's artistic director had involuntarily insinuated this within seconds of our meeting, with his little story about having worked with the father. Karl Paryla was terrific; Michael remains a project. Secretary to the King in *Der Kaiser from Amerika*, Michael, The Son Of. The Lost Son of Karl Paryla.

The Son Of.

Behold, the lost son of Karl Paryla.

Was the realization—*That was how I got my job here in the palace*: words put in his mouth—deflating, heart-sickening, a kind of death to him? Picture Michael, in rehearsal, day after day. Punctured. He once had promise, could have played any part, any number of roles, but is picked for a role which keeps him down. Not, this time, opposite Herbert Steinmetz from Stuttgart. Opposite his own father, a sort of spectacular artist, who lurked behind every scene.

Before leaving the theatre, I ask my host if I may take her photograph.

"Sure, why not?" Sandra is flattered. She crosses her arms, leans heavily on the wall.

The better to serve my memory of Michael.

*

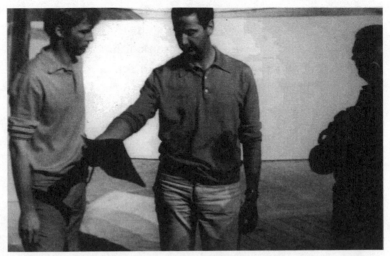

Michael (left) in rehearsal for *Der Kaiser von Amerika* (Thalia Theatre, 1966).

There is something else, before I leave Hamburg: grey Hamburg of the ashen canal water, melancholy Hamburg, pale sky Hamburg, colours weak as my knowledge of Veronal, which was or was not his barbiturate of choice. Maybe it was Luminal. Maybe Lethe. Let's decide it was Veronal. Let's have that decided. Little Verona in a pill bottle. Veronal, and Verona for Shakespeare, the setting of *The Two Gentlemen of Verona* and the setting of *Romeo and Juliet*. Verona like Venice like Hamburg, city of canals.

There is something else. I forget who told me, it may have been The Filmfuehrer. *Whether a person looks good on camera or not is unpredictable.* I must say I'm intrigued by this. It must be important enough, *whether a person looks good on camera or not is unpredictable* has a certain ring.

Another thing. In each scene that you appear, you should ask yourself, 'What does my character want?' Here, if it's not already obvious, the answer is: I want to become Michael. His Doppelgänger. His double-goer and paranormal twin. I'm learning a few tricks and finally know what it is like when artifice eats at the face. What is at the source of our fierce resistance to become the other? Is there some innate inability to be untrue? I see that the struggle to become an actor is in us all. I first sensed it in the garde robe at the Thalia Theatre, seated before the mirror.

I see that what went through you, Michael, was a flaming arrow of indignity lit by ambition. Acting is an annihilation and a gift. There is danger in it. Of this I am sure. I have no doubt.

Deutsche Bahn ice 164

THE TRAIN LEAVES THE STATION, breaks from the platform like a long ship, and the oft-dazzling Michael Paryla is quiet. His crossed-arms to chest, an outline without core, Michael is transported in a casket along these rails, upon this straight line, to his resting place south of Munich. A bizarre attraction, an impressive plaything, exaggerated excess—no longer. No more the sparkling fool, Junker Bleichenwang. No more Sempronius. Final moments, on stage, in character, a fool and a royal secretary.

Underling, underling.

He died three days after the *Hamburger Abendblatt* notice appeared, and only a week before the ensemble for *Der Kaiser von Amerika* was scheduled to shift locations and ready themselves for a guest appearance at Wiener Burgtheatre. Art Nouveau Vienna. Red Vienna. Anschluss Vienna. *Wien Judenrein* Vienna. Waltzing Vienna. Mozarthaus Vienna. The City of Dreams. Old Freud Vienna.

Then was Vienna the trigger?

Vienna belonged to his father. Karl Paryla was born in Vienna at the turn of the century—Austro-Hungarian Empire Vienna, Habsburg Vienna. His father made his home in the Austrian capital with his second wife. More to the point, Karl Paryla owned the stage. But then Vienna was also Michael's city.

Michael was born in Vienna in 1935. In Vienna, his mother and father had grown apart, but on the eve of the Anschluss and on the edge of a precipice known as *Wien Judenrein Vienna,* they struck a deal and decided they would stick it out, for Michi's sake, and separate only after the escape, if they made it safely to Switzerland.

There were many reasons for Michael to avoid going to Vienna in 1967. Every one of them had to do with his father.

Perhaps this is the moment to tell the tale I alluded to earlier, concerning the family's flight from Vienna.

"He wore the black," Eva described one of her brothers-in-laws, Hrolf Kramm, this way when I spoke to her in 1994. She implied Hrolf Kramm was a member of the SS. *We were stuck in Vienna in 1938 and needed to find a way out. Hrolf came to Vienna and made contact with me. He knew we were trapped.*

"Oh yes, he wore the black." Eva swore to it. *He came to me, alone, and Karl never knew anything about that. Karl and I, we had no money for a bribe. So Hrolf came in secret and took me to an apartment and afterwards he said, Good, the directions are simple. Go to such and such a place. There is a barn, hide inside. Wait there. Someone will come. Someone will come and guide you across the mountains.*

"And sure enough there was an escape chain over the mountains to Switzerland. Sure enough, I paid the price."

Vienna is where Michael's story meets Hrolf's shadow and the words mostly die away except for some bare phrases. *He wore the black.* Eva told me, *Karl never knew anything about that. That.* Safe transit in return for a sexual favour, blackmail perpetuated by her brother-in-law. Karl never knew? That's hard to believe. *He did not want to know?* Less kind but more credible. And what about Michael? He was only three years old at the time. But was it something he learned about in due time without ever having been told? Did he know it in his heart in the way we know all about the pain of the people we love? *Karl never knew about that.* I don't know. There are not two sides to this story unfortunately. What remains are Eva's words.

Not all of what I know about my family history is rooted in fact. Lots of it I invented as a child growing up in Canada. For years, when I played army in the yard with neighbour-hood boys, I squinted and saw myself as my great uncle Abelard Kramm, fighting in a trench on the Russian Front. Abelard and Hrolf are brothers, my grandmother's siblings. When my grandparents fled Germany to South America in 1935, the brothers Kramm stayed put. Abelard died in 1941 of sniper fire on the Eastern Front; Hrolf Kramm not until 2003, in Switzerland, of septicaemia—or blood poisoning, which sounds about right.

In my early adolescence, after reading about the Battle of Stalingrad, I would transport Abelard in my mind to this bat-tle, famous for its number of casualties. It became part of my own private legend that Abelard had died fighting in Stalingrad, when in reality, as I know today, he died thirty kilometres south of Luga. *Dorfes etwa 30 km südlich von Luga,* stipulated the let-ter from his field officer.

Stalingrad seemed important, though. The city's name struck a chord in me. Saying 'Stalingrad' provoked an eerie sense of the inevitable meeting the systematic; to my ears, the battle was engineered to end as many human lives as possible. And so it was in Stalingrad that I placed Abelard at dusk: first lighting a cigarette—hands cupped around the orange flame: stupid, stupid—then standing to remove his wool sweater.

The sniper aims. He fires and the bullet passes into my heart.

This is how I died for Abelard, when I was in my early teens. Abelard's death story—dark, unsung, dangerous—might excite a young boy, and it did me. Even now, in my late forties, I cannot remove my sweater in winter without getting trapped in a weave of obscure emotions. In the middle of the afternoon, alone, anywhere, I'll think directly of Abelard. He cannot see out when he is shot. He falls face down in mud, wet clothes soon swollen. Sometimes, I let myself go a little further; I imagine myself kneeling beside him and take his hand in my own and slide his gold ring with the family emblem off his finger. At such moments I feel very alive, full of thanks not to be a soldier; especially not one of *their* soldiers, buried kilometres south of Luga.

The photograph I remember best of Abelard—it survives as a kind of shadowy family icon—portrays him in his Wehrmacht uniform. Abelard is striking: clear-eyed, full lips, strong jaw, but he is hardly masculine-looking. Instead, he gives a feline impression. There is a rumour that Abelard was gay, and that his anxious father used his societal connections to expedite Abelard's path to the Eastern Front. The first time I saw Abelard in pictures I thought of David Bowie from *Heroes*.

But that's enough romantic invention. What is real and what is hard fact is that Abelard and his brother Hrolf fought for *them*. The fact that great uncle Abelard was killed fighting for 'the Germans' definitely was ominous. More than ominous, this fact seemed wrong, plain backwards. But was I ever really ashamed of him? No. What did it have to do with me picking off the twins who lived next door to us in Dorval, using my sleek and just-bought carbon copy of an Enfield Rifle Musket? And anyway, what was there to fuss about since Abelard was deceased? In the natural history of my feelings toward him, the latter fact is key: Abelard was good and dead before I'd even heard his name mentioned in family conversation, killed on a day when no other soldier in Battalion 48 had lost his life. The original notification of death, dispatched from the office of the Oberkommando der Wehrmacht, contained a private letter from Abelard's field officer to his next of kin.

> Your son died in a tragic manner. A shot that struck his ammunition pouch caused the bullets to explode without injuring him. He sought cover to see if everything was in order. As he took off his pullover, he stood up too straight, and a shot to his heart killed him. He was the only loss that the company had suffered on that day.

I recently acquired a photocopy of this odd, which is to say, rather touching letter. On the back side is a diagram of the battlefield, hand-drawn by Abelard's field officer. The diagram—rudimentary, but carefully composed—shows roads and a bending river, and it pinpoints the battalion's position on the day Abelard died. Reading the letter again, I realize that the detail of Abelard standing absurdly "too straight" to remove his pullover is something that I had heard repeated many times. That is, in the telling of the story, at different times and over the years, this detail had stuck. It appears to be authentic, after all.

Killed on a day when no one else in Battalion 48 had lost his life. There is a rightness to this statement, another element of the story that I seem to have known about from the beginning. It is as though on 11 December 1941, Abelard paid a price. He was chosen to die; and to die young; Abelard for his company of men. All the more reason I would whisk my naïve boyhood image of him away from the battlefield into my imagination for polishing, possibly for safekeeping.

The stories about Abelard and Hrolf struck a chord in me, dissonant but romantic, that would ominously resound years later when I learned more about Michael, and Michael's spin as a Gestapo agent in *The Great Escape*. Michael became a fascination, and the irony is that Michael's experience of the war always seemed more vital for me, and he the actor more real to me than the other two, Hrolf and Abelard, who in fact were soldiers, if we are still calling *them* soldiers.

When my nuclear family left Canada to live two years in East Africa in the late 1970s, we stopped off in Germany on the way over to visit with relatives. One day, my parents took me and my brothers and sister to the concentration camp at Dachau, easily accessible by train from Munich. We entered the camp the same way the first prisoners—these first were political prisoners—entered in 1933, through the Jourhaus and through the rod-iron gate upon which the Nazis had affixed the phrase *Arbeit macht frei*. Inside, we spent the afternoon, in hard-to-break silence, touring the grounds of the memorial site. We saw an exhibit of photographs, the barracks, the crematorium, and I remember a vast area which was called roll-call square, where up to forty thousand prisoners could assemble and would be counted each morning and each night. *Arbeit macht frei* might be the first German sentence I remember reading. The literal translation—'Work Makes Freedom'—did not come close to conveying the cruelty of the Nazi policy of extermination through work, nor was such sinister irony fathomable to the ten-year-old tourist I was. I need not properly remember the moment—and I don't—to be certain that my father that day took us children aside for a good fifteen minutes to explain what the words really meant. He took a long time with us, I'm sure he did, and we understood the gravity without probably understanding him.

After Munich, we travelled to see uncle Hrolf, still in Constanz. My parents never had anything good to say about him, but off we went to visit anyway. Like him or not, he was family, seemed to be the message. Hrolf was part of the package.

The central family myth about Hrolf Kramm is that he used his rank in the military and his geographic position—he was stationed in southern Germany, on the border with Switzerland—to help Jewish families escape Germany. Hrolf was a good Nazi. He did what he could to help. He was one of them but not really one of them. Competing myths or the apocrypha suggest that Hrolf's prime motivation was never 'to help the Jews'. After the war, he was set up for life. Where did his money come from? It is speculated that Hrolf took bribes from Jewish families in return for safe passage to Switzerland. Not everyone in the family believes this to be true. I'm not absolutely sure I believe it myself.

What is most striking about Hrolf Kramm at first glance has nothing to do with bribes or blackmail. During the war he had lost an eye. On the few occasions I met him, I spent my time trying to guess into which socket his glass eye had been inserted: the left, or the right? As a boy, I poorly understood the mechanics of a glass eye, but what strikes me as significant today is how Hrolf's ocular prosthetic altered *how I saw him*. I must have believed that his prosthetic *functioned*, or else did it just lie there like a marble in a hole and block his sight? For me, as a child, there was so much anxiety bound to the foreignness of the thing itself—Might it crack? Was it breakable?—that it has taken me years to realize that really, it wasn't the glass eye that bothered me so much, it was his *absent eye*. The missing one. Unconsciously I must have equated the injury with some form of penalty. Missing an eye was his punishment for being a Nazi. Was he a Nazi?

But then, what if the wound was self-inflicted? I didn't think of this possibility until much, much later. I wished for all the related Steinmetzs and Kramms that I was right about this. But no. It had been an accident. Shrapnel from a grenade explosion. So I'd heard, friendly fire.

My train car is boisterous. Laughter erupts down the aisle. A party of six are sharing lunch. Cold cuts, cheese, dark rye. The DB ticket collector enters and walks toward me, slowly like a lazy bee swaying between seat rests and passengers. The mission is cross-pollination, and during the return trip to Munich I am set up with my laptop. I cannot stop looking at him, the Gestapo from Breslau, at him from the movie especially, who put a spell on me. He who blossoms despite the sadists in the wardrobe department. Fifty-seven seconds all counting—before we lose sight of him for good, on-screen and off, stardust to rust, so it goes and so it must.

STOP PAUSE PLAY

PLAY
He speaks the existential discourse of border guards and customs officials. What is your age? Why have you come here? A
song and dance: Michael sings with the philosophers of frontier
authority. What is the purpose of your visit? Who in hell are
you? Dialectics of flesh and spirit, a chorus-line to-and-fro that
springs forth laconic data of the self. Are you French?

PLAY-REWIND
I press stop then play-rewind and Michael is sucked backwards-
a-blur into the film's unconscious. I press play—and just in
time: Michael re-emerges. Reconstituted, assembled in colour,
he is himself again, in Neustadt.

PAUSE
Now look. I press pause, and watch: left foot frozen, forward knee uplift, locked-but-stepping aboard train 78185 at
2:08:37.

Fedora. Lips parted, front teeth prominent. Appalling. Even a
split-second pause disturbs his nature. Paused, Michael suffers

a seizure. Pause-him-and-he-jitters. He surrenders free will. Becomes a monster. One of them.

PLAY!
He enters the coach. He spots the lazy pair of SS officers. It must be either the black uniforms or their higher-functioning evil that makes them drowsy so.

Michael takes it all in. In the near row of camera-facing benches, the orchard-fresh Nazi Youth fixes a squalid place in history. He is wearing the brown shirt and a bright red armband. His handkerchief is joined under his chin by a wooden ring. What does Michael see in him? In age and putty face, he is the Doppelgänger of the young master Michi, resident of the Lahr DP camp. His double-goer. Does he notice?

Germany floats freely outside the window. His paranormal twin is mesmerized by what mumbo jumbo now?

> A. The Jungvolk Oath: "In the presence of this blood banner which represents our Führer, I swear to devote all my energies and my strength to the saviour of our country, Adolf Hitler. I am willing and ready to give up my life for him, so help me God."

> Or B. One of the Hitler Youth 'Prayers' : "Adolf Hitler, you are our great Führer. Thy name makes the enemy tremble. Thy Third Reich comes, thy will alone is law upon the earth. Let us hear daily thy voice and order us by thy leadership, for we will obey to the end and even with our lives. We praise thee! Heil Hitler!"

Or C. "Führer, my Führer, given me by God. Protect and preserve my life for long. You saved Germany in time of need. I thank you for my daily bread. Be with me for a long time, do not leave me, Führer, my Führer, my faith, my light, Hail to my Führer!"

Or perhaps in his reverie the youth recites D., one of the many buoyant mottoes for boys: "Live Faithfully, Fight Bravely, and Die Laughing!" "We were born to die for Germany!" "You are nothing—your Volk is everything!"

Michael takes a moment to reminisce. What does he make of it all?

PAUSE

Michael is no stranger to trains. No stranger to the calling, to delivery or travel, no stranger to leaving nor to arriving, no stranger to taking a little time off, some metaphysical flux-enfer as an excuse for being.

PLAY

Richard Attenborough and Gordon Jackson's documents are false. That much is certain, *psst, ihre Pässe ist* counterfeit. The audience knows. Michael knows it. The ensuing dialogue may as well be gibberish: *Vous êtes Francais? Oui. Oui. Merci. Oui. Moi aussi. Later, I film Gandhi!*

But like the professional he is, Michael speaks his lines in a clear register. Michael repeats the syntax string, without ecclesiastical sing-song, from subject to verb, engine to caboose: *Ihre. Paesse. bitte. Vous. Etes. Francais?*

FAST FORWARD

I fast forward now and Michael swims by the escapees at a high speed of hundreds of frames per second, which is humorous but surely is also dangerous. The visual gag quickly becomes annoying. More tiresome than pause and play. More fatiguing than play-rewind. Tiresome for me and—you'd expect—for him. But not at all. He performs splendidly. Fast forward is his element. Does he not see the fast track for what it is? Fast forward is dangerous, reckless as predestination.

'All is grace.' Yes. Oui! All is grace, except in hindsight, Michael, wherein some things are an intractable disgrace.

When I ease off, gradually, equilibrium is restored. Michael regains composure. He finds himself wherever he is. But no matter how many times I've done this—blindly fast-forwarded him—I can never predict his exact position. There is a limited range of possibilities, true enough, and Michael eventually surfaces within this range, between Munich and Hamburg (or Breslau and Berlin for the sake of the film), but never at the same spot and never the same Michael.

STOP

Achtung! You there! Your Great Emanation. Stand and unfold yourself. You come most carefully upon your hour. You and your historical accuracy. You sham, you florid sham of light waves.

Is it you? Is it really you? Him?

Your material trace, your buzzing emanation, is all there is left.

REWIND

I rewind, then hit play. You arrive at Neustadt, impossible-to-find Neustadt, the old station located in impossible-to-locate Geiselgasteig. You step out of history and crunch the itching gravel. You walk the station platform, step aboard the train. I observe closely as you enter your passage of time through *The Great Escape*. Your uncredited fifty-seven seconds.

PAUSE

I pause him often, at different intervals, at random: as he boards as he looks left as he looks to his right as he advances up the aisle and when he stops to chat with the British and American actors.

I gently apply pressure: suspended, under my thumb, shivering in disbelief. Act you little Michael.

Then I unfreeze him and he always says *Danke*. Never 'Thank You'.

REWIND

The boy is first-class. He puts up with these experiments. He is tireless. What I mean is, over time, he does not deteriorate. Michael is sharp. He comes from good stock, that's right. Even after fast-forwarding, slow-reverse, pause, and plain-old play time, Michael is crisp. Intact. He does not fade. Just the opposite: he blooms under the microscope.

Here, instead of using a live specimen for investigation, I study dead Michael on film.

STOP
When I stop to measure his position in reference to the running time of the film, it is obvious that I have lost something.

The more precisely I can measure his position, the less precisely I know him this instant, and vice versa. This is the gist of the Heisenberg Uncertainty Principle. I cannot know him at any fixed point. He is elusive after all. Stranded within a range of possibilities. Missing in action. Abandoned in a moving picture. Draped in naturalism. Earth shifting beneath his feet.

So I play.

PAUSE
Look at yourself, Michael. I've caused trouble, I have. I've paused you again and I've really done it, you're trembling in your tan trench coat, wavelengths pouring through your Goonskin. What is it that terrifies you? Who are you hiding from? Son, you're blushing.

He's self-conscious. Red in the face. Michael has method, but he's vain. Is this, the basis of the uncertainty principle, sub-atomic vanity?[38]

Self-consciousness goes undetected unless you fix the image. Molecules, observed, change behaviour.

---

38   There could be something else going on here under the skin. Though his father contends Michael was most interested in making it in the theatre, he and others, including Michael's cousin Sybille, have stated that Michael might have looked at the movies as a 'fast track'. The nuance here is that having success in the movies is crass and was frowned upon. So perhaps Michael here, knowing his father is watching along with the whole world, is feeling sheepish. Shamefaced because he is appearing in a Hollywood movie and not even in a leading role, but as an uncredited hack. And then there is the fact of playing the part of a blond bimbo.

Vanity, pure vanity. Nature is shot through with it.

PLAY

That on my flat screen is the quantum aspect of him. The smallest discrete amount of Michael. A single frame fixed for the eye. Jittering as vibrations and pixels and dots per inch pour through him. Act little Michael. *Acht du lieber!*

Look at the boy. He shakes and trembles. What have I done? Wavering between future and past, between rewind and forward, between fast and slow speed, what have I done?

I said he came from good stock, but is that enough? Perhaps he is like the actors his father Karl Paryla loved so much, one of Brecht's human puppets who were instructed to perform self-consciously, as though, at every moment, they know the beginning, middle, and end of the play.

Michael has full knowledge—beyond his seconds on film—of the span of his life. That is why he shakes and trembles so. He knows about the beginning, middle, and especially he knows the end. He knows and it has all gotten to him. He's frayed. His nerves are shot. He doesn't know once upon a time from ever after.

*

He does a fine job. He speaks fluently. But at the end of the line, when the credits begin to tumble, his name is nowhere. Michael is all lost—already lost: you can see it in his eyes— but the role playing continues: there is Junker Bleichenwang and Sempronius and many others, Francisco, Fred Nicolls,

Cosimo de Medici. He is many and none. Alas, the sick seagull cannot find sleep without milk and barbiturates. And despite his rising star he is down on himself. It's all in his head, but he exists in his head. He naps in the afternoons. A few hours here and there. When he comes to, he remembers Konstantin Gavrilovich Trepliov, the Russian Hamlet, in Chekhov's play. Michael was twenty when he played the role. The character Trepliov has a complex relationship with his mother, and commits suicide at the end of the play. Maybe Michael found a little of himself in Trepliov. His Trepliov is a young man, a budding playwright with a fragile ego and heart, who is needy and, above all, seeks his mother's approval. Approval for what? To be himself. At McGill in 1955, Michael is away from home, learning to be a man, learning to act, girlfriend Janine Blum at his side. And Trepliov's mother, Arkadina, in the play, is a celebrated actress from the old school of Russian drama. Much like Eva, Michael's mother. The Arkadina of the play is forty three years old. Eva's exact age, the year that Michael played Trepliov. What is more, Trepliov misses his father, a well-known actor, who is perpetually 'away'. As is the case with Michael, Trepliov's father's absence creates a void in his life.

When he awakes from his nap, it all seems strangely familiar. It's uncanny. More than a decade later, Michael can cite the stage manager's traffic directions, which precisely mark his own physical whereabouts for the duration of the action of the play.

Between Acts 1 & 2 exit left, wait for curtain fall, open door to warn Nina, then change costume. 12 minutes.

Between Acts 2 & 3 wait stage left: bandage applied to the head by Paulina.

Between Acts 3 & 4 once more wait stage left, be patient: young Masha will change you.

End of Act 4, remain offstage when the gunshot is fired, and wait for curtains and applause. Trepliov, you've taken your life.

I lean my head against the glass. I don't want a suicide for an ending. I don't think it was.

WALDFRIEDHOF

THE TRAM PASSES OSTFRIEDHOF, then Tegerseher Platz. Waldfriedhof, the cemetery at the end of the line, is a thirty minute ride. The Bavariafilmstadt three stops before that. There's a transit map by the sagging exit doors.

This old electric tram has its charm. The ride is precisely slow and slowly precise, and for days I have used a single ticket which I punched myself when I boarded the first time. It's the honour system, Michael. Is this news? An honour system. Wherein citizens act in good faith according to the law and their own principles. There are no Sicherpolizei and likely no fugitives on Tram 25. The morning-showered businessman in the seat ahead holds the *Süddeutsche Zeitung* like a full windshield. The Party paper used for a prop in the movie—that's history, long gone and good riddance. There are no bloody losses nowadays to report, except on Wall Street. Next stop Grodner Strasse. Nobody wears a Fedora. No more. Fedora, leather trench coat, are passé. Now ADIDAS. The black tracksuit and white stripes make it official: society has demilitarized. Materialism is the new fascism. Leisurewear is supreme. It's altogether a different world. The Berlin Wall fell more than twenty years ago. Outstanding, isn't it? Altogether different, and yet on cue, up stands the gentleman at his stop—Tiroler Platz—wearing (no kidding) a green felt cap with a feather and all. Well, this is Munich and Bavaria. Some things never change. From the southern limits of the city you can see the Alps. And up there, invisible to the eye, is the former Nazi resort and residence Berchtesgaden, where Hitler and his top darlings received the first Gestapo report of the escape sixty-six years ago.

Am Wildwechsel. You are buried at the deer's pass, a street named for a timid creature, under a canopy of pine trees. Beside you, the family Moser—*Ruhe in Frieden:* Rest in Peace—and Benno Martin 1898-1967. The stone is roughly hewn, a sturdy mass; it looks to have punctured the earth's crust from below. Moss and lichen have taken to it, and the pine, planted by your father days after the funeral, has matured and must have deep, tangling roots in the grave itself. There are no dates engraved—not your year of birth, not your year of death—and no inscription except *Michael Paryla* and *Margaret Jahnen.* You escaped with hardly a scratch.

Is any of this news?

Insofar as arrangements made with the cemetery administration are concerned, the plot is taken care of by your father, who took out a fifty-year lease on this ground.

And then?

I don't know, Michael. And then—who knows? You better than me. I'll go pester one of the gardeners. They should have an idea. Meanwhile, I confess the cemetery itself is very peaceful. Serene and humid and green. The stones and pebbles and bushes and the trees. The earth and sky. I've come to pay my respects. But the route has not been easy, and what I've uncovered, the little I know, is a burden. For example, your father did not attend the funeral. Overcome with grief, Karl could not make himself come. I understand, but I still think that, no matter how unpleasant, for fathers as well as for sons, there is such a thing as your duty, obligations you must perform. Yes, like an honour system. I'm also saddened to inform you that your mother did not travel from Canada to be at your funeral, and nor did she ever take a trip to Munich in all the years she outlived you. After leaving Germany in 1949, she would not set foot again in this country. In 1967, she wrote her sister and your aunt Irene that she did not have the 'means' to come. Financial, or moral? Does it make a difference? The fact remains that neither of your parents were at your side during the funeral. I find that hard to believe, and difficult to accept. Margaret came, and her son Jerry, and your grandfather Emil, and Irene. But not your own parents. How could they act so shoddily? Why couldn't they pull themselves together for your sake, and for their own?

You need the dark, I know, and you crave the quiet. But Michael, our roots are mysteriously bound together. You've had enough time alone, undisturbed by light and words. What is keeping you?

Karl did come several days *after* the funeral. He described his experience to Eva. How he visited this place and held you in his arms. He wrote a sympathetic letter about the afternoon he spent here at Waldfriedhof. He describes holding the deceased Michael (sorry) in his arms and addressing your memory. He imagined you alive. He resurrected you, for an hour, a guilty hour—for a communist like him—but it was relatively easy for him to do: so strong was your living memory in him. You had presence and *je ne sais quoi* after the curtains closed. Isn't that the story of your life? The first time I read his letter from 1967, it brought me to the edge of tears. I let them go. I'm not at all religious, nor a communist—not even an actor, but flesh and blood and a human being —and therefore I feel Karl and Eva's crushing pain as I stand here.

How should I put it?

How to unravel and disentangle the household textiles, work loose the old bed sheets and garments? How to read between layers and layers of resin-soaked regret, and not miss the amulet or the wax plaque placed over the incision upon your heart? How to go about it? How to unravel being from nothingness? Where stop? At which station? Breslau, Vienna, Zurich, Berlin, Sault Ste. Marie, Montréal, Munich, Hamburg.

And here in Munich again, the end of the line.

I haven't forgotten your question: *And what then?* After fifty years. I'm thinking about this while I walk the moss, past your neighbour Benno Martin: 1898-1967, to speak with the gardener, who is tending to a family plot occupied by five.

"Please, I have a question."

He turns from the ground and grimaces, a stout man in brown overalls with a seamstress's pin pad for a chin and deep red lips.

"No English," he says, and makes himself upright from a kneeling position. He steps unsteadily, and the boxes of plants roll onto their side. "*Bulgarisch,*" he points to himself, and then goes about wiping the dirt from his hands and from the front of his overalls.

"Cigarette?" He will find someone who can help me, his boss speaks English. Meanwhile, killing ourselves slowly by the same filthy habit is the best way I have ever found to break through walls, build mutual trust. He points: there she is, driving a miniature pickup truck, laden with plants, down the narrow path. He yells out her name, which I don't catch. She stops the truck and jumps out of the cabin. She reaches into the cargo bed, turns and marches over to our smoking party—an earthy blonde, wearing high rubber boots, tugging a watering hose.

The Bulgarian points: he wants to talk to you.

"Bitte," I begin.

"Yes," she nods. "What is it?"

I point to the grave at our feet. "I am family."

"His or hers?" she interrupts.

"His. Michael Paryla."

"This grave is taken care of by another gardener. But maybe I can help you."

"I hope so."

"What is it?"

"The plot was paid for by his father for 50 years. But what happens after that?"

"He is dead when?" she asks, taking the cigarette from the Bulgarian and raising it to her lips.

"1967."

"So in 2017 … " She is doing the math. " … Is that right: fifty?"

"Ja," the Bulgarian breathes sharply.

"For as long as it is paid, the gardener will come to keep the plot. But in 2017, then, the stone comes down. The ground is dug. And another one goes in."

"Really?"

"That's the way it is," the blonde gardener smiles compassionately at me. "When you die, you lose your spot."

"Yes." The Bulgarian knows it all too well.

"Except, if you are very famous." She drops the Bulgarian's cigarette and destroys it under the heel of her boot. And continues: "If you are famous, then you are important to history. And your place is kept for visitors. Or maybe, you have lots and lots of money?" The woman points to a solid structure on the other side of a stone boundary fence. There it is: a grand mausoleum built with black granite, a piece for the permanent collection.

Did you hear, Michael? When you die you lose your spot. The mighty stone comes out, the ground is dug, and another like you goes in. *Alles in Ordnung!* Except if you are famous.

Or *very* famous.

That's not you, I'm afraid. You're not very anything. You're very underground, okay yes, but very famous, no. Steve McQueen, that one is uber-very famous. Richard Attenborough is Knighted. James Garner, TV loved Garner. These are examples of the very famous. McQueen, Attenborough, Garner, and Bronson, Jackson, Leyton and McCallum. You're the very opposite. You are extremely unknown. So you see the great irony is not that you played a Gestapo officer despite your background—the irony is that everybody has seen that film, and so everybody has seen you, but nobody knows you or remembers you or ever remembers seeing you. And if you really do have a father-complex, more people, many more people, millions in fact, have seen you in *The Great Escape* than ever watched Karl perform on a stage.

What does this have to do with anything? I'm working on that, trust me. I'm following every trail to the end, shifting links und rechts, Hansel and Gretel, left and right.

What comes to mind is that your memory is alive despite what the gardener said. In 1967, when Karl, your father, stood where I am standing, in front of your stone, he held you in his arms. He had his method, a thespian's method, granted. He held your face close to his and kissed you, your living memory, because he could not imagine you dead. He could not fathom you gone. I find myself in the opposite similar position. I, who never had the pleasure, hold you, the dear dead boy, the dead boy, dear.

I stood an hour at the foot of your grave.

You gave me no sign. Weren't you even listening? *Acht du!* Act you little Michael. Assume a virtue. Because we're not done.

Toughen up. We depend on each other. This has as much to do with my escape as it does with yours. Michael, neither of us is going anywhere until we get this straight.

I'm writing a letter, to be read aloud, to you, my so-called dead cousin.

DEAR MICHAEL

LIEBE MICHAEL, THE COMPLICATIONS of childhood are limited to the heart.

Always.

So much depends on the little red wheelbarrow.

*

I am making a death mask. Of you.

*

How should I begin?

*

Want to know what I think? You were exhausted, through, and at such a juncture, cardiac massage was useless.

And anyway, they could not get in, the door was locked. *Hamburg is a wild city.* You locked yourself in, and you hid. You shut out your mother, you were on unstable footing with your father, there is something pathetic in your choice of Margaret as a partner, and you were callow in your treatment of Jerry. You came out only for a night of theatre. How each role…touched you…how together they deformed you. If you had survived all that, allegedly you would have become some kind of nutcase.

*

You did not leave a note. Amateur. Instructions would have been a nice gesture. And what about your method? Did you even have one? Amateur.

*

I have the autopsy report, letters from your Karl, Irene, and Emil, newspaper clippings, photographs and oral reports, and I have a list of plays and a list of theatres, and the movie—I have that on DVD: The Mirisch Company Inc., Presents *The Great Escape*—and recently I got my hands on a Penguin edition of *The Seagull* and located an online source for GB Shaw's *The Apple Cart*. I have your Souffleurbuch. I have that you died in the afternoon. I have that at 8:00 PM you had not showed up at the theatre. And yet I have nothing.

*

Since early days you were coached to avoid confrontation, and schooled not to speak about the past. These days what do you have to lose?

*

I've read your diary from 1949 and I know about Lahr, the DP camp, and your first crepe-sole shoes and about your first mole. I know about the YMCA dance and the diphtheria outbreak, and about the water purification plant. I know about *The Mikado*. I know about your dog Romeo. I know about basketball and smelts and the clarinet, I know a lot about Eva. I know you had the mumps, and you had your tonsils out. I know your final marks for Grade 13. I know about the professor's wife at McGill University, I know about The Adonis and Trepliov and Claudio, I know about your chilly audition for The National Theatre School, I know about Janine and about Lois and Ken, I know about meeting your father in the park in Munich and eating strawberries. I know about Margaret and Jerry (but not everything and hardly anything at all). I know about your financial worries and friction with colleagues, and I know you loved the nightlife. I know about your insomnia. I know about the milk and barbiturates and about the whiskey. I know about your collapse in Bremen. I know about that one testicle and about an episode of jaundice. I even know things you don't know about yourself: the findings of your autopsy report, your burial place, what people have said about you since. Yet I don't really know too much. I don't know your insides at fourteen when you arrived in Canada. After several years, did you feel German still, or Canadian with a difference? I don't know what you expected when you arrived back in Germany. I really want to know if Romeo bit you on the face. Did you lift your arm? What about your stepfather, Antoine? Allegedly he was serene, a Zen-like person. Why didn't any of that rub off on you? Was it a moment of mad despair?

Lastly, Michael, how deep was your Goonskin?

*

Not everyone is calling it an accident.

Maybe you could no longer breathe. Simple as that.

*

I am inserting below The Case of Michael Paryla. Please have your experts read it, and send me any questions you have about it. As you can see for yourself, it is thorough and professionally done.

WHAT THEY SAY ABOUT YOU: A REVIEW

"He only ingested four pills, which should not have been lethal."
–Your aunt Irene, in a letter to Eva

"I had a death mask made of Michi, it turned out beautifully."
–Your father, Karl Paryla, in a letter to Eva

"Michi's life is behind him—he had a good heart and that is probably what's most important. He will not be forgotten, and we all will go the same route in the end."
–Irene

"Certainly, a grown man is no longer a child that one can raise."
–Karl

"Michael's name of course was Paryla and no one would assume anything."
–Janine

"I think he was unhappy because he could not be like his father."
–Gerhardt, your cousin Johanna's husband. (You might remember meeting him in the lobby of the Kammerspiel in Munich.)

"Michael was such a straight, honest person. And he wasn't anymore. He did things later … I just shudder."
-Eva, with the magic hands.

"He was tapped for a leading roll in a theatre production. The premier performance was very successful. He received rave reviews. The celebration of his success lasted into the wee hours of the morning."
–Sybille (You might remember your cousin, who visited Munich that summer of 1962.)

"It's difficult for the son of an actor to become an actor. And his father, Karl Paryla, was such a strong actor, too. But this is not a story about acting. More it is the story about a son and a father, a father and a son."
–Dr. Giesing of the Hamburger Theatersammlung. (You would not have met her, but she is organized and quietly keeps your memory alive.)

WORDS THAT DESCRIBE THE PREDICAMENT OF BEING YOU*
*From my perspective, not yours

Displaced. Envious. Gifted. Lost. Lost Son. Disenfranchised. Dethroned. Underdog. Underling. Underprivileged (Versus European half-brothers). Prodigal. Unproven. Non-entity. Insignificant. Role-player. Practical joker.

MAKESHIFT DEFINITIONS FOR WORDS WHICH DESCRIBE THE PREDICAMENT OF BEING YOU

Displaced—It's obvious you never belonged anywhere.

Envious—Of your half-brothers, of your father's affection, of your father's talent and success.

Gifted—Your je ne sais quoi.

Lost—It's obvious you didn't know who you were or wanted to be.

Lost Son/Prodigal Son—In your dreams you were the great one, you left home and would return home a triumph, lost and found.

Disenfranchised/Dethroned—Your father left when you were four. You grew up in exile from the skilful affection of your father, although you were the rightful heir.

Underdog—It was the North American in you. What can I say. You attended Sault Ste. Marie Collegiate and fooled around with *The Mikado* while your half-brothers were raised in Vienna, in the shadows of a great theatre family.

Underling/Underprivileged—It was the European in you. You seethed that Canada did not 'value' art.

Unproven—Isn't it obvious.

Role player—You played one of the watchmen in Hamlet, not Hamlet.

Practical Joker—Mixing milk and whiskey, marrying your mother, playing some blond bimbo on the train. What more can I say.

Non-entity/ Insignificant—See your STARmeter ranking below.

STARMETER RANKING
"STARmeter rankings provide a snapshot of who's popular based on the searches of millions of IMDb users. Updated

weekly, these rankings also graph the popularity of people over time and determine which events affect public awareness."

Michael, your STARmeter ranking is a dismal 3,802,520.

AUDITION

Til Kiwe. Robert Graf. Hannes Messemer. And then there was you. The King of America.

There was something about you, and there still is something about you, Michael. The casting directors did not care about Him. About KP. Your father Karl Paryla. Certainly not John Sturges, who is renowned for casting excellent actors in secondary roles. Not Lynn 'Never Forget a Face' Stalmaster, Hollywood's Casting Fuehrer. You earned your spot, Michael. What I cannot understand is how things ended up without you getting your credit. What did you sign? Did you make a deal? There's some hint of the ignominy in the trench coat you'd been assigned by the sadists in Wardrobe. The sleeves that end just below your elbow are designed to shrink your ego. They must have been laughing it up in Make-up and Costumes. Rollickin' in Make believe and Forgery. The insult is highly apparent. The message clear. You won't be on-screen more than a minute. You're not worth the bother. It was humiliating, wasn't it?

But what could you say?

Danke.

You needed that role.

Vielen Dank.

In a way, your life depended on it.

THE STALMASTER

It would be something to find hard copies of your agency contract and the autopsy report from your casting audition. But there's no way, Michael. Stallmaster Lister Inc. came by the name honestly. I can't get through to them. And as for the United Artists, who hold the movie rights, the website is a Wall, a big fat HTML FLASH anti-fast-loading JAVA script shit wall.

WHAT THE CRITICS SAY (Revisited)

> They bravely play above the conventional ... Steinmetz only a bit, but Michael Paryla clearly goes above and beyond (goes to excess).

You go above and beyond, of course you do, Michael. You've got method for brains. And you're becoming a star. Meanwhile, *der kanadische Schriftsteller*—like Herbert from Stuttgart: like a good Steinmetz—I stray 'only a bit' beyond the conventional. Why? Because my intimate group of advanced readers caution me to play your memoir straight; because I have a fictional editor who kills footnotes for breakfast; and because recycled sermons abound about the depressed marketplace; because 'prospective publishers' reply to the underground route of unsolicited submissions with hate literature against my literature. Still, there is nobody in this more real than you, Michael. I won't forget that. I won't let you down. But I won't go easy on you, either. They say you go above and beyond—to great excess—show me some of that same spirit now.

> Michael Paryla's hesitant, inhibited and dumb Bleichenwang has a bizarre attraction.

Translation for deaf ears: You seemed out of your mind.

FATHEROLOGY

You were unhappy because you could not be like your father. This is the accepted wisdom, Michael: that you lived under intense pressure. But did you invent that, or were you born into it? Did the fatherology ensnare and entangle you? And yet you never had a mature relationship with him. He abandoned you when he abandoned your mother. What does it mean when the son is unhappy because he cannot be like his father? It's a very squalid situation. It's dirty, cheap and infertile in the imagination department. Shall we conclude, Michael, that you felt a certain impotence vis-à-vis your father? Dr. Franz, while digging around and making his pathology report, *discovered an active gland in the pituitary region, which, according to him, 'should stop functioning after puberty and may signify a continuing infantilism'.* You were possibly envious of your father's success and jealous of the intimacy he kept for your half-brothers, Stephan and Nicolas. What does it mean when myth and psychology collide in one person, i.e. your person?

From the outside it looks like you lost your will.

STATUS
Refugee. Displaced person. Stateless. Undetermined nationality. Actor. Not very stable. Not very convincing.

SUICIDE
Never at the nadir. When the solution to a long-standing problem appears, then.

When, out of darkness, your star is rising.

So this fits.

THE PURSUIT OF HAPPINESS
The Nightlife. In Hamburg you exploited it. To seek pleasure is not in the German constitution like obedience and loyalty and discipline and the rest: punctuality, efficiency, rigidity, denial, cleanliness, arrogance, persistence, responsibility. It was the North American in you. Or, the happy face of despair.

YOUR COLLAPSE AND THE FAINT CRACK
In my experience, Michael, the faint crack before the collapse
is barely audible, but it is audible, and seemingly comes from
within, an echo of the delayed manifestation of the world col-
lapsing upon you from without, giving you just enough time to
get the hell out.

Were you confused by this phenomenon? Many a tunnel
man has had to be pulled out by the ankles.

BREAKDOWN: ESCAPE CONSTRUCTION
A breakdown of the materials used for your great escape: 4 bed
boards; 0 beading battens; 1 blanket; 2 pillow cases; 0 chairs; 0
20-man tables; 0 double tier bunks; 0 knives; 0 spoons; 0 shovels; 0 feet of electric wire; 0 feet of rope; 1 bed cover; 0 towels; 0
bed bolsters; 0 benches; 0 water cans; 0 forks; 0 lamps; 1 alarm
clock; 3-4 sleeping pills; ½ glass of milk; 1 bottle of whiskey.

YOUR ENTOURAGE AND THE GERMAN CIRCLE
Eva held the German circle responsible for your death. This I
conclude from aunt Irene's letter, dated 15 April, 1967. The
entourage included Margaret, Jerry, and Karl. Who else? Your
doctor, maybe. Hearing news of your death, Eva claimed she
had no energy to 'write back and forth' between Canada and
Germany. She wanted to cut all contact. Germany was dead to
her. After leaving the country in 1949, she would never return
to Europe. And she couldn't forgive you, Michael, for choosing
Germany over Canada, your father over your mother, the ego's
entourage in place of true love. This is how I read the letters.

MOTHEROLOGY
Eva's estrangement needs to be understood. At the end of her
life, she was angry, still. Angry at you. And at what happened
to you. But her resentment started much earlier. What started it

all? You wanting to become an actor like him? For your mother Canada was a good enough stage. She had quit the theatre in Germany but never stopped acting. She was a regular-life thespian. But you had to do it the old-fashioned way. You had to audition. You had to prove yourself. You raised your nose and returned to Europe. You had forgiven what she could not forget, and forgotten what she could never forgive. Germany was wrapped up in Karl, and Karl in Germany. Eva wanted baby back.

THE STORY OF JERRY
Karl in a letter to Eva: *The story of Jerry also drove us apart.*

What was the story of Jerry?

I MARRIED MY MOTHER
When your aunt Irene asked you, in 1959, during the early days of your courtship, what kind of a person Margaret Jahnen was, allegedly you responded: "Just like Eva! I married my mother!"

Did you really say that?

THE F-MATH
To recapitulate, Michael, you were most sad because your happiness depended on impressing your Viennese father. You did your best to catch his eye. You 'married' a woman who reminded you of your mother. By marrying this woman you became more like your father. Now, Margaret's son Jerry struggles in life without his father. And when you come along you are no good to Jerry. You treat Jerry badly, which is in character: Karl, leaving in 1938, treated you shoddily. The mysterious Jerry visits Eva once in Canada. Perhaps you saw in Jerry a twin, competition, another displaced son. Perhaps you saw in Jerry a boy without his father, a suffering creature, pathetic as yourself. When Eva met Jerry she felt strongly

that he was a crank, lost and confused. She decided this was enough evidence to prove that his mother Margaret must not be a good person. His mother, according to you, Michael, was just like Eva.

BLAME
Specifically, Eva blamed Margaret for your death. Margaret, the woman who stole your affection. Margaret, who you compared to your own mother. In blaming Margaret for your death, Michael, Eva was laying blame at her own feet. Margaret was a proxy. Eva blamed herself.

KARL AS WELL
Karl, as well, blamed himself for your death. (Everyone wants credit.) Specifically, he blamed himself for not intervening, when he could, between you and Margaret. He mused that perhaps, together, he and your mother (your real mother: Eva) could have influenced and altered your course. He regrets that *the right thing to do was once very simple* and is *immensely reproachful* toward himself.

LIEBESTOD, HIGHLY OPERATIC
He who is too closely associated with death will be homeless on earth. Were you part of the delicate minority, smitten with life but unable to endure it? There is a word for this in German, *Liebestod*. Michael, did you suffer from made-for-the-opera Liebestod? Were your days on earth haunted? You, born in exile, a refugee, displaced since the day of your birth? You, travelling through? Only child of separated thespians, not part of this or that adopted country for long: as if your only sweet tradition was the absence of a place you could call home? Because of this condition you struggled in every moment to invent the fragile architecture of the present.

BARBITURATES

Downers. Why take them? Oblivion. For the gratification of oblivion. For the love of liebestod. Your aunt Irene and others acquainted with your case explained that after giving a performance you were high, high on yourself, and it was always late at night, and you couldn't fall asleep. So you took pills to come on down from up high. Taking pills is an occupational hazard that you were not fit for. This is the accepted wisdom.

INTRINSIC MYSTERY

Outlines but no core. All talent and no substance. Gorgeously corrupt.

I'm thinking of one another's individual enigma and intrinsic mystery.

In the end you were captivating, and captivated.

NARCOTIC YEARNING

In exile on stage in bed.

You were restless and very tired at once. Exhausted from narcotic yearning. What a pastime. Pining for annihilation. What an exhausting leisure-time activity.

CHILDHOOD: EVA

You didn't have the right of return. You didn't have the shelter of, the security or even the insecurity of, childhood.

There was no other-place, no haven or idyllic realm, to which to return.

The closest thing in your mind was Germany.

Eva knew it would be a mistake to return there, to return to zero. She knew that it would be a mistake to play at a homecoming. Michael, going home is not as simple as that. You can't escape that way. Life is not that easy. You can't just make it up.

She knew your time would be wasted. That your time would be short.

CHILDHOOD: ACT ONE
It was unfortunate that you had set your sights on the same career as your father. Being the son of a great actor might have had its advantages, but, Michael, wasn't it also an oppressive burden, a permanent insult to your ego?

To seek approval from him was to lower yourself into a jam of fear, envy, pride, jealousy, kindness.

DIFFICULTY IN BEING
Was there some difficulty in being, for you? Difficulty being you? Wherever you went melancholy followed, back from the theatre, to your apartment, descended from on high, out of the darkness, onto the flatness of your chest. Did you try reading, propped up by pillows, until you couldn't keep your eyes open any longer?

We have all read of artists who ended it because they felt sure they could not practise their art anymore. Michael, did you feel that? That you could not act anymore or any better— you had reached the pinnacle and had decided to rest where no one could reach you—and that was the end? You couldn't live without acting and you couldn't act without drugs and alcohol and milk.

That was neither living nor was it acting, but escaping slowly to death.

WE DIDN'T KNOW
This is what many Germans claim. 'We didn't know.' 'We suffered, too.' Look Michael, you're not responsible for the Holocaust, but you are responsible for your own reaction to it. I have heard that Eva taught you to keep quiet about the past, which amounted to

your keeping quiet about childhood and Germany. She schooled you to keep quiet about who you were and where you came from. There had been exile and immigration, and there had been assimilation. Denial and identity repression could have fucked you up really badly. But it's no excuse.

BACKGROUND TO YOUR JEWISH BACKGROUND

On paper you were Paryla. But Eva was née Steinmetz. And if you search 'Steinmetz' in the Central Database of Shoah Victims you'll find an Eva Steinmetz from Hungary. There is even a Michael Steinmetz born in 1861. I found Hermann Steinmetz, same as your uncle's name. How real was your Jewish background? Here are the number of registered murdered Steinmetzs by country: Poland 304; Hungary 168; Germany 61; Austria 20. Bertha Steinmetz, who was murdered in Auschwitz, was your first cousin once removed, same as I am to you.[39]

BEING NOT GERMAN NOT JEWISH

It turns out you were neither German nor Austrian, not really Jewish, not Canadian, and no Steve McQueen. You were not really anything.

BEING NOT STEVE MCQUEEN

With all your uncertainties, mysteries, doubts, you were a natural at Being Not Steve McQueen. And in my book Being Not McQueen is just as obercooler as Being McQueen.

OBERCOOLER STEVE MCQUEEN

You remember him surely. His StarMETER ranking went through the roof. In 1974, McQueen was the highest paid movie actor on the planet. On set, I bet you got on easily with McQueen—you who had mastered basketball and YMCA

---

39   I gather it's understood, there was a War on Steinmetz before the War on Michael.

dances, had America down. And you shared something with McQueen. Maybe you discussed the matter. McQueen's father was a stunt pilot. McQueen Sr. abandoned Steve and his mother when Steve was six months old. He was brought up by his grandparents, since his mother was an alcoholic. What did Steve get out of this? An unquenchable thirst for speed. McQueen once claimed that he could only relax when he was going fast. As a matter of fact, he badly wanted to jump the frontier fence into Switzerland at the end of the movie. I bet he had it in him, too. But there was insurance to consider. Insurance is a bitch when you're uber-famous.

ACTOR'S BLOCK

What is actor's block? Depression, maybe. Lack of will and the inability to make decisions. Loss of drive and interest in sex. Not wanting to be you when you *are* you. They say unless you feel the fire to act, do not become an actor. Because you will need it. You need that fire to pass over the threshold of self-consciousness into the essence of the character.

I understand that you once *had* fire. Once upon a time you had it, the same way many writers profess the existential-must to write. True or faux?

MAMA'S BOY

In the afternoon, as is well-known, you liked to take a short nap. To catnap. Which is a form of pretend-sleeping, or anyways it is less threatening than a good night's sleep, for an insomniac.

At night, it was different. In the dark, you pulled off petals one by one, and the whirlwind of characters made the bed spin.

You may call me Francisco. 'Tis bitter cold. And I am sick at heart.

You may call me Sempronius, secretary to the king.

Cosimo de Medici.

Stand and unfold yourself. You come most carefully upon your hour.

My father was a sort of spectacular artist. He arranged the last two coronations. That was how I got my job here in the palace.

You see, my mother doesn't love me. She wants to have love affairs, to wear light-coloured blouses. My father was a member of the petty bourgeoisie, as you know—although he was a well-known actor too.

I was despicable enough to kill this seagull today.

When I see the curtain rise on a room with three walls, when I watch these great and talented people, these high priests of the sacred art depicting the way people eat, drink, make love, walk about and wear their clothes, in the artificial light of the stage… when I'm presented with a thousand variations of the same old thing, the same thing again and again—well, I just have to escape, I run away.

It was a moment of mad despair, when I had no control over myself.

I've got magic hands.

You may call me Konstantin Gavrilovich Trepliov, the Russian Hamlet.

In modern parlance, a Mama's boy.

1956: YOU

Behold Mike. Momma's boy. Trepliov. Behold: you are lost.

So.

You leave because Canada is a desert and you will never be found if you stay.

You leave to find your footing.

You, a non-entity, will impress them all.

1967: YOU

You were en route to the top! You were on the right path. You had matured. You were becoming a success, becoming a real star. Nothing could stop you. You had the chops, handsome looks, language facility. You had it all and some kind of malleable face. Some unnatural trace of your race. Nothing could slow you down, unless—one little thing, Michael—unless you had crashed, and were broken inside. Unless you were some kind of mental cripple. I'd like to share with you my conclusion about this, drawn at length, from Karl's letter to Eva, dated April 29, 1967. A letter principally about the autopsy report and your war scars.

CARPE DIEM

These scars to your myocardium, and the question of whether or not you, Michael, suffered from jaundice in childhood, beg further research.

SCARLET FEVER

Scarlatina, a streptococcal infection. You may have been exposed about the time Eva volunteered in a DP camp—Switzerland: 1943-45. An outbreak was confirmed one day when she was on duty; and your mother was placed in quarantine. The problem was there was no one at home to take care of Michi. You would have been seven or eight, a ripe old age for developing rheumatic fever as a complication from scarlet fever.

RHEUMATIC FEVER

An inflammatory disease. Rheumatic fever may develop after an infection with streptococcus bacteria, such as scarlet fever. It usually affects children between the ages of six and fifteen. Sequelae are limited to the heart.

DIPTHERIA EXPOSURE

Do not forget the acute infectious disease caused by the bacteria *Corynebacterium diphtheriae.* Do not forget the diphtheria outbreak in 1949 at the DP camp in Lahr. You were fourteen. All you had to wear on your feet were those crepe-sole shoes. No defence against bacteria that can spread through your bloodstream to other organs, such as the heart, and cause significant damage. More precisely, with an infection of this sort the fibres of the myocardium—the walls of the heart—are thinned and its cavities dilated.

Michael, I'm thinking of you in these terms: thin walls of a cavernous heart, a cavernous heart of thin walls.

MUMPS
No one remembers what these are. Mumps might come from 'mumble' or from 'lumps'. In any case, the mumps are what you had a severe case of as a child, this according to your pal Ken Taylor. The mumps are characterized by a painful swelling of the salivary glands. Again an inflammation of the heart known as myocarditis is a rare sequelae of the mumps. Other complications include orchitis, which is the painful swelling of the testicles. Likely you experienced this in spades. In teenage males, infertility is common.

TONSILS
Yours were taken out. In the opinion of Dr. Franz, a doctor of pathology from Hamburg, the scars to your myocardium could have resulted from an infection following an operation to your tonsils.

VITAL SIGNS
Did you cry? The doctor did not remark on it. But then he'd have been busy, occupied with your vital signs—pulse and breathing and lack thereof—to have had the presence of mind to take a picture of your emotional health. For goodness sake, you were cold.

PHYSICAL FINDINGS AND PATIENT HISTORY: SUMMARY OF THE EVIDENCE

You had your tonsils taken out, one testicle is smaller than the other, and at time of death there was a rogue gland functioning in your pituary region. To make matters worse you were possibly infertile due to your teenage case of the mumps. Them's the lumps. Still the origin of those scars to your myocardium are bewitching, the etiology ranges from scarlet fever to diphtheria to an infection to your tonsils. Enter signs and symptoms and cue the storm clouds: episodes of insomnia and anxiety. What caused these? What causes a mature person to lose the ability to sleep? Worry. Adrenaline. Loneliness. Uppers. Did you simply bite off more than you could chew?

The Upstanding Young Doctor at ASKLEPIOS KLINIK ST GEORG

Doctor Franz is without doubt an ideal follow-up candidate if it comes to a more in-depth exploration of the rheumatic fever/jaundice hypothesis. But Dr. Wuehler, the attending at St Georg's, he ultimately might be the one to contact for more facts about the last hour of your great escape. He is our best bet for the whereabouts of you, Michael, for the upstanding fellow from St Georg's in Hamburg was the last person to have laid hands on you, the last of all to apply pressure to your by now much maligned heart valves (which, it must be said, were not equal to the task).

NADIR OR ZENITH

You were not tapped for a leading role as your cousin Sybille once told me, were you? The champagne did not flow after a successful opening night. No, probably not. Sybille's version of events doesn't add up. Much of the evidence about you is misleading. The type of life you lived in Hamburg is your business.

But again, I don't suppose you were on the way up, as Karl claims you were. Or were you? I just don't know. Were you at the nadir or the zenith? Had you finally found the solution to a long-term problem, or had you dug yourself deeper into the hole? The question remains: Michael, were you digging yourself out, or under? Did you feel like a failure at art and at love? I'm beginning to see how nothingness and emptiness and impotence were leitmotifs for you all of your life. You were not German, not really Jewish, not Canadian, and neither on the rise nor in decline, not at your Nadir nor perched at the Zenith. For all that, or because of all that, you had a cavernous heart. For sure you had that, and thin skin. I can hear it, and you beating yourself up, over nothing, underground.

BUBBLES

I have taken a couple of lessons, and have made progress. My teacher told me about 'the bubbles', i.e. on stage the actor fully exists inside three spheres; the bubble of 'I': internal monologues and soliloquy; the bubble of 'You and I' : dialogue; and the bubble that contains 'You and I and the world': no question this last bubble is a big ugly bubble, and a messy place. I have learned also about timing and beats.

GUARDS

They—the guards and gardeners, the critics and ferrets, the sentries, the goons en masse—have every advantage but the urge to escape.

YOU PUT A SPELL ON ME

Yes you did. My paranormal twin. All along there has been identity repression and assimilation, acting and becoming, diaspora, exile and escape, stateless persons of undetermined nationality, immigration and assimilation anew, sublimation and trials of

self-actualization, and the hopeful hard suffering of the birth
of the true.

ESCAPE COMMITTEE
It's basically you and me, Michael. We make a plan and flip for
who goes first.

ESSENTIALS OF PLAN
Do some reconnaissance and find the blind spots in the fence;
forge a new identity; pick the location and conceal the trap;
sign up a good selection of stooges and diversionists; wear long
woollen underpants; use a spirit level; paste a fat lamp to your
forehead; tunnel like hell.

SECURITY PRECAUTION # 1
Keep your plan a secret. At Stalag Luft III only twelve men
out of the hundreds involved making the tunnels had actually
known the entire escape plan. Roger Bushell and the escape
committee held the cards close to their chests. Similarly,
Michael, you kept your Hamburg plan secret; secret from
your wife, from your peers and from your parents. I expect
you were not yourself aware of the ending. You never let on,
anyway. If you'd let the cat out of the bag, you might have
tried to stop yourself. You might have modified your diet of
barbiturates and milk and whiskey. But Michael, you didn't
let it out. You kept it from yourself until that faint crack that
seemed to have come from above, but was issued from deep
within, signalled the end.

RECAPTURE
Für dich ist der Krieg nicht vorbei. Michael, for you the war is
not over. Trust me, and try to show the same resourcefulness
the prisoners did. You're not the only one in history to have

been put in an escape-proof situation. Think of Goering's luxury camp with its machine-gun nests and soil impregnated with microphones and seismographs. By comparison Waldfriedhof is a state-run spa.

DUTY

For the Allied airmen escape was no game. They were duty-bound to create havoc and disruption behind enemy lines. It was part of their code of ethics. Same thing here and now, Michael. It is the duty of every prisoner never to give up free will. It is our duty, at least to attempt escape. Even unsuccessful breakouts upset the familiar and disturb the marketplace.

AUTOPSY REPORT, REVISITED

Before ending (with a little drama), I would like to return once more to my understanding of the pathology report and the elegant phrase *Neubens im Herzmuskel*. Michael—you know what this means? YOU WERE NOT WELL. It means you were hurting. Karl raises the worry of childhood exposure to yellow fever. He means scarlet fever. This fits with your case history. But I'm unimpressed by the science.

Neubens im Herzmuskel, scars to your myocardium, these are technical terms.

Your heart was broken.

It was cavernous. It had thin walls. It was easily breached.

UNFORTUNATE PASSING

Karl's letter of 21 April, 1967 stresses you were unwell for quite a while, and that your poor health, i.e. your broken heart, 'decisively contributed' to your 'unfortunate passing'.

Your scars were the result of an original insult, but which?

Scarlet fever, your doting mother, your absent father—how can we be precise about the natural history of the broken heart?

IN MY OPINION
I have taken the best of eight years to reflect, and in my opinion the kicker was not sleeping pills and alcohol. I would trace your killer to the half-glass of milk—the child's drink, the infant's soda—which you imbibed for your worrying stomach. In my opinion, you died from exhaustion from a child's heart broken in 1938. A broken heart launched by the separation of your parents, the little red wheelbarrow of heaviness which you locked from the inside.

PLAUSIBLE DENIABILITY
All that talk earlier about the danger of mixing pills and alcohol when dealing with a narrow therapeutic index suggests you could have deliberately killed yourself in such manner to rescue for your parents some plausible deniability.

THE FIRE
When did the fire go out? At the threshold of consciousness you passed into essence.

CURIO-HAUS
In the movie, Michael, you kindly assist the Nazi assassins who were tried at the Curio-Haus in 1948, and hung at Hamelin Gaol.

 And in 1967, twenty years enigmatically *später,* Hamburg is where your life ends. Coincidence? The jury is out.

STURM UND DRANG
The alarm sounded. No one came running to find you. There was no manhunt. No grand Grossfahndung. No teamwork, no networking Nazis grinning cheek to cheek. The clock stopped at 6:00 PM—the alarm sounded and then: the connected springs, levers, and cogs wore themselves out, singing and ringing, sturming and dranging.

Then it was hours before the firemen broke down the door to your apartment. What they found is the territory of medical science. You were in a state, semi or unconscious, in and out of it. Sullied. More than halfway down the rabbit hole. Still: emergency workers with the best intentions rushed you to St Georg's, where the attending physician, a fine young man, plunged his weight into your ribs, fracturing, splintering, flushing blood, and chasing you, through four chambers of your heart.

Doing all work possible until all the good went out of that.

CUT

Now backtrack. Fast-rewind. To the film—THE MOVIE—release in '63. Shhh, Michi. *It is Germany, March 1944, the 11th anniversary of Hitler's rise to the chancellorship, etc. Ja, Ja. Das ist Deutschland* and Michael you are the blond bimbo on the train. See how you ambulate, no fuss, single-mindedly, with the casual swagger of your superior face. Swaying not much, not much at all because at this point, after a day of shooting, running up and down the Munich-Hamburg line, you've got your sea legs beneath you, and your future well ahead and your past bloodless on the tracks.

FREEDOM

It must taste great.
It's the real thing, no?

MUNICH

You're not at peace. This is the accepted wisdom. Munich is your resting place, but how do you sleep? Not well, if I know a thing or two about you. You were never at ease in your goonskin. Gather yourself together then.

TRAPFUEHRER
I'll push over your stone. And call down the shaft, All Clear! [40]

UNDERGROUND
It must be exciting. You're part of the underground. Not the French underground, but anyway. You're part of a big secret. It's hard work, the unravelling and disentangling. Use the fat lamp and a prismatic compass. And a spirit level. Now suppose I avert my eyes as you come up for air. Suppose I look the other way at self-slaughter and dismiss what your mother Eva suspected, and what your father Karl would not authorize himself to believe. Suppose I give the all clear, then will you come out, wherever you are?

You must spit black all day.

I warn you, I'll pull you out by the ankles!

IMPROVISATION
Follow this rope into the forest. Improvisation is our strength. Gather your things, therefore. We meet at the Sagan station. That's Neustadt to you. Arrive by dawn.

OPENING NIGHT
It's no use. You live in the past. *What time is it?* It is past eight. And where are you? Michael, you're late. *Typisch.* This evening's performance will go ahead without you. Neither the flow nor the understanding of the play... This is sad. But show business is show business.

ALARM
Have you overslept? Dream of me as I dream of myself, liberated, in Hamburg, pacing the sidewalk of Mühlendamm street

---

40   I'm no trapfuehrer, actually. I don't like the sound of that word. I'm more like the camp forgers who work in relative safety under a window, using the daylight and an old fashioned typewriter and making the hand-lettered passes and tracing the juvenile insignias, without ever setting out on the journey itself.

below your window, measuring the length between lamp posts, just occasionally pausing like POW David McCallum on the station platform to read from *Die Völkischer Beobachter. Another Day of Bloody Losses.* Every day is a loss, Michael. Every dawn and dusk, behold some bloody man at loss. You. Me. Me. You. You. Me. Behold. Behold we are lost and never found. Behold bloody lost souls. Understand? Then, if you please, stroll past the front window. That's all I ask. Proof I have not imagined everything. Proof I'm no crazypants. Ten more minutes. That's all I can give you. What are you playing at tonight?

BLOND IS PASSÉ

Now Michael, only the unsteady percussion of the train's wheels and the tracks and the carriages, shush and shunted, the buffeting panes and the tripped slosh of metal to remind me that I am rolling through memory as well as time.

1989

INT-TRAIN. The Author is Dead—First episode. Aboard the overnight train to Berlin. Berlin not Hamburg. Not yet Hamburg. All of twenty-four, I sit by the train window, chin in hand like some wise critic of ghostly reflections. Pupils agape, my eyes drink and pull, darkness within wishing for a match without. Over the hours, I slip down the seat and my organism shudders before gliding deeper. Before reaching Berlin, I open my eyes and immediately in the darkness I am conscious of a field of energy neither created nor destroyed: I have company, this is unambiguous. The borderguard—border police, who?—parts the sliding steel door and emerges from my sleep, a totalnightmarian. Wearing leather boots cap belt holster. Short black hair. Blond is passé. I come to consciousness with him speaking the iron-curtain dream language. *Passkontrolle. Ihre Pässe bitte.* The same old song. A Golden Oldie. The same Anti-Fast-Entry/Exit

Wall of Shit. Why have I come? What is my purpose? Passport, visa, ticket. He hums and thumbs my spine: he compares portrait to face, face to portrait, human to race. What if I'm not him? But it cannot be otherwise. *I am the one on this train tonight,* I begin in a whisper, gaining in confidence, *I am the one sitting by the window. Here is my head. This is my head leaning like a book on the glass. And by my nose is my reflection. Trite as I shall ever become, stark as a death mask.*

Now, go away Passkontroller. Go away Nightmarian. Now that same old tripped slosh of metal, to remind me.

Then to Berlin itself. I buy myself army boots near the Brandenburg Gate. Black leather lace-ups. American or British or French. Russian or German. Old masters or new masters. Punk rock! I slip them on and sit by the wall and wait for an opening. Everything lines up from here. I watch the skies. I compose in my famous blue notebook: *The self reports to no one in particular.* And date it. Berlin. November 1989.

Citizens go at the wall with picks and hammers and screwdrivers. Gouging out chunks. Breaking off pieces. The wall spits back stones and cement. I stand aside for the grand wrecking ball to swing (from where it is hung, high, out of sight, aloft) to swing low, through the present, toward the future and back through memory along the return arc.

Graffiti-crabbed ingots: in purple, in green, in white and black. Fragments from slogans profane and political. Promises private and public. I examine a few pieces and stuff them away in my shoulder bag and start walking. I walk away from that once impenetrable partition, casually, nonchalant as that charlatan POW James Coburn, the manufacturer and bike thief, who slips away in Füssen. In Berlin and without the benefit of Elmer Bernstein's soundtrack, I walk for hours and hours in a daze of unknowing and already gone: not underground, but like a mole burrowing blind in search of sight before I knew the first thing about you. Gone and forgotten and no one is qualified to come after me, to round me up, and bring me back, except someone like you.

But you never came, Michael. Therefore.

PLAY

Let me bring you up to date. October 2012 from Ottawa. A typed note. Ordinary paper, no black border, standard postage. Forget Express. Forget I have been on the Autobahn driving eight hours a day. Forget I need a vacation. Forget I have terrible news. Forget 'our Michi died last night in Hamburg'. Forget I made a death mask of you. Forget if there is something stuck in your ear. Forget you don't like worms. Forget grubs. Forget ants. Forget Piglet Lamond. Forget Roger Bushell. Forget Wally Floody. Forget the Mirisch brothers of The Mirisch Brothers Inc. Forget Steve McQueen.

How shall I put it? Forget the odds. Forget the sad and insane. Escape.

CUT

To be a witness, true, detached and devout, of free will, predestination, faith and doubt.

TICK-TOCK

We do our bit, we tick and tock, until (you'll never guess the ending, I dreamt this up):

Michael: The Last Escape

A New Production

Hamburg-Ottawa
23 October 2010

I am to play you. Not an escaped POW, not one of the snob RAF, not some straight-bang Nazi. But the real you. Michael Paryla. I'll live with the pressure. No bouts of insomnia. No fear of failure. No barbiturates. No milk. Nary a scar to my myocardium. I promise: eight o'clock, tomorrow, on location I will be. Look out the window onto the street. Look for a man your height. Pull back the curtains—eight-thirty at the latest—if not I'll do this without you.

The situation calls for an understudy.

INCOMPLETENESS

ON THE EVENING OF 20 JANUARY 1967, Michael Paryla was slated to perform in the role of Sempronius, a royal secretary, in Shaw's *The Apple Cart* at Hamburg's illustrious Thalia Theatre. Instead, that same evening, he was found in a coma in his apartment and rushed to the St Georg Hospital, where he died. On the bed table the firemen discovered a bottle of pills and a glass half-full of whiskey mixed with milk. He did not leave a suicide note and the police investigation into his death found no evidence of foul play. After the autopsy, his body was transferred from Hamburg by train to Munich and buried at Waldfriedhof, in a plot only kilometres from the giant sound stages at Bavaria Film Studios, where the camp interiors for *The Great Escape*, including the tunnels sequences, were filmed.

Three years after my trip to Germany, I often revisit the hour I spent at Waldfriedhof. I remember, I stood by the side of his grave and, as his father had, many years before, I spoke to his memory. What did I 'speak to his memory'? Alas, poor Michael, something less Shakespearean than Karl Paryla might have contrived on the spot. Still, there I stood, smoking a cigarette and looking up at the sky, when I hit an impasse, staring too long at his headstone. He had escaped with hardly a scratch. *Michael Paryla*. No date of birth and year of death. So I addressed some final words to him and then, as I was leaving the spot, I kissed my hand and pressed my palm to the stone. *Ruhe in Frieden*. I felt my tears coming and I let them go. Sleep in Peace.

Well, the point is, it is no longer a reliable memory. I have put myself back there, so many times, under different guises, it is a wonder I have not been left in Waldfriedhof in place of Michael, and him returned instead of me, to finish the story, one way or other, once and for all.

His life, like many true stories, feels incomplete. That's the thing. Not because of how he died, under circumstances I have done my best to describe, and not because he departed young without making good on his promise and potential. I don't believe his life was cut short; hadn't it already begun to reveal a recurring pattern? We might retrace his steps—we may owe it to him to follow every trail to the end—and try to guess at the meaning of his life, but the fact of the matter is some truths are unprovable, and maybe our fundamental dissatisfaction with open endings has to do with this: our desire for closure exceeds what is knowable. More devastating, perhaps, is that neither physical or circumstantial evidence nor proof of cause or natural history can be relied upon for human understanding.

Whenever I feel lost, I read from Paul Brickhill's memoir *The Great Escape*. On page 121 begins Brickhill's Ode to Al Hake and Stalag Luft's Compass Factory.

Al Hake made his compass production line in a room in 103. He made the compass casings out of broken gramophone records, heating bits until they were soft as dough then pressing them into a mold. Artists painted the points of the compass accurately on little circles of paper, and they fitted neatly into the base of the casings. He sank a gramophone needle in the center of the base for the needle pivot. The direction needle itself was a bit of sewing needle which he rubbed against a magnet. With a great delicacy he soldered a tiny pivot socket to the center of the magnetized needles. (The solder came from the melted joints of bully beef tins, and he dug the resin for the soldering out of the pine trees, and after the pine trees were cut down, out of the resinous wood of the huts.) Valenta even got him some luminous paint for the needles so they could be used at night without the danger of striking matches. [41]

Glass for the compass tops he took from bits of broken window. If there weren't any broken windows handy, he broke one himself and then cut the pieces into circular disks under water so the glass didn't crack or chip. He made a little blow lamp out of a fat lamp and some thin tubing rolled out of old food tins. Through the tube he blew a gentle jet of air against the flame, playing it around the rim of the compass case, and when it was melting soft he pressed in the glass and there it set, tight and waterproof.

Al Hake's factory produced more than 250 compasses in this manner. The POWs professionally engraved an inscription in the bottom of the casings, 'Made in Stalag Luft III'.

I sit at a table with the book flat before me using a pencil to underline text, drawing my own subterranean network for emphasis, until I realize how useless that is: with Brickhill there is nothing superfluous. What is, is, and what is not, is not there. When I turn back several pages, I read aloud about how the POW's hid the tools they had amassed while digging the tunnels and working on their escape plan. False walls and trap doors concealed storage spaces. In hut 110, Brickhill tells us, a prisoner nicknamed Little S "cut out bits of the inside of books so the chisels and pliers fitted flush inside and were never noticed unless the book was opened; and the ferrets, fortunately, never went in for literature."

*

---

41   Flight lieutenant Ernst Valenta was one of the tunnel specialists, and was one of the 50 shot by the Gestapo after the March 1994 escape.

There is no saving Michael Paryla. I accept, I do accept that. Off camera, he was free to make the world his stage—at liberty to play the clown or fool or tragic hero, the prodigal son, or an absurd minor character in search of meaning and his creator. I appreciate the old Stanislavski trick that the first truth in acting is circumstance, and understand that off the mark circumstances can be difficult, for some, unbearable, prohibitive, agonizing. I do understand, I do, that at times to continue moving forward, through the day, and through the night, amounts to a severe challenge on par with tunnelling 350 feet horizontally under the watchful eyes of a tight-knit community of Hundfuehrers and Ferrets, from inside a camp built by a group of future Hall of Fame War Criminals.

What comes to mind is Michael's grand exit, his all-time-forever escape from money problems and bouts of insomnia, from simmering insecurity and feelings of inadequacy, from stage fright and sideswiping gusts of despair. His escape from a broken heart, for too long locked from the inside.

Escape. What is it about escape? Appell is taken early at my desk in the forgery factory. I pass the hours in the compound of this desire. How shall I put it? I remember well that it is every prisoner's duty to attempt escape. In Brickhill's world, this was part of 'carrying on the war by other means.' Prisoners were bound by a sense of duty and tactical motivations: escape attempts created chaos inside the enemy territory, and diverted attention from the front lines. The more brazen an escape attempt, the more it invited reprisals from the enemy power, often in the form of harsh collective punishments.

In 1929, the International Committee of the Red Cross drew up a draft of the Convention Relative to the Treatment of Prisoners of War, and presented it at a high-level diplomatic conference meeting in Geneva. Germany was one of the first nations to sign the Geneva Convention, expanding upon the protective rights of prisoners of war and making escape attempts from prison camps legitimate. Article 50 of the treaty stipulated: "Escaped prisoners of war who are re-captured before they have been able to rejoin their own armed forces or to leave the territory occupied by the armed forces which captured them shall be liable only to disciplinary punishment." The fair-minded language of Article 50 is a long way from the verbal communication of the Sagan Order, commissioned in 1944 by Heinrich Himmler, the head of the SS. The Sagan Order sealed the fate of the recaptured prisoners of Stalag Luft III. The murders were premeditated. The executions were to be justified under the false pretence that the recaptured officers "were shot while trying to escape." Would it be too much now to borrow the wording of this specious defence to describe Michael's death, i.e. Michael was 'killed while trying to escape', which, if not a hapless description of suicide, is a useful variation on the theme? Thus we might understand that Michael was not trying to end his life, only trying to escape it. There is a difference. A legitimate difference.

Art. Art carries on with life by other means. That's what I say. Even failed breakouts free the spirit.

In 2017, when stone comes down, I plan on being there, in Waldfriedhof, to see that everything goes according to plan. And when another goes in, after Michael comes out, he just might want to read from this.

*

2017

-Ihre Pässe bitte?

-Yes, of course. Here they are. My papers. Naturally I cannot say no. Take them from me at once.

ACKNOWLEDGEMENTS

This book contains quotations from multiple sources, beginning with *The Great Escape* by Paul Brickhill, Faber & Faber, 1951; for my uses I referred to the Cassell Military Paperbacks edition of 2004. Line quotations from "The Seagull" are from *Anton Chekhov Plays* translated by Elisaveta Fen, Penguin Classics, 1951. Quotations from George Bernard Shaw's "The Apple Cart" are taken from Project Gutenberg. Quotations from Ursula Hegi are from *Tearing the Silence: On Being German in America* by Ursula Hegi, Touchstone, 1998. Additional background information on the escape came from various sources, including *A Gallant Company: The True Story of 'The Great Escape'* by Jonathan F. Vance, I Books, 2003. For a knowledge-base and information on most everything and anything: Wikipedia. For an update on the so-called dead I visited the Rudolf Steiner Archive at www.rsarchive.org. For a guide to the making of the movie, I read Steven Jay Rubin's *Combat Films. American Realism: 1945-1970*, Jefferson: McFarland, 1981. I visited time and again Rob Davis' excellent website The Great Escape: www.elsham. pwp.blueyonder.co.uk/gt_esc/; and Don J. Whistance's wonderful The Great Escape Locations Site: www.thegreatescapelocations. com. My time signatures in the chapter Movie Time refer to the 2004 MGM Home Edition Collector's Set Special Edition. *The Great Escape © 1963 Metro Goldwyn-Mayer Studios*. For a history of barbiturates I would like to acknowledge Dimitri Cozanitis' "One Hundred Years of Barbiturates and their Saint", *Journal of the Royal Society of Medicine*, Volume 97, December 2004.

Over the 'war' years, I relied on many people for their support, knowledge, and generosity. I would like to thank and acknowledge the professionals who helped me tunnel through the research material: Mary E. Houde (McGill University Archives), Eric Berthiaume (Goethe-Institut Montréal), Edward Ned Comstock (USC Library), Dr. Christian Riml and Helma Türk (Tiroler Filmarchiv), Dr. Michaela Giesing (Hamburger Theatersammlung), Sandra Asche (Thalia Theatre). I wish to express my sincere gratitude to the members of the escape committee: Dan Birkholtz, Simon Dardick, Mark Frutkin, Christoph Geyer, Joan Harcourt, Stephen Henighan, Robert Hutcheon, John Koensgen, Alen Mattich, my agent Hilary McMahon, Merle Moja, Ruediger Müller, Alice Petersen, Michael Robinson, for translation Claudia Rathjen, Carmine Starnino, PJ Tarasuk, Sonya Eva Tarasuk and Emil Tarasuk, Miriam Toews, Jonathan F. Vance, my parents Nicolas and Birgitta Steinmetz. For their openness and witness, I owe a special debt of gratitude to Michael H. Kater, Ken Taylor, Lois Rodger, Buddy Yukich, Sybille Sidden, Janine de Salaberry (Blum), Robert Carmichael, Terry Taft, Stephan Paryla-Raky, Nicolas Steinmetz, and Eva Stehr (in memoriam). Special thanks to John Leyton, aka Willie 'Tunnel King', for answering my call. And, for a cameo and his many truly astonishing insights and comments on an early draft, thank you so much Clayton Bailey.

I could not have endured the long winters without camp serenaders, most of all Tallest Man on Earth, Bon Iver, Frank Ocean, Chopin, Gonzales, Miles Davis, and The Necks.

There would not have been light at the end of the tunnel without the inspiration and encouragement of Dan Wells, and the care and craft of Chris Andrechek, Tara Murphy and Kate Hargreaves of Biblioasis.

Most of all, I owe this great escape to my wife Jill Tarasuk for her encouragement and love and strength, and for making a fine martini.

I gratefully acknowledge financial support from the Canada Council for the Arts, Ontario Arts Council, and City of Ottawa Arts and Culture Funding.

ABOUT THE AUTHOR

BORN IN MONTRÉAL, Andrew Steinmetz is the author of a memoir (*Wardlife*) and two collections of poetry (*Histories* and *Hurt Thyself*). His novel, *Eva's Threepenny Theatre*, tells the story of his great-aunt Eva, who performed in one of the first touring productions of Bertolt Brecht's masterpiece *The Threepenny Opera* in 1928. An unusual fiction about memoir, *Eva's Threepenny Theatre* won the 2009 City of Ottawa Book Award and was a finalist for the 2009 Rogers Writers' Trust Fiction Prize. Steinmetz is also the founding editor of Esplanade Books, the fiction imprint at Véhicule Press.